Translated Texts for Historians

This series is designed to meet the needs of students of ancient and medieval history and others who wish to broaden their study by reading source material, but whose knowledge of Latin or Greek is not sufficient to allow them to do so in the original language. Many important Late Imperial and Dark Age texts are currently unavailable in translation and it is hoped that TTH will help to fill this gap and to complement the secondary literature in English which already exists. The series relates principally to the period 300–800 AD and includes Late Imperial, Greek, Byzantine and Syriac texts as well as source books illustrating a particular period or theme. Each volume is a self-contained scholarly translation with an introductory essay on the text and its author and notes on the text indicating major problems of interpretation, including textual difficulties.

Editorial Committee

Sebastian Brock, Oriental Institute, University of Oxford
Averil Cameron, King's College, London
Henry Chadwick, Peterhouse, Cambridge
John Davies, University of Liverpool
Carlotta Dionisotti, King's College London
Robert Markus, University of Nottingham
John Matthews, Queen's College, Oxford
Raymond Van Dam, University of Michigan
Ian Wood, University of Leeds
Jan Ziolkowski, Harvard University

General Editors:

Gillian Clark, University of Liverpool
Margaret Gibson, University of Liverpool
Christa Mee, Birkenhead

Already published

Gregory of Tours: Life of the Fathers
Translated with an introduction by EDWARD JAMES
Volume 1: 163pp., 1985 (reprinted 1986) ISBN 0 85323 115 X

The Emperor Julian: Panegyric and Polemic
Claudius Mamertinus, John Chrysostom, Ephrem the Syrian
Edited by SAMUEL N.C. LIEU
Volume 2: 153pp., 2nd edition 1989, ISBN 0 85323 376 4

Pacatus: Panegyric to the Emperor Theodosius
Translated with an introduction by C.E.V. NIXON
Volume 3: 122pp., 1987, ISBN 0 85323 076 5

Gregory of Tours: Glory of the Martyrs
Translated with an introduction by RAYMOND VAN DAM
Volume 4: 150pp., 1988, ISBN 0 85323 236 9

Gregory of Tours: Glory of the Confessors
Translated with an introduction by RAYMOND VAN DAM
Volume 5: 127pp., 1988, ISBN 0 85323 226 1

The Book of Pontiffs *(Liber Pontificalis to AD 715)*
Translated with an introduction by RAYMOND DAVIS
Volume 6: 175pp., 1989, ISBN 0 85323 216 4

Chronicon Paschale 284–628 AD
Translated with notes and introduction by
MICHAEL WHITBY AND MARY WHITBY
Volume 7: 280pp., 1989, ISBN 0 85323 096 X

Iamblichus: On the Pythagorean Life
Translated with notes and introduction by GILLIAN CLARK
Volume 8: 144pp., 1989, ISBN 0 85323 326 8

Conquerors and Chroniclers of Early Medieval Spain
Translated with notes and introduction by KENNETH BAXTER WOLF
Volume 9: 176pp., 1991, ISBN 0 85323 047 1

Victor of Vita: History of the Vandal Persecution
Translated with notes and introduction by JOHN MOORHEAD
Volume 10: 112pp., 1991, ISBN 0 85323 127 3

The Goths in the Fourth Century
By PETER HEATHER and JOHN MATTHEWS
Volume 11: 224pp., 1991, ISBN 0 85323 426 4

Translated Texts for Historians
Volume 11

The Goths in the Fourth Century

by
PETER HEATHER and JOHN MATTHEWS

Liverpool
University
Press

D
137
.H434
1991

First published 1991 by
Liverpool University Press
PO Box 147, Liverpool, L69 3BX

Copyright © 1991 Peter Heather and
John Matthews

All rights reserved. No part of this
book may be reproduced in any form
without permission in writing from the
publishers, except by a reviewer in
connection with a review for inclusion
in a magazine or newspaper.

British Library Cataloguing-in-Publication Data
A British Library CIP Record is available
ISBN 0 85323 426 4

Printed in Great Britain at the
University Press, Cambridge

CONTENTS

PREFACE

In the seven chapters of this book we present literary texts and other sources on the material and cultural history of the Goths in the period from their first attacks upon the Roman empire in the mid-third century, to their crossing of the Danube to enter Roman territory in the mid-370s and 380s. We do not extend to the period of Gothic settlement in the Roman west in the fifth and sixth centuries, except in one respect: in order to make intelligible, and do justice to, the work of Ulfila as evangelist and teacher of the Goths, we trace the history into the later period, from which it actually survives, of the Gothic Bible of which he was the originator. In our last chapter we give some selected passages of the Gothic Gospels, with a parallel translation from the Greek (that of Tyndale) and enough comment to make possible at least a first acquaintance with the language to those who have not met it before, and would not easily know where to find it. Gothic is the earliest Germanic language of which we have any extensive knowledge, and without insisting that it should be widely known we feel strongly that it would be a very incomplete selection of texts on the Goths that gave no indication of its character.

Nearly all the texts we have chosen for translation are either unavailable, or are very inaccessible, in English. Most of them were written in Greek. We begin in Chapter 1 with the *Canonical Epistle* of the third-century bishop in Pontus, Gregory known as Thaumaturgus, the 'Wonder-worker', which is extremely revealing of the circumstances and aftermath of the earliest Gothic incursions into the Roman provinces of Asia Minor. Then follow, at some distance in time, two speeches of the orator Themistius, *Orationes* 8 (in part) and 10. These speeches are invaluable in defining Romano-Gothic relations in the reign of the Emperor Valens (364-78), and are also used in this book to provide the context for a survey of these relations in the course of the earlier fourth century. They have been translated by David Moncur, with annotations by him and by ourselves. We are grateful for the opportunity to incorporate these texts in our book, and look forward to the completion of his selection of other speeches of Themistius for a future volume in this series.

In Chapter 3, which is in many ways a counterpart to that on

Themistius, we describe and illustrate the archaeological culture which represents the period of Gothic settlement in the territories covered by the modern Soviet Union and Romania, and is divided between the archaeological research of these two countries. This chapter contains much descriptive material that might have been presented as part of an introduction to the entire volume or in many separate places in the course of it, and it offers more interpretative comment than one might expect of a collection of sources. However, we are not aware of any comparable, and certainly not of any accessible, attempt to synthesise the material and archaeological culture of the Goths. We think that it would be wrong to adduce the archaeological evidence merely in support of the literary texts we have translated, and that the attempt to describe it in its own right – as a sort of text composed of physical objects and situations – is well worth while. Our mode of reference has here been adapted to suit the particular nature of this material, and we present a full bibliography of archaeological material at the end of this chapter: all other bibliography is classified at the end of the book.

The fullest ancient literary text with any pretensions to describe Gothic society as if from within is the martyr-act known as the *Passion of St. Sabas*, and this forms the central document of Chapter 4 (it was with this text, in fact, that our idea for this book began). It is followed by the three letters of Basil of Caesarea that are the best evidence for the genesis and diffusion of the *Passion*, and do much to explain its character; and it is preceded by the brief narrative of the church historian Sozomen which both attempts to summarise Gothic history in the 370s, gives the fullest surviving description of the Gothic persecutions of Christians at that time, and introduces us to the figure of Ulfila. We have also taken the opportunity in this chapter to translate some briefer martyrological material surviving in Greek, and a fragment of a Gothic calendar commemorating martyrdoms and other events. At this point we introduce the Gothic language, by presenting the text of the calendar in both Gothic and English, and give also a schematic facsimile of the original document.

Chapter 5 presents evidence on the life and work of Ulfila, in the form of a fragment of the neo-Arian (or more exactly, Eunomian) church historian Philostorgius, which in its original form was probably the source of the passage of Sozomen mentioned above, and of a vigorously combative letter, preserved in a single fifth-century Latin manuscript, written after Ulfila's death by his pupil and admirer, Auxentius of Durostorum.

Material relevant to the textual history, methods of translation and vocabulary of the Gothic Bible is presented in Chapter 6, together with representations of the Gothic letters devised by Ulfila and a short extract of continuous text shown in facsimile and in its conventional transliteration. This prepares the way for the selection of passages of the Gothic Gospels in Chapter 7.

Two authors are conspicuously absent from our selection, in the first case only because his work is readily and recently accessible. We strongly recommend readers of our book to the Penguin translation, by the late Walter Hamilton, of the great Roman historian, Ammianus Marcellinus. The relevant passages of Ammianus are Books 27.5 and 31.3ff., at pp. 336f. and 414ff. of the Penguin volume. As for the Gothic historian Jordanes, we are sceptical of the value of this infinitely lesser writer as authentic evidence for the fourth-century Goths, of whom he wrote from an anachronistic and ideologically selective sixth-century standpoint. With the exception of a paragraph about the 'Lesser Goths' apparently descended from the community of Ulfila in Moesia translated at Chapter 5, n. 32, we refer the reader to the translation of the *Getica* by C. C. Mierow (2nd ed., Princeton, 1915; repr. Cambridge and New York, 1966).

Many readers of this book will already be familiar with the vigorous and highly distinctive work on the Goths, and on the barbarian world in general, of E. A. Thompson, notably in *The Visigoths in the Time of Ulfila* (Oxford, 1966). They should also know of Herwig Wolfram, *Geschichte der Goten von den Anfängen bis zur Mitte des sechsten Jahrhunderts* (2nd ed., Munich, 1980) in the English translation by T. J. Dunlap (Los Angeles and London, 1988), and should be warned of Peter Heather's forthcoming *Goths and Romans, 332-489* (Oxford, 1991). There is also a considerable body of specialised literature, on a subject that has not entered as fully as it should into the mainstream of historical study of the later Roman empire. Historical writing on any subject or period cannot and should not be separated from discussion and controversy, but this should be on the basis of a direct presentation of the evidence which, in the present case, is not so well known or easily available that it can be taken for granted. Both Thompson and Wolfram discuss the *Passion of St. Saba*, but neither offers a translation nor refers to one. Part of the contribution of our book will, we hope, be to have made accessible some primary evidence to enable the reader to control, and in general to read more constructively than would otherwise be possible, the interpretations offered by modern writers on the Goths.

We have tried to restrict our introductions and annotations to explaining the nature of the texts translated and particular textual and linguistic difficulties attending them, and to presenting essential circumstantial and background information; and we have refrained from pressing our opinions (not that we have always hidden them) on matters of historical interpretation which it is properly for the reader to decide. We have proceeded by separately preparing draft translations of specific texts or chapters and the annotations on them, and exchanging the result for discussion and improvement. We would like to put on record the enjoyment and benefit we have gained from these discussions, and particularly the working sessions on Themistius, which we have shared with David Moncur. In addition, we thank Neil McLynn for help in interpreting the letter of Auxentius and the Brixian preface, Robin Lane Fox for valuable suggestions on the *Passion of St. Saba*, Philip Beagon for advice on Gregory Thaumaturgus and Basil of Caesarea, and Bryan Ward-Perkins for help with the archaeological material presented in Chapter 3. Other improvements have been suggested by Margaret Gibson, Robert Markus, Ted Nixon and Mark Vessey, and we thank Dariusz Pajor, who visited Oxford from the Jagiellonian University of Cracow in 1989-90, for his assistance in translating the Russian publication referred to at Chapter 4 n. 12. We also acknowledge the contributions of members of the seminar on the Goths held in the History Faculty in 1988, at which we tried out some of our texts and ideas. The maps and the archaeological illustrations were drawn by Alison Wilkins of the Oxford University Institute of Archaeology, and the book has been printed from camera-ready copy prepared in Times Roman by WordPerfect 5.1 on the Olivetti laser-printer in everyday use in the College Office at Queen's College. We are grateful to the Murray Fund of the Faculty of Modern History, and to the Governing Body of Queen's, for financial grants towards publication.

Oxford, 16 April 1991.

P. J. H.
J. F. M.

LIST OF MAPS AND FIGURES

ABBREVIATIONS

AE	*L'Année Epigraphique*
ANRW	H. *Temporini, W. Haase (edd.) Aufstieg und Niedergang der Römischen Welt*
BAR	*British Archaeological Reports*
Blockley	R. G. Blockley, *The Fragmentary Classicising Historians of the Later Roman Empire* (see Bibliography, s. Eunapius)
CC	*Corpus Christianorum* (Turnholt)
CIG	*Corpus Inscriptionum Graecarum*
CIL	*Corpus Inscriptionum Latinarum*
CSEL	*Corpus Scriptorum Ecclesiasticorum Latinorum* (Vienna)
CTh	*Codex Theodosianus*
GCS	*Die Griechischen Christlichen Schriftsteller der Ersten Drei Jahrhunderte* (Berlin)
GRBS	*Greek, Roman and Byzantine Studies*
HAColl, Bonn	J. Straub & others (edd.) *Bonner Historia-Augusta-Colloquium* (Bonn, 1964-)
Jacoby, *FGrH*	F. Jacoby, *Die Fragmente der Griechischen Historiker* (Berlin, 1923-)
Jones, *LRE*	A. H. M. Jones, *The Later Roman Empire, 284-602: a Social, Economic and Administrative Survey* (1964)
JHS	*Journal of Hellenic Studies*
JRS	*Journal of Roman Studies*
JTS	*Journal of Theological Studies*
MGH, auct. ant.	*Monumenta Germaniae Historica, scriptores antiquissimi*
MIA	*Materialy i Issledovniya po Arkheologii SSSR*
Müller	C. Müller, *Fragmenta Historicorum Graecorum* (see Bibliography, s. Eunapius)
Mus. Helv.	*Museum Helveticum*
PG	*Patrologia Graeca*
PIR^2	*Prosopographia Imperii Romani (2nd ed.)*
PL	*Patrologia Latina*
PLRE I	A. H. M. Jones, J. Martindale, J, Morris, *The Prosopography of the Later Roman Empire*, Vol. I (1971)

RE	Pauly-Wissowa, *Realencyclopädie der Classischen Altertumswissenschaft*
SA	*Sovetskaya Arkheologiya*
SChr	*Sources Chrétiennes*
SCIV	*Studii ši cercetari de Istorie Veche ši Arheologie*
Sirm.	*Constitutiones Sirmondianae*
YCS	*Yale Classical Studies*
ZKG	*Zeitschrift für Kirchengeschichte*
ZPE	*Zeitschrift für Papyrologie und Epigraphik*

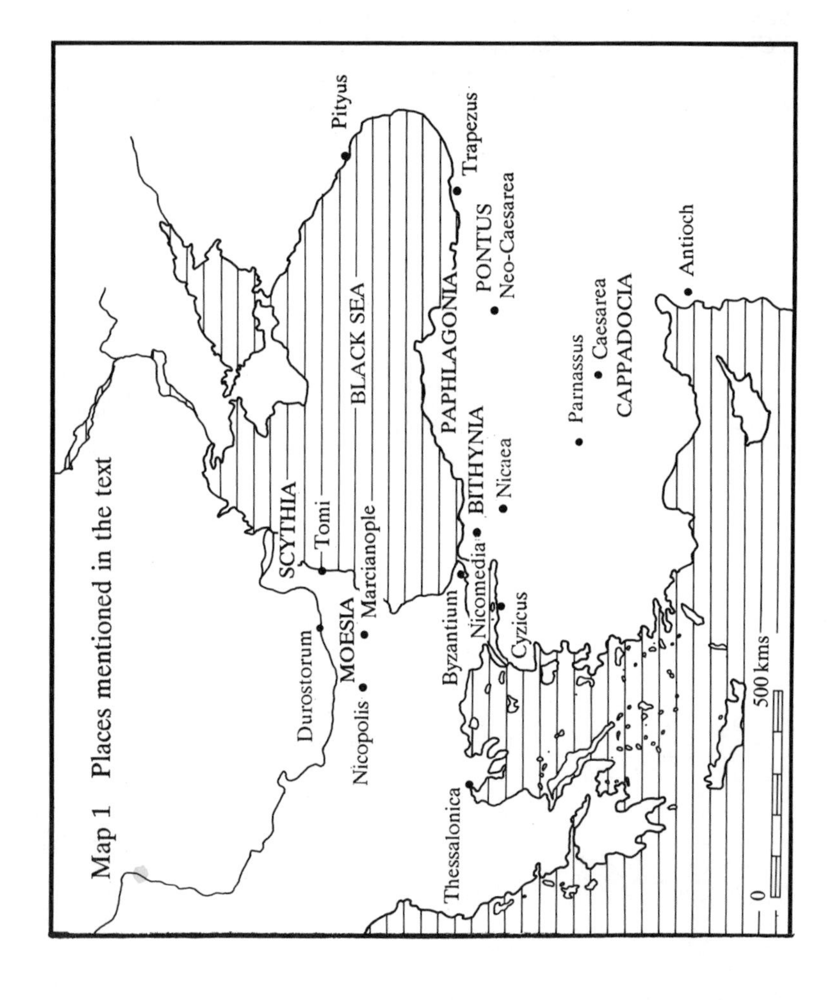

Map 1 Places mentioned in the text

CHAPTER ONE

THE CANONICAL LETTER OF GREGORY THAUMATURGUS AND THE THIRD-CENTURY INVASIONS

INTRODUCTION

Gregory, later known as Thaumaturgus, was bishop of his home city of Neocaesarea (formerly Cabeira: modern Niksar) in Pontus in the middle years of the third century. The exact dates of his episcopate are not known, but there fell within it the Christian persecution of the Emperor Decius (initiated in 249/50) and the invasions of Goths and others in the 250s which are the subject of his *Canonical Letter* translated here. It is possible, but not certain, that Gregory attended a council at Antioch in 264 or 265, at which Paul of Samosata was convicted of heresy, and that he lived on until the reign of Aurelian (270-5).[1] The *Canonical Letter* responds to queries addressed to Gregory by a neighbouring bishop, possibly of Trapezus, concerning the conduct of Romans during and after the Gothic invasions of Pontus and the breakdown of law and order that attended them.[2]

These invasions were a manifestation of the wider pressure building up on the Danube frontier of the Roman empire in the second and third quarters of the third century. Individual Goths, and perhaps even whole units composed largely of Goths, seem to have served with the Roman army in the east throughout the third century (the earliest evidence so far come to light is an inscription of A.D. 208).[3] Such recruitment is probably a sign that the movement of

---

[1]On the background and career of Gregory, see Robin Lane Fox, *Pagans and Christians* (1986), 516-42; Ray van Dam, 'Hagiography and History; the life of Gregory Thaumaturgus', *Classical Antiquity* 1.2 (1982), 272-308, at 272-4; F. L. Cross and E. A. Livingstone, *The Oxford Dictionary of the Christian Church* (2nd rev. ed., 1983), 600-1.

[2]Trapezus is suggested as the possible see of the recipient of Gregory's letter on the basis of Zosimus 1.33; below, n. 5.

[3]M. P. Speidel, 'The Roman army in Arabia', *ANRW* II.8 (1977), at 712-16, with full refs. The Greek inscription, the text of which was reported in *AE* 1911, 244, shows a detachment of what look like Gothic *gentiles* at a fort in the southern Hauran. Speidel translates (p. 712): 'Monument of Guththa, son of Erminarius, commander [*praepositus*] of the tribal troops [*gentiles*] stationed among the Mothani. He died at the age of 14 years. In the year 102, Peritius the 21st [= February 28, A.D. 208]'.

Goths (and other peoples) south and east from central Europe into the northern hinterland of the Black Sea was already under way by the beginning of the third century (for the relevant archaeological evidence see Chapter 3). These movements eventually precipitated conflicts not only between Goths and Romans, but also between Goths and other tribal peoples.

The Goths' first major incursion into Roman territory seems to have come in 238, when the city of Histria at the mouth of the river Danube was pillaged; for the next decade or so fighting was concentrated in and around Trajan's province of Dacia (encompassing Transylvania and the Carpathian mountains) and the Roman frontier along the lower Danube. This phase of fighting culminated in the defeat and death of the Emperor Decius at Abrittus in 251.[4] After this success, raiding became more widespread. In particular, the Goths and other tribes were able to force the cities of the northern Black Sea coast to provide them with ships (and presumably sailors) to enable them to raid the opposite shore of the Pontus. For the raids which followed in the 250s, Zosimus' *New History* (1.27 and 1.31-6) provides the clearest and fullest ancient account. Zosimus here describes three raids, the first two undertaken by the (to us) mysterious Boranoi, an initial and unsuccessful attack on Pityus on the north-east coast of the Black Sea (1.31.1-32.2) being followed by a more successful one which sacked both Pityus and Trapezus and ravaged large areas of the Pontus (1.32.3-33.3). This success encouraged other tribal groups, particularly the Goths, to undertake a third raid which devastated large areas of Bithynia and the Propontis (1.34-5). These raids perhaps occupied three successive years, which have been alternatively dated 254-6 and 255-7.[5]

The Goths might have been recruited by Septimius Severus after c. A.D. 196, when abortive movements of 'Scythians' are mentioned in a fragment of Cassius Dio (75.3; ed. Loeb, vol. 9, p. 198). In a later and better-known reference, troops from the Gothic and German ἔθνη (i.e. again *gentiles*?) are mentioned in the army of Gordian III in 244 in the *Res Gestae Divi Saporis*, edd. E. Honigmann and A. Maricq (1953), p. 12 (line 7); tr. Speidel, at 714: 'Gordianus Caesar raised an army from the entire Roman empire, and from the lands of the Goths and of the Germans, and marched to Assyria against the land of the Arians and against us'.

[4] See further Wolfram, *History of the Goths*, 43ff. with refs.

[5] For full discussion of the evidence of Zosimus, see nn. 53 and 59-63 in the ed. of F. Paschoud, identifying the ultimate source as the *Scythica* of the Athenian historian Dexippus: on whom, see F. Millar, *JRS* 59 (1969), 12-29, with a translation at 27f. of fr. 28 (Jacoby, *FGrH* II.A, pp. 472f.), in which Dexippus encourages his countrymen in their resistance against the invading Heruli. See also Wolfram, *History of the Goths*, 48f., and D. Magie, *Roman Rule in Asia Minor* (1959), 705-7 with refs. One

According to Zosimus, the aim of all these raids was booty – both human and material – which was taken back across the Black Sea. This fits very well with the kinds of situation envisaged by Gregory in his *Canonical Letter*. If the 'Boradoi' of Canon 5 can, as seems very likely, be read as 'Boranoi', then we have a second direct point of contact between Zosimus and Gregory, since this group of people is not otherwise mentioned in historical sources.[6] It is possible that it was in these raids of the 250s that the ancestors of Ulfila were taken from Cappadocia to Gothic territories beyond the Danube, as described by the fifth-century historian Philostorgius (below, Chapter 5). The references in the *Letter* to Roman captives taken by the Goths, and even (Canon 7) staying with them voluntarily, certainly illustrate the kind of circumstances in which such movements of populations and communities could occur; and, as we shall see, Philostorgius would at face value suggest that Ulfila's ancestors were captured before 260 (Chapter 5, n. 17). However, Philostorgius survives only in fragmentary form, and uncertainty must attend any inference which requires too precise a reading of his text. That Gothic raids into Asia Minor continued into the 260s and 270s is certain. In these years, the main focus of Romano-Gothic warfare was again the Balkans and adjacent European lands (including Italy), where the Emperors Gallienus (259-68), Claudius Gothicus (268-70) and Aurelian (270-5) won a series of victories which eventually curtailed the inroads. At the same time, sea-borne raids involving

---

of the most vivid individual items of evidence for reactions to the invasions is the Greek inscription from the oracle of Zeus Panamaros near Stratonicea in Caria mentioned by Magie, p. 706 (*CIG* 2.2717 = Le Bas-Waddington, No. 518, now revised by M. Çetin Şahin, *Die Inschriften von Stratonikeia* II.1 [1982], No. 1103):

> '[Oracle of Z]eus Panêmêrios. [The city, under the instructions] also of Sa[ra]pis, asks through Philokalos the son of Philokalos, *oikonomos*, [whether] the sacrilegious barbarians will attack [the ci]ty or its territory in the coming year. The god gave his oracle: I see that you are troubled but am unable to understand the cause of this. For I have arranged neither to give your city for sacking nor to make it slave from free nor to deprive it of any other of its good things'.

Since the inscription was actually put up (in the Council House), presumably the oracle was proven accurate. The cult of Zeus Panamaros is described (without mention of the oracle) by Ramsay MacMullen, *Paganism in the Roman Empire* (1981), 46f.

[6]Wolfram, *History of the Goths*, 50, adopts the same emendation. He considers the Boranoi to have been Sarmatian, but there is no explicit information in any source to this, or any other, effect. It is conceivable that the word simply means (from the Greek) 'men from the north' – in which case it will not be what they called themselves. Paschoud, n. 53 at p. 148, is not strictly accurate in saying that Zosimus is the only source to mention the Boranoi.

Goths and others (particularly Heruli) spread as far as the Aegean, and tribes from the northern Black Sea littoral were still raiding Asia Minor in the time of the Emperor Tacitus (275-6).[7]

Even if Gregory's letter may therefore not necessarily be associated with the precise moment at which Ulfila's ancestors were taken from Cappadocia, it is still a powerful evocation of the general circumstances relevant to this, and to Romano-Gothic relations in the mid-third century.

Our translation of the *Canonical Letter* is from the text printed in *PG* 10.1020-48; it is given there with the Byzantine commentaries of Theodore Balsamon and John Zonaras. The interest of these writers in the *Letter* reflects the fact that it came to be accorded authoritative status within the eastern church tradition.[8] This derived its canon law (rules governing the church and church procedure) from four main sources: from ancient tradition, most notably the collection of second- and third-century texts on church practice compiled in the fourth century as the *Apostolic Constitutions*;[9] from the rulings, or 'canons', of church councils, as collected from the early fourth century onwards; from public legislation, as preserved for example in Book 16 of the Theodosian Code; and from certain letters – the 'canonical letters' – of twelve Greek fathers, together (in Greek translation) with writings of Cyprian of Carthage. The most important of these fathers was Basil of Caesarea, who set out some 84 canons in a series of such letters.

Precisely when the status and form of the canonical letter were fully worked out is a matter of debate. It is however likely that the extant form of Gregory's *Letter* has been influenced by its later role in eastern canon law. This is most obviously so in the case of Canon 11, which is certainly a later addition to the text of Gregory, under the influence of the 'canonical letters' of Basil of Caesarea, or perhaps as part of a developing 'canonical' tradition that itself

---

[7] The sources for the raids of the 260s and 270s are much less straightforward than for the earlier raids. For an introduction to the problems, see Wolfram, *History of the Goths*, 52ff., with refs. The raid of 275-6 is recorded by Zosimus 1.63.1.

[8] The authoritative treatment of this subject is P.-P. Joannou, *Discipline Générale Antique (IVe-IXe s.)*, t. II, *Les Canons des Pères Grecs* (1963); text of Gregory, with introduction and French translation, at pp. 17-30.

[9] See the brief notice in F. L. Cross and E. A. Livingstone, *Oxford Dictionary of the Christian Church* (2nd rev. ed., 1983), 75f.

contributed to the form of Basil's pronouncements.[10] Of the Byzantine commentators referred to above, Zonaras has nothing to say of this Canon - which lacks manuscript authority - while Balsamon is content with a brief allusion to Basil. The division of the text into a number of separate Canons may also reveal the hand of a canon lawyer, seeking to facilitate reference to it. The separation of Canons 2 and 3, for instance, is artificial; the story of Achar in Canon 3 merely illustrates the point made in Canon 2 that unpunished theft will bring ruin to the whole people and not merely to the thief. It is also noticeable that Canons 6-9 all adopt the same opening formula ('Concerning those who . . . '), followed by a summary of the content of the Canon. In consequence the shorter Canons (6, 8, 9) are repetitive, the same thing being said twice. The explanation of this may be that what now appears as the first sentence of these Canons is in fact a descriptive title added later for ease of reference; this is indeed how these canons are set out and translated in the standard discussion of P.-P. Joannou (n. 8 above). It thus seems not unlikely that Gregory's letter was originally continuous, and that it was broken up into a number of Canons, some with titles, when its authority was recognised.

TRANSLATION

Canon 1

The question of the meat,[11] most holy father, does not weigh upon us, if the prisoners simply ate what their captors put before them: particularly since it is agreed by everyone that the barbarians who overran our regions did not sacrifice to idols. For the Apostle says, 'Meats for the belly and the belly for meats: but God shall bring to nought both it and them' [*I Cor.* 6.13]; indeed, the Saviour also, who purifies all meat, says, 'Not that which entereth into the mouth defileth the man, but that which proceedeth out' [*Matt.* 15.11]. So too in the case of women captives defiled by barbarians who offered violence to their bodies. If a person's past way of life convicts this person, as it is written, of going after the eyes of

[10] See Joannou's introduction, pp. xiii-xvii, with p. 17 on the 'inauthenticity' of Canon 11.

[11] The Greek text has here the plural βρώματα 'meats', more generally, 'food'. Our translation is an attempt to preserve acceptable English while retaining the allusion to *I Cor.* 6.13, cited in the following sentence.

fornicators,[12] then clearly the state of fornication is suspect even in a time of captivity; and one ought not readily to share in one's prayers with such women. But if a woman has lived in the highest chastity, and in her former life has shown herself pure and beyond all suspicion, and now falls into a wanton act through force and compulsion, we have an example to teach us in the book of Deuteronomy, in the story of the young maiden whom a man found in the field, offered her violence and lay with her: 'Unto the damsel', it says, 'thou shalt do nothing; there is in the damsel no sin worthy of death: for as when a man riseth against his neighbour, and slayeth him, even so is this matter: the damsel cried, and there was none to save her' [*Deut*. 22.26-7]. This is how these things are.

Canon 2

Covetousness is a terrible sin, and it is not possible in a single letter to set out the divine writings, in which not only is robbery proclaimed shocking and awful, but in general all passion for gain, and grasping after the belongings of others for immoral profit. Any such person is to be excommunicated from the Church of God. But that in the time of the invasion, amid such grief and lamentations, some should go so far to regard the crisis that brought ruin to all as the opportunity for gain for themselves, is the work of men impious and hateful to God, and their wickedness is beyond all measure. Therefore it seems right to excommunicate such men, lest wrath descend upon the whole people and first upon those in authority over them, who make no inquiry. For I fear, in the words of Scripture, that the impious man may destroy the just man together with himself: 'Through fornication and covetousness', it says, 'cometh the wrath of God upon the sons of disobedience. Be not ye therefore

12 'This person': the Greek word αὐτόν at this point is idiomatically correct, grammatically masculine because conveying a general application though referring in practice to the female sex. The context makes the literal translation 'him' unacceptable, but 'her' would be too specific for the Greek. The phrase 'going after [i.e. 'seeking'] the eyes of fornicators' (πορευομένου ὀπίσω ὀφθαλμῶν τῶν ἐκπορνευόντων) is a variation on *Jude,* v. 7, ἐκπορνεύσουσαι καὶ ἀπελθοῦσαι ὀπίσω σαρκάς ἑτέρας (R.V. 'Having given themselves over to fornication, and gone after strange flesh'), with the substitution of πορευομένου for ἀπελθοῦσαι for the sake of the word-play with ἐκπορνευόντων. πορεύεσθαι is in any case sometimes used in Classical Greek (esp. Herodotus) in the sense of men 'going to' women (and vice versa); cf. Liddell and Scott, s.v., II.2. The context in *Jude* of Sodom and Gomorrah also gives resonance to the idea of conviction for past sin expressed by Gregory; cf. also *II Peter* 2.10.

partakers with them; for ye were once darkness, but are now light in the Lord. Walk as children of light (for the fruit of light is in all goodness and truth), proving what is well-pleasing unto the Lord; and have no fellowship with the unfruitful works of darkness, but rather even reprove them; for the things which are done by them in secret it is a shame even to speak of. But all things when they are reproved are made manifest by the light' [*Eph*. 5.5-13]. So speaks the Apostle. So then, if certain people, even while paying the penalty for their former covetousness in time of peace, now, in the very time of wrath, again turn aside to covetousness, taking advantage of the blood and ruin of men who have been laid waste, taken captive, or killed, what else should we expect than that those who are so driven by covetousness should pile up wrath both for themselves and for the whole people?

Canon 3

See, did not Achar the son of Zara 'commit a trespass in the dedicated thing' and wrath descend upon the whole congregation of Israel [*Josh*. 7.1ff.]? He was one alone in sinning, but he did not die alone in his sin.[13] For us, too, everything that is not ours but belongs to another, which is a source of profit at this time, it is fitting to reckon a 'dedicated thing'. For that man Achar took from the spoil, as do these men of our time take from the spoil: but he took what was the enemy's, while these now take what belongs to their brothers, reaping a ruinous profit.

Canon 4

Let no man delude himself, and say that he has found (*sc*. something that is not his); for it is not right, even for a man who has found a thing, to derive profit from it. For it is said in Deuteronomy, 'Thou shalt not see thy brother's ox or his sheep go astray in the road, and disregard them: thou shalt surely bring them again to thy brother. And if thy brother be not nigh unto thee, or if thou know him not, then thou shalt bring them home [to thine house], and they shall be with thee until thy brother seek after them,

---

[13]Achar stole a garment, 200 shekels of silver and 50 shekels of gold from the spoils of Jericho which were dedicated to God. As a result the Israelites lost their next battle and 36 of their number against the men of Ai. Achar and his entire family were stoned to death and then burned along with all their possessions, in expiation of the sin. Our translation, 'dedicated thing', departs for clarity from the R.V.'s 'devoted thing' (A.V. 'accursed thing'); Greek ἀνάθεμα.

and thou shalt restore them to him again. And so shalt thou do with his ass, and so shalt thou do with his garment, and so shalt thou do with every lost thing of thy brother's, which he hath lost, and thou hast found'.[14] So Deuteronomy [22.1-3]. And in Exodus, it is said that not only if a man finds what is his brother's, but what is his enemy's, 'thou shalt surely bring these things back to their master's house again' [*Exod*. 23.4]. If then it is not right to take advantage of a brother or an enemy when he is living at ease in peace and comfort and unconcerned for his possessions, how much worse is it when a man suffers misfortune or is fleeing the enemy and is forced by necessity to abandon his property?

Canon 5

Others delude themselves by keeping the property of others which they have found, in place of their own which they have lost, in order that, since the Boranoi and Goths worked on them deeds of war, so they may become Boranoi and Goths to others.[15] I have therefore sent my brother and fellow-senior[16] Euphrosynos to you with this purpose, that he may deal with you according to the procedure we adopt here, and advise you whose accusations you should accept, and whom you must excommunicate from your prayers.

Canon 6

Concerning those who forcibly detain captives (who have escaped) from the barbarians. Something quite unbelievable has been reported to us as having happened in your country,[17] which can only be the work of faithless, impious men who do not so much as know the name of the Lord; and this is that men have reached such a point of cruelty and inhumanity as to detain forcibly some captives

---

[14]We show the Revised Version, with amendments of detail to conform to the literal sense of Gregory's Greek, which also differs in detail from the Septuagint. The phrase 'to thine house', present in the Septuagint (and in the Authorised and Revised Versions), is omitted by Gregory.

[15]We read Βοράνοι for Βοράδοι, given in the printed text of Gregory; see our Introduction and n. 6 above. Zosimus (1.27.1, 31.1) adds Goths, Carpi and 'Ourougoundoi', describing them all as people from 'beyond the Danube'; cf. Paschoud's n. 53 at p. 143.

[16]'Fellow-senior' is for the Greek συγγέρων, lit. 'fellow old man'. Gregory does not use the word 'presbyter', so 'fellow-elder' might be misleading.

[17]'Your country'; cf. n. 2 above for the possibility that the recipient of the *Canonical Letter* is the bishop of Trapezus.

who have escaped from the barbarians.[18] Send men out into the countryside,[19] lest divine thunderbolts descend upon those who perpetrate such wickedness!

Canon 7

Concerning those who have been enrolled among the numbers of the barbarians, and have performed outrageous acts against those of their own race. As for those who have been enrolled among the barbarians and followed after them as prisoners,[20] forgetting that they were men of Pontus, and Christians, and have become so thoroughly barbarized as even to put to death men of their own race by the gibbet or noose, and to point out roads and houses to the barbarians, who were ignorant of them;[21] you must debar them even from the ranks of Hearers, until a common decision is reached about them by the assembly of saints, with the guidance of the Holy Spirit.

Canon 8

Concerning those who brought themselves to attack the houses of others during the barbarian invasion. As for those who brought themselves to attack the houses of others, if they are convicted after accusation, let them not be fit even to be Hearers. If however they confess their own guilt and make restitution, they are to prostrate themselves among the ranks of the penitent.[22]

Canon 9

Concerning those who found in the fields or in their own houses

---

[18]The situation recurs in the invasions of the early fifth century; cf. *CTh* 5.7.2 and *Sirm*. 16, a law of 10 Dec. 408; *CTh* 10.10.25 of the same date, referring to Illyricum. Cf. *CTh* 5.6.2, of 23 March 409, restored by Mommsen to refer back to the law of December 408.

[19]'Send men out'; viz. as a commission of enquiry.

[20]Literary sources show that different tribes did supplement their numbers by making some prisoners full members of the group (see below, Chapter 3), but Canon 7 seems to be concerned with people who followed the raiders only while they were on Roman soil, since they remained within the scope of Roman episcopal jurisdiction.

[21]This too is a situation that recurs later – in the aftermath of the Gothic crossing of the Danube in 376: Amm. Marc. 31.6.6f. (the miners of Thrace). See G. E. M. de Ste Croix, *The Class Struggle in the Ancient Greek World* (1981), 477 and 479, also connecting the passages of Gregory and Ammianus.

[22]For the grades and conditions of penitence mentioned in this and the following Canon, see below, n. 26.

objects left behind by the barbarians.[23] Those who found in the field or in their own houses anything left behind by the barbarians, if they are convicted after accusation, let them likewise be included among those who prostrate themselves. If however they confess their own guilt and make restitution, let them also be worthy of participation in prayer.

Canon 10

Those who fulfil the commandment should fulfil it without any ambition for base gain, demanding reward neither for the giving of information, for returning a runaway slave, for restoring lost property,[24] nor recompense of any kind.[25]

Canon 11

[As explained in our Introduction, this Canon is a later addition to the text. It is translated here for the sake of completeness, and because it helps to explain the grades of penitence and forgiveness mentioned in some of the previous Canons.]

Lamentation (*prosklausis*) takes place outside the door of the house of prayer; and the sinner standing there must beg the faithful as they enter, to pray on his behalf.[26] 'Hearing' (*akroasis*) takes place inside the door in the narthex, where the sinner must stand

---

[23]What is meant is evidently property of other Romans, taken but then abandoned by the barbarians.

[24]The translation preserves the meaning of the Greek by expanding its different terms for specific forms of reward or recompense; μήνυτρον is for giving information, σῶστρα (neut. pl.) for returning a runaway slave, εὕρετρον for giving back lost property.

[25]Cf. *Sirm.* 16 (above, n. 18); a captive redeemed for money from the barbarians was expected to restore his purchase price to his redeemer. If he did not have sufficient money, he was to work for 5 years for his redeemer, and then regain his free status.

[26]For these grades of penitence see the Canonical Letters of Basil of Caesarea, esp. *Epp.* 199 can. 22; 217 can. 56, 61, 75. *Ep.* 217 can. 56 sets out the grades of penitence for a confessed murderer in a period of 20 years' excommunication regulated as follows: 'for four years (the penitent) should "mourn" (προσκλαίειν), standing outside the doors of the house of prayer, and begging the faithful as they enter to offer prayers on his behalf, while confessing his violation of the law. After four years he shall be received among the "hearers" (εἰς τοὺς ἀκροωμένους), and for five years shall leave (the church) with them; for seven years he shall leave the church praying in the company of those in prostration (ἐν ὑποπτώσει); for four years he shall merely stand (συστήσεται) with the faithful and shall not take part in the offering. When all these years of penance have been completed, he shall participate in the sacraments (μεθέξει τῶν ἁγιασμάτων)'.

until the catechumens leave, and then depart. For, it is said, the sinner may hear the Scriptures and the teaching but must then be put outside, and must not be thought worthy to participate in prayer. Prostration (*hupoptôsis*) means that one stays inside the door of the church and departs with the catechumens. Reunion (*sustasis*) means that one stands together with the faithful, and does not depart with the catechumens; and the last grade is participation in the sacraments (*methexis tôn hagiasmatôn*).

CHAPTER TWO

THEMISTIUS, *ORATIONS* 8 AND 10: GOTHS AND ROMANS IN THE FOURTH CENTURY

INTRODUCTION

Orator, philosopher, politician, Themistius is one of the most remarkable figures of the fourth century. Of Paphlagonian origin, he was apparently born, in about 317, at Constantinople (or, as it then was, Byzantium).[1] He spent his boyhood and youth in that city, and although there is some evidence that he travelled fairly widely in search of an education, he had returned to Constantinople by 337. The first part of his adult life seems to have been spent in academic pursuits; he quickly published an extant *Paraphraseis* of Aristotle, and began to teach in what was now the capital of the eastern half of the empire in the late 340s. His first known opportunity to make an impact on the political stage came in 350 when he delivered an oration before the Emperor Constantius II. Success soon followed; in 355 he was adlected to the senate of Constantinople, and was proconsul of the city in 358/9, the last city governor to hold that title before it was replaced by that of *praefectus*. Although public office came his way again only in 384 when he became prefect of Constantinople, in effect for the second time, Themistius had nevertheless spent almost the whole of the intervening thirty years intimately involved in imperial affairs. Though a pagan, he played a major role in the regimes of a succession of Christian emperors: Constantius II, Jovian, Valens, and Theodosius I.

Over a period of many years, Themistius delivered a series of political orations, or 'logoi politikoi', some 19 of which are extant; many were framed for occasions of the greatest importance, celebrating imperial consulships and other significant anniversaries.[2]

---

[1]On Themistius' background and upbringing, see *Or*. 17, 214c; *Or*. 34, §§12, 16 with *PLRE* I, pp. 889ff.

[2]See esp. the important study of G. Dagron, *L'Empire romain d'orient au IVe siècle et les traditions politiques de l'hellénisme: Le témoignage de Thémistios*, Travaux et Mémoires 3 (1968), 5ff. Photius, *Bibliotheca* 74, mentions 36 political orations, but it is not unlikely that he was in fact referring to the combination of public and private orations currently extant. Both the orations and Themistius' extant

Of these, we have chosen two - *Orations* 8 and 10 - to provide a framework for a description of Romano-Gothic relations in the fourth century before the arrival of the Huns.[3]

The choice of *Oration* 10 requires little justification. Like the vast majority of Themistius' speeches, it has never been fully translated, and its contents are central to our concern.[4] Entitled 'On the Peace of Valens', it was delivered in January or February 370 before the senate of Constantinople, in the presence of the Emperor Valens himself. Its subject-matter is the war between Valens and the Goths (or 'Scythians', as Themistius, like many other ancient writers, chooses to designate them) which had occupied the years 367-9, and the orator is particularly concerned, as his title implies, with the peace agreement which had brought conflict to an end. What emerges clearly from the speech, is that Valens' initial idea had been to defeat the Goths decisively, but that he had eventually decided to make a compromise peace. According to Themistius, this decision was taken from a position of dominance, and Valens had been persuaded to it by repeated embassies from the senate of Constantinople which Themistius himself had led.

The selection of *Oration* 8, or rather the second half of it, requires a little more explanation. The speech celebrates the opening of the Quinquennalia (the fifth year of the reign) of the Emperor Valens. If it was delivered on the correct day - and there is every reason to suppose that it was - then Themistius aired the speech in public on 28 March 368; we also know that it was given at Marcianople, the military base from which the Gothic war was being conducted, at the moment when the troops were being prepared for a second year of campaigning against the Goths (cf. *Or.* 8, 174/116; Themistius had witnessed military manoeuvres the day before he gave his speech).

---

philosophical works have been published in the Teubner series (ed. H. Schenkl, as revised by G. Downey and A. F. Norman); *Orations* 8 and 10 are both from Vol. I of this edition (1965). Our translations are based on this text, and our form of reference (e.g. *Or.* 8, 170/113) gives first the page reference to the Teubner edition and then the form of reference used by both this edition and the older one of W. Dindorf, *Themistii orationes* (Leipzig 1832, photographic reprint Hildesheim 1961).

[3] *Orations* 14-16 also shed light on Romano-Gothic relations after the Huns had forced the Goths into the Roman empire in 376; *Orations* 15 and 16 will be translated in the forthcoming TTH volume on Themistius by David Moncur.

[4] Some isolated extracts appear in translation in L. J. Daly, 'The Mandarin and the Barbarian: the response of Themistius to the Gothic Challenge', *Historia* 21 (1972), 351-79. Of the political orations, only *Oration* 1 has been translated, by G. Downey, 'Themistius' first Oration', *Greek and Byzantine Studies* [subsequently *GRBS*] 1 (1958), 49-69. An annotated translation of the private orations (20-34) is being undertaken by R. J. Penella of Fordham University, New York.

The speech sheds much light on the tax reductions of Valens and Valentinian (an important historical topic in itself), and contains also some references to the Gothic war. Of more fundamental importance, however, is Themistius' explicit connection of Valens' tax reforms with the conduct of foreign policy, with the argument that a reduction of the tax burden is of greater importance to the empire as a whole than winning great victories on the frontiers, which benefits only the particular area in which warfare is being waged (172f./114ff.). Given that Themistius was speaking in front of Valens in the emperor's military headquarters, there can be no doubt that this argument was meant – and would have been taken by its audience – as more than of merely general interest. It is to be read as a specific comment on the implications of financial policy for the Gothic war which was then in full swing.

Oration 8 is thus no less relevant than *Oration* 10 to the Gothic war of 367-9. It also raises the fundamental question of how we should read Themistius' speeches. This question will be more fully explored in the forthcoming volume translating a wider range of Themistius' political orations (cf. n. 3), but it is necessary here to define a basic approach to the orator's work with reference to the two speeches on the Gothic war.

Themistius consistently presents himself as an independent commentator upon the actions of different emperors. *Oration* 8 is devoted to a comparison of the Emperor Valens with Plato's ideal king, and in *Oration* 10 Themistius presents himself both as a philosopher commenting on Valens' conduct of war and peace (esp. 196f./129), and as the leader of an autonomous senatorial delegation, which argued that the Gothic war should not be pursued to its end (esp. 203/133). Commentators have taken Themistius' self-representation at face value, reconstructing his personal vision of the conduct of foreign affairs and discussing the orator's influence on the formation of foreign policy over the years.[5]

Once the texts are set in relation to the sequence of events on which they comment, however, it becomes clear that this view of Themistius cannot be sustained. Despite his absence from political office for thirty years, he must be seen as a publicist for successive imperial regimes. The speeches themselves make clear that Themistius spent a great deal of time at Valens' court, and was often involved at politically crucial moments. *Oration* 10, 197f./130 shows

---

[5] E.g. Daly, 'The Mandarin and the Barbarian', *passim*; Dagron, *Thémistios*, 95-112.

that Themistius was at Valens' side during at least one of the winters separating the campaigning seasons of the war, and the orator thanks Valens for the favour shown to him. It also appears that Themistius accompanied Valens' two senior generals on the diplomatic mission which paved the way for the 'summit meeting' between the emperor and Athanaric, leader of the Goths (202/133; see below). The extravagant degree to which he was willing to praise Valens is also evident. This is not to deny that the speeches reflect Themistius' own highly individual approach; his trade mark was a distinctive development of the concept of *philanthropia*, which made it applicable to a wide variety of political contexts.[6] It seems clear, however, that Themistius was saying things that successive imperial regimes wished to have said: presenting imperial policy in a way that had been agreed beforehand, rather than providing an independent commentary. The key to his success over such a long period was not only his oratorical skill, but also the adroit way in which he adapted himself to a number of regimes, some of which were antagonistic to predecessors whom Themistius had also served. The pose of philosophical freedom was most useful in this regard, allowing Themistius to swap masters the more easily because he could claim never to have been subject to one.

In *Oration* 8, we at once find Themistius very willing to disparage his former employers. Barbed references to forty years of steady tax increases (171/113), and to the unfitness for office of one descended from three generations of emperors (173/115) are aimed at the Emperor Julian in particular, and the house of Constantine in general. Yet it was Constantine's son Constantius II who had initially raised Themistius to prominence. Through his favour, Themistius entered the senate of Constantinople; we know too that he was allowed to share the emperor's table, and four speeches in favour of Constantius are extant.[7] But the second year of Valens' reign (365-6) had seen a dangerous revolt against him which aimed to put a member of the house of Constantine – Julian's uncle Procopius – on the throne. Valens survived, but it seems to have been a close run thing,[8] and Themistius' new employer had every

[6]For an introduction to Themistius' use of this term, see Daly, 'The Mandarin and the Barbarian', 354ff.; G. Downey, 'Philanthropia in Religion and Statecraft in the fourth century after Christ', *Historia* 4 (1955), 199-208.

[7]*Orations* 1-4; cf. *PLRE* I, p. 889f. on his career under this emperor.

[8]Cf. for a recent account, J. F. Matthews, *The Roman Empire of Ammianus* (1989), Chap. IX, at 191-203.

reason to wish to hear the age of the Constantinian dynasty presented as very far from a golden one. With the same adroitness, Themistius was later to attach himself to the house of Theodosius I after Valens' death at Hadrianople. Themistius' political speeches have a distinctive vocabulary and style, but they are not the commentaries of an independent philosopher.[9]

This is reflected in the fact that Themistius was criticised in his own lifetime for misusing philosophy - for pretending to be a philosopher, when he was in fact a flatterer, who used certain aspects of the discipline to further his personal ambition. The accusation is implicit in the Emperor Julian's letter to him (esp. 254B-C), and Themistius was allowed to play no part in this imperial regime, even though Julian regarded himself as a philosopher, and Julian's letter indicates that Themistius had already made a initial approach to the new emperor.[10] We might even detect some personal bitterness in Themistius' disparaging reference at the end of *Oration* 8 to Julian's having been awed by a miracle worker (Maximus of Ephesus), rather than paying heed, as Valens now did, to true philosophy.[11] When Themistius accepted the urban prefecture of Constantinople in 384, it was again claimed by some that his philosophy was a mask for personal gain.[12] Contemporaries knew that Themistius was more deeply implicated in the politics of successive regimes than he himself was wont to claim.

THE WAR OF 367-9 AND ROMANO-GOTHIC RELATIONS IN THE FOURTH CENTURY

As we saw in Chapter 1, many of the third-century invasions of Roman territory by Goths (and other tribes) were launched from bases on the northern coast of the Black Sea. Gothic raids penetrated imperial territory in the Balkans as well, but the Goths were not at this time the main enemy immediately beyond the

---

[9]We would thus see Themistius fulfilling a similar function for eastern regimes as that performed for the *magister militum* Stilicho in the west by the poet Claudian; cf. Alan Cameron, *Claudian: Poetry and Propaganda at the Court of Honorius* (1970).

[10]For references to the sources and discussion, see Dagron, *Thémistios*, esp. 36-49, 60-75, 218-235.

[11]180/120. Compare similar remarks in *Or.* 5, delivered before Jovian, 92f./63ff.

[12]Cf. Dagron, *Thémistios*, 49ff. esp. on the epigram of Palladas, in *Anth. Pal.* XI.292 (tr. Dagron, 51); in *The Greek Anthology*, ed. and tr. by W. R. Paton (Loeb, Vol. IV, p. 206), or by R. Aubreton (Budé, Vol. X, p. 173).

defended frontier; the Carpi, amongst others, were more of a direct threat.[13] By the second decade of the fourth century, however, the Goths were the major threat to the lower Danube frontier of the Roman empire (that is, the length of the Danube east of the Iron Gates, where the river breaks through the Carpathian mountains). The Romans had by now abandoned the province of trans-Danubian Dacia (essentially modern Transylvania) and set their frontier once again at the river Danube, where it had been before Trajan's conquests.[14]

As we shall see in Chapter 3, the Goths in the fourth century dominated a large area of what is now the southern USSR (cf. Map 2), but this area was not united under a single political authority. Ammianus mentions two political units, the Tervingi and the Greuthungi, and it is possible that there were more.[15] We do not know how far Roman interest extended into this territory, but the imperial authorities were naturally most concerned with that Gothic political entity which was closest to the actual frontier. From Ammianus' account of events of the 360s and 370s, we know that this group was called the Tervingi, and there is some indication that its authority extended from the Danube north-eastwards to the river Dniester.[16] It is thus usually assumed – we think correctly – that, when the sources talk of 'Goths' in general dealing with the empire at earlier points in the century, before Ammianus' detailed narrative begins, we should understand the action to have involved primarily the Tervingi. (In the secondary literature the Tervingi are almost always called 'Visigoths', as though they were the same group who later established a kingdom in southern Gaul and Spain in the fifth

[13] See Bichir, *Archaeology and History of the Carpi*, esp. chaps. 9-11.

[14] The title *Carpicus Maximus* seems to have been taken for the last time as late as 317: Bichir, *Archaeology and History of the Carpi*, 172, based on *CIL* 8.8412 (we find unconvincing the reading CA<P>P(ADOCICUS) for CARP(ICUS), supported by T. D. Barnes, *ZPE* 20 (1976), 153f.). Goths are attested beside the frontier in the 320s (see note 18), and, to judge from victory titles, some may have been in direct contact with the frontier by the 290s: J. Kolendo, *Eirene* 5 (1966), 144 and 148 n. 232. See, in more detail, Wolfram, *History of the Goths*, 57ff. On the abandonment of trans-Danubian Dacia, see the articles by A. Bodor, D. Tudor, and R. Vulpe in *Dacoromania* 1 (1973).

[15] See further, Heather, *Goths and Romans*, chap. 3.

[16] See esp. Amm. Marc. 27.5 and 31.3. At the time of the Hunnic invasions (mid-370s), the leader of the Tervingi advanced as far as the Dniester to meet the threat, and encountered some retreating Greuthungi who had made their camp there (31.3.3-5). The river may thus have formed a boundary between these two Gothic groups.

and sixth centuries. This is a demonstrable anachronism,[17] and we prefer to use the name given them by Ammianus. The reader will need to take account of this when relating what follows to other secondary accounts).

We know of three periods of military or diplomatic confrontation between Romans and Goths in the fourth century, before the arrival of the Huns overturned the established order beyond the Danube. The first period preceded a major peace agreement in 332. In the 320s Goths intervened on behalf of Licinius in his civil war with Constantine, provoking a full-scale military response by the latter after his victory over Licinius. This reached its culmination when the Goths were trapped and defeated by Roman forces in Sarmatian territory in 332. The peace which followed was disturbed in the second outbreak of unrest in the late 340s, by what seems to have been largely a diplomatic confrontation. We know little of its circumstances, but Libanius suggests that it was solved by Constantius II by negotiation rather than battle. This may also have been the occasion when Ulfila was forced to leave Gothic lands (see further, Chapter 5 below). Finally, the 360s saw a third phase of confrontation, the pattern of which was not dissimilar to that of the 320s and 330s. Valens' rule was challenged shortly after his accession by the rebellion of Procopius, a member of the house of Constantine. As in the 320s, the Goths intervened in imperial politics, again on the losing side, and, after defeating Procopius in 366, Valens turned his attention to the Danube frontier. Three years of military activity followed in 367-9, at the end of which another peace agreement was formalised, Valens meeting the Gothic leader Athanaric on board a ship in the middle of the river.[18]

Of these confrontations, we know most about that of the 360s because of the information provided by Ammianus Marcellinus and the two speeches of Themistius translated below; supplementary material can be found in Zosimus, in a fragment of Eunapius' history,[19] and in an oration of Libanius. These sources make clear that the peace agreement of 369 inaugurated relations of a much more distant kind than those which had prevailed before the war.

---

[17] For an introduction to this problem, see Wolfram, *History of the Goths*, chap. 3; and for a more radical approach, Heather, *Goths and Romans*, chaps. 1 and 3-6.

[18] The major sources are *Anon. Val.* 5.21-8; 6.31-2 (the 320s and 330s); Libanius, *Or.* 59.89f. (the 340s); Amm. Marc. 27.5 (the 360s). For refs. to other sources, see Wolfram, *History of the Goths*, 57ff.

[19] Zosimus' account (4.10-11) is likely to have followed Eunapius very closely, but all that we possess of the latter's original is frag. 37 Müller/37 Blockley.

Tribute or annual gifts were sent to the Goths before the war, but not after (Themistius, *Or.* 10, 205/135). The new agreement ended the arrangement whereby the entire length of the frontier was open for trade, confining it henceforth to two designated emporia (ibid. 206/135). Before the 360s, Gothic troops had also served with Roman expeditionary armies in the east (see below), but this was not the case in the 370s, and Themistius' *Oration* 10 puts tremendous emphasis on the importance of a heavily defended frontier to maintain security on the Danube (206ff./136ff.). All this suggests a change in basic strategy; before the 360s, the imperial authorities saw close relations – the economic, military, and political linkage of the Tervingi to the Roman state – as the key to peace, whereas, after 369, separation and a strongly-defended frontier were the order of the day.[20] It is probably no coincidence that the leadership of the Tervingi let loose a persecution of Christians immediately after the new peace came into force (see below, Chapter 4). Christianity was clearly associated with the advancement of Roman interests, and the persecution indicates a hardening of Gothic attitudes in the changed circumstances.

If the overall effect of Valens' Gothic war is clear, we also need to ask whose will the new peace expressed; the answer to this question will underly any interpretation of Romano-Gothic relations in the period before the Hunnic invasions. According to Themistius, Valens was dominant in 369; both militarily (*Or.* 10, 201ff./132ff.) and diplomatically (202/132; 203ff./134ff.). Themistius focuses his attention especially on the question of tribute, emphasising that payments, of gold coin and supplies, were stopped (205/135). Since it seems natural to suppose that the Goths would have wanted the payments to continue, Valens and the empire have been seen as the gainers, and the Goths the losers, from the war and the new peace agreement.[21]

This view of events cannot stand without challenge. In the first place, our evidence indicates that it was the Goths, and not the Romans, who were the real aggressors in the 360s. Even before Procopius' usurpation, Valens had sent troops to the Danube because the Goths were threatening the frontier (Amm. Marc. 26.6.11f.). Trouble had been brewing since the reign of Julian (Amm. Marc. 22.7.7f.; Eunapius, frag. 22.1 Müller/27.1 Blockley),

[20] All commentators agree on the basic effect of the 369 agreement; eg. Wolfram, *History of the Goths*, 68f.; Thompson, *Visigoths*, 13ff.

[21] E.g. Wolfram, *History of the Goths*, 66f.; Thompson, *Visigoths*, 13ff.

and Libanius (*Or.* 12.78) records that in 362 a Gothic embassy came to Julian asking for alterations to the terms of their treaty. The emperor dismissed the embassy, saying that the treaty could only be changed by war. No clash occurred in Julian's reign, and some Goths served on his Persian campaign, but the accession of Valens offered the Goths more hope of changing the relationship by force. There is no inconsistency between this hostility and the Goths' decision to assist Procopius, when they responded to a request which stressed the usurper's relationship to the Constantinian dynasty (Amm. Marc. 27.5.1). The Goths presumably intervened in the civil war (as they had done for Licinius in the 320s), in the hope of winning concessions from a victorious Procopius.[22]

Gothic aggressiveness is only at first sight surprising. Although we might expect the Goths to have been content to accept their subsidies in return for peace ('exacting tribute for staying their hand', as Themistius said; *Or.* 8, 179/119) and the freedom which they possessed to trade at any point on the Danube frontier, there were other matters, not mentioned by Themistius, which were a source of grievance to them. They were required, for instance, to perform military service for the empire. Gothic troops fought under imperial command against Persia in 348, in 360, and on Julian's ill-fated expedition.[23] After the Goths were forced by the Huns to enter the empire, the obligation to serve in Roman armies was a real source of friction.[24] It is also worth recalling that the relationship prevailing before the war with Valens was the result of Constantine's great victory in the 330s, which the emperor had celebrated with a victory column and annual games.[25] Eusebius and Libanius both assert that the subsequent peace agreement turned the Goths into Constantine's 'slaves',[26] and we must doubt whether its

[22]Wolfram, *History of the Goths*, 66f. views the close relations and tribute payments as welcome to the Goths, and has to make Valens the aggressor. He fails to take proper account of Amm. Marc. 26.6.11ff., and does not refer to Libanius, *Or.* 12.78. Similar is Chrysos, *To Byzantion*, 97ff. Thompson, *Visigoths*, 17f. makes the Goths the aggressors, but does not explain why the Goths should have wanted to change a relationship which, in his view, basically satisfied their demands.

[23]Respectively, Libanius *Or.* 59.89f.; Amm. Marc. 20.8.1; 23.2.7. The Goths claimed that the aid they sent to Procopius followed the precedent set on these occasions: ibid. 27.5.1.

[24]Cf. Heather, *Goths and Romans*, chap. 5.

[25]Wolfram, *History of the Goths*, 62 with refs.

[26]Eusebius *Vit. Const.* 4.5; Libanius *Or.* 59.89; cf. Brockmeier, 'Grosse Friede', 93f. with further refs. The sixth-century Jordanes presents the agreement as very favourable to the Goths, but this is another anachronism: Heather, *Goths and*

arrangements can really have satisfied them.[27]

To turn our attention to the Roman side, despite Themistius' claims in *Oration* 10 it does not appear that Valens had achieved a position of dominance by 369. In 367, most of the Goths escaped to the 'montes Serrorum' (Amm. Marc. 27.5.3f.), probably the south-eastern corner of the Carpathians;[28] only a few stragglers were cut off. In 368, an unusually high flood of the Danube prevented any major Roman attack, presumably because the necessary pontoon bridges could not be constructed. In 369, although Valens penetrated quite a long way into Gothic territory, encountering Greuthungi as well as Tervingi, there was again no major engagement. Athanaric resisted Valens' troops for a while, and fled after only light skirmishing (*leviora certamina*) (Amm. Marc. 27.5.3-6). Themistius (*Or.* 10, 201f./132f.; 211f/138-140) explicitly confirms that Valens won no major military victory over the Goths in these years.[29] This is important, because such a military success was what Valens initially had in mind. One of Themistius' aims in *Oration* 10 is to explain why the emperor had changed his mind and decided not to destroy the Goths when it was in his power to do so (esp. 198ff./131ff.). According to Themistius, he was dissuaded by senatorial embassies led by the orator himself (*Or.* 10 200ff./132ff.), but failure to inflict a decisive defeat on the Goths is a far likelier explanation.

We should not exaggerate the extent of Valens' failure. The Goths did not defeat him, nor even attempt to. He disrupted their harvests and halted all commercial transactions. They were thus anxious to end the war, and Valens agreed to peace only after turning away several Gothic embassies (Amm. Marc. 27.5.7-9; Themistius, *Or.* 10, 202/133). Yet Themistius explicitly admits that

---

Romans, chap. 3.

[27]Thompson, *Visigoths*, 13ff. argues that tribute payments were not part of Constantine's treaty, but this cannot be maintained. Julian confirms that these payments had been instituted by Constantine in the 330s (*Caesares* 329A); cf. Wolfram, *History of the Goths*, 63. On tribute, see further below.

[28]Cf. M. Cazacu, *Dacia*, n.s. 16 (1972), 299-302.

[29]Ammianus' account of 369 (27.5.6) is problematic, seeming to describe Athanaric as leader of the Greuthungi, and not making explicit the relationship of the skirmishing to the activities of Athanaric's force; we interpret them as the same, not separate incidents. Others (especially Thompson, *Visigoths*, 18f.) read Ammianus to suggest that there was a battle which Valens won, but Themistius, *Or.* 10, 201f./132f. and 211f/138-140 explicitly supports our interpretation. If Ammianus contradicted Themistius, we would follow the former (so Thompson, *ibid.*, 19 n. 1), but this is not the case here.

the peace of 369 incorporated something of the Goths' wishes (*Or.* 10, 205/135). This is hidden away in a passage devoted to the masterly fashion in which Valens dominated his summit encounter with Athanaric, but the point is of critical importance.

Valens' decision to compromise with the Goths should also be seen in the light of trouble in the east. In the late 360s, the Persian Shah Sapor ousted the rulers of Armenia and Iberia, who had been Roman allies, and replaced them with his own nominees. These manoeuvres are described by Ammianus after his account of the Gothic war (27.12.1ff.), but Sapor clearly began his intervention while Valens was still occupied on the Danube. Indeed, a reference in Themistius' *Oration* 8 to the arrival of the Iberian prince Bacurius in the Roman camp may indicate that Sapor had already made his move by winter 367/8 (174f./116). The Persians were a far greater threat to crucial Roman interests than the Tervingi, and it seems likely that Valens decided to make a compromise peace on the Danube rather than allow Sapor to pick off Roman satellite states at will.

There remains the question of tribute payments. The fact that the Goths received them before the war seems to contradict the notion that they were attempting in the 360s to change the nature of their relationship with the Roman state. Why should they have wished so to change a situation that was already in their favour, and does it not follow that the Romans are the more likely to have attacked the Goths than vice versa?

This is precisely the argument that Themistius wishes us to accept; it is however not conclusive. Gifts to foreign peoples were a constant feature of Roman diplomacy, used in different ways for centuries, and to interpret them as 'tribute', a mark of submission to the barbarian incompatible with Roman supremacy over him, is in some ways to miss the point. A display of generosity – giving more than the recipient can afford to return – is in itself an assertion of superiority, and gift-giving and exchange have long been a means by which relationships are maintained.[30] Such gifts increased the powers of patronage available to the foreign leaders to whom they were granted, and so reinforced the position of those with whom the

[30] For gift payments as a standard feature of Roman diplomacy, see for instance J. Klose, *Roms Klientel-Randstaaten am Rhein und an der Donau* (1934), 138; D. C. Braund, *Rome and the Friendly King* (1984), 62f. The classic study is that of M. Mauss, *The Gift: Form and Functions of Exchange in Archaic Societies* (1925; tr. R. Cunnison, 1954).

treaty had been made. This was to Rome's benefit, since the loss of face inherent in a surrender might otherwise have led to the ousting of these leaders in favour of others less amenable. Ammianus similarly refers to treaties whose form was dictated by native custom; the gain once more being greater security, since tribal groups were more likely to uphold relationships which they understood.[31] Even Julian's subjugation of the Alamanni in the 350s seems to have left them with rights to annual gifts, and Julian had been in a position to enforce his will much as he chose.[32]

The question is partly one of semantics. Gift-giving, while a standard feature of Roman diplomacy, could be labelled 'tribute', with all the pejorative implications of the term, if to do so were useful in any given circumstances. Even though he himself used payments on the Rhine frontier, Julian could disparage Constantine's payments to the Goths as 'a kind of tribute', using them as a stick with which to beat an emperor whose achievements he desired to minimise (*Caesares* 329A). In Themistius' case, the emphasis on 'tribute' has a different purpose. Like Julian, Themistius has to admit that the gifts provided for the Tervingi were not strictly 'tribute', but claims that this is what they *should* be called. So he is able, in *Oration* 10, to present the ending of the payments as a measure of Valens' success in the war (esp. 205/135).

As Michael McCormick's book has recently re-emphasised, the emperor as victor was one of the most fundamental images presented to the people of the later Roman empire.[33] They were fed on a diet of victory, and came to expect no less. Along with this, in imperial propaganda and in the Roman mind, went an entrenched belief in the superiority of the inhabitants (particularly the upper classes) of the empire as inheritors of Graeco-Roman culture, over the 'barbarians' who inhabited regions beyond the imperial frontiers. Thus Themistius can state that Romans are more rational than 'Scythians' (i.e. Goths) or Germans (*Or.* 10, 199/131 with note 80 below). This conjunction of expectations of victory and a sense of moral superiority, made it undesirable for a Roman emperor to be seen as in any way having been dictated to by so-called barbarians. Even a compromise peace had to be portrayed as entirely

---

[31] Amm. Marc. 14.10.16; 17.1.13; 17.12.21 (cf. 17.10.7, 30.3.6).

[32] The Alamanni revolted in 365 because Valentinian I reduced their gifts (Amm. Marc. 27.1.1ff.); Ammianus gives no indication that Julian's arrangements had been revised before this date.

[33] *Eternal Victory*, esp. chaps. 1-3.

determined by the emperor. This is the central message of Themistius' *Oration* 10, a subtle argument which removes from the Goths any control over events, and provides for its audience (the leading members of the political classes of the eastern empire gathered in the senate of Constantinople) the ending of the so-called 'tribute' as the criterion of imperial success.

An earlier phase of this propaganda is already visible in *Oration* 8 of 28 March 368. This speech identifies the ending of tribute as a potential mark of imperial success (179/119), and puts forward the argument that money is much better spent on a general tax reduction than on frontier warfare. This suggests that, as early as spring 368, Valens was preparing public opinion for the possibility that expectations of a total defeat of the Goths might not be satisfied. March is when the annual thaw on the lower slopes of the Alps and Carpathians feeds the tributaries of the Danube. By the end of the month, it was probably already becoming apparent that the Danube flood was going to be too great to allow a large-scale campaign north of the river in that year. Themistius was thus speaking after one year of fruitless campaigning, at the exact moment that the Danube was threatening hopes for the next. Valens may not yet have decided definitively to extract himself from the war by making a compromise agreement, but his propaganda was already beginning to allow for the possibility that, under the additional pressure of events in the east, he might be forced to.

We end with a brief word about the peace ceremony which ended the war, and which took place on board ship in the middle of the Danube. Ammianus tells us that this occurred because Athanaric claimed to be barred by a fearful oath and his father's order from crossing into Roman territory, and because he could not be forced to (*adigi non poterat*) (27.5.9). This remark is one of the most explicit indications which we possess in our sources of the limitations of Valens' ability to dictate to the Goths. The symbolism of the peace ceremony seems to confirm the point.

It was more usual for an emperor who had achieved a significant victory either to make the enemy come to him on Roman soil, or to parade imperial standards in the defeated people's territory, compelling their leaders' attendance upon him there.[34] This second means of displaying Roman power remained open despite Athanaric's oath prohibiting the first, but the leaders instead met in

---

[34] Cf. e.g. Amm. Marc. 17.12.9-16, 21; 18.2.15ff.; 30.6.1f.

the middle of the river, in a ceremony which would thus seem to have accorded Athanaric a symbolic diplomatic equality.[35] Themistius diverts our attention by picturing Goths beside the river cowering in fear (202/132ff.), and praising Valens' fortitude for standing in the sun (203/134), but Ammianus was not misled. Discussing later events, he noted that Athanaric feared that the ceremony of 369 would have left Valens with a grudge (31.4.13).

The episode strongly recalls a treaty of friendship made between Valentinian I and the Alamannic king Macrianus in 374. Valentinian had twice previously failed to destroy Macrianus' power: in 371 (Amm. Marc. 28.5.8ff.), and 372 (ibid. 29.4). In 374, he needed to deal with troubles in Illyricum, and courteously summoned Macrianus to a meeting on the Rhine (30.3). Like Valens, Valentinian conducted negotiations by boat, providing a second example in which a meeting in the middle of a frontier river is linked to an agreement where the relevant 'barbarian' king is in a less than subservient position to the Roman state. The similarities are obvious, both in the summit meeting and the pattern of events (frustrated Roman plans for domination) which led up to them. Seen in this context, the peace ceremony is a confirmation that Athanaric did indeed throw off some elements of Roman domination in the 360s.[36]

TRANSLATIONS (by David Moncur)

1. *ORATION* 8, 170/113ff.

[170/113] This then is the gist of my speech; that the less the king exacts, the more he bestows.[37] It is this that had long been absent from the Roman empire; rather the opposite tendency was established. Each and every year the taxes increased in size, with the

---

[35] Wolfram, *History of the Goths*, 68.

[36] Ammianus notes that the Goths 'sent submissive deputations', and given the heavy emphasis placed on imperial victory (see above), it is likely that the Goths had to make some kind of submission. No source describes a formal surrender, however, and Valens certainly conceded some of the Goths' demands; any submission was thus much more notional than the surrender of 332.

[37] Themistius often summarises in this way the main point he is about to make (cf. *Or*. 10, 198/130); it is conventional in Greek and Latin writing of the late empire, and indeed generally, to introduce an argument with a 'sententia', or pithy statement of its content.

year gone by easier to bear than the present one, and that awaited more onerous than both. Arresting this pernicious growth, you first held it in place against expectation and for three successive years the affliction did not make its usual advance; and in the fourth you reduced the level of the imposition. Decrees that were beyond belief were published: 'The measures of grain and wine you shall pay in taxes shall be reduced by such and such an amount, and for the future also shall fall short of what is customary by equal quantities'.[38] What can you say? When the king marches against the Scythians, when he stirs up total war, with no limit set on the issue of supplies, is it not welcome that we actually make no additional contribution to what is required?[39] In fact it will be incredible if the prevailing need does not double the taxes. But now when the occasion **[171]** demands lavish expenditure, you bring us back to our ancient frugality, not piecemeal, but all at once, considering well and with absolute wisdom that while it is preferable to increase hardships gradually – for so the application of the hardship may escape notice – in relieving difficulties, the more complete it is, the more obvious the change for the better. Because of this, those who made continual impositions of insignificant amounts over a forty-year period got away with doubling the taxes[40] while the contributions we shall make over to you next year shall be halved, if the measures of the return turn out according to expectation.[41]

---

[38]Valens' tax reductions are also mentioned by Themistius, *Or*. 10, 196/129, and confirmed by Amm. Marc. 31.14.2. His brother Valentinian pursued a similar policy. Themistius' account of these reforms is precise: taxes have already been reduced by a certain amount, and will be reduced by the same amount again in the next year (cf. n. 41 below) to achieve a total reduction of up to 50%.

[39]Zosimus 4.10.3f. likewise notes that, despite the need for war provisions, taxes were not raised unjustly in 366/7. Zosimus gives much of the credit to Auxonius, praetorian prefect of the Orient from 367-9 (*PLRE* I, p. 142f.). Eunapius, *V. Soph*. p. 479 (ed. Loeb, p. 454), reports that Auxonius was appointed to this office through the influence of Clearchus, who had been a friend of Themistius in Constantinople since the 350s (Libanius, *Epp*. 241, 508, 1430, 1452; cf. *PLRE* I, p. 211f.). Themistius alludes to a proverbial saying attributed to the Spartan king Archidamus, 'War is not supplied at a fixed cost' (ὁ πόλεμος οὐ τεταγμένα σιτεῖται); cf. Plutarch, *Life of Cleomenes* 27(48).3, *Life of Crassus* 2.8 and in other passages (cf. ed. Budé, Vol. XI (1976), pp. 70-1). The saying is also referred to by Synesius, *De Regno* 25 (ed. Terzaghi, p. 54; *PL* 66.1101A; tr. Lacombrade, *Le Discours sur la Royauté de Synésios de Cyrène* (1951), p. 70).

[40]A reference to the house of Constantine which held sole sway over the empire from 324 to the death of Julian in 363.

[41]For the tax strategy, see n. 38. 50% is an enormous cut in tax rates, and one wonders whether this is an early example of the economic theory whereby tax rates

Shall I tell you the reason for this? It is because you had charge of a household before a palace, and transferred your experience from the lesser to the greater field.[42] The comedy has it [Aristophanes, *Knights*, 542] that one should first hold the oar before taking the helm in hand. But there is no need for you to seek men to teach you with how much sweat farmers earn a hemiekton, an amphiekton and an amphoreus,[43] a single bronze coin or a stater of **[114]** silver or – what most men dearly love to see – of gold. You know how great an evil is dishonesty in a tradesman, bad workmanship in a scribe, corruption in a public official – all traits which multiply hardships. You came to this dais raised in the school in which Cyrus was raised in Persia, Philip in Macedon and Numa among the ancient Romans, whom the Roman senate snatched from his team as he ploughed in his shirt, and clothed in the purple.[44] Because of this you can look over this great empire from afar as if it were a single household and see its annual **[172]** income, its expenditure, its deficiencies, its surpluses, where things run easily, where with effort.

And so you alone among emperors do not raise those put in charge of the accounts above the military commanders, nor do financial officers go about looking down their noses at the generals, nor are public affairs dependent on their seals, but now they rival

are cut drastically in the expectation of maintaining revenues by stimulating extra economic activity. The full reduction is promised by Themistius only if the figures work out properly. It may also be relevant that Valentinian and Valens reconfiscated the independent endowments of the cities. This had gone on to some extent under Constantius II; Julian had returned all the city lands, but Valentinian and Valens renewed Constantius' policy, agreeing in the end to leave the cities with one third of their income (*CTh* 4.13.7; 15.1.18; cf. Jones, *LRE*, 732f.). The confiscated city lands were perhaps used to help fund a general reduction in overall imperial tax rates. A crackdown on corruption was also part of the strategy, cf. nn. 54, 64.

[42] Themistius is making a virtue of necessity. Valens was *protector domesticus* under Julian and Jovian (*PLRE* I, p. 930), but both Ammianus (31.14.5) and Zosimus (4.4.1) comment on the fact that he had held no great public office before being made emperor by his brother. Themistius is perhaps disarming in advance the objection that over-rapid promotions are of themselves undesirable (e.g. Eunapius, frag. 48 Müller/46.1 Blockley).

[43] The ἐκτεύς was equivalent to one Roman modius of wheat. As a liquid measure, it is the equivalent of about 2 gallons (imp.) and in ancient measures equals 8 χοίνικες and 32 κοτύλαι). The ἡμίεκτον (a genuine measure attested elsewhere) is thus half a modius of wheat; the ἀμφίεκτον ('double ἐκτεύς') would be 2 modii, but is otherwise unattested, and may be an invention of Themistius. The ἀμφορεύς was a liquid measure of about 9 gallons (thus 4.5 modii), 1.5 times the size of the Roman *amphora* measure.

[44] Themistius' knowledge of early Roman history is at this point faulty. It was not king Numa but L. Quinctius Cincinnatus who, according to legend, was summoned from the plough to become consul or dictator.

Aristides of old in the justice of their exactions.[45] In this way you show yourself to be more perceptive at understanding, anticipating and making light of technical intricacies, than those other emperors who just did the work and nothing more.[46] To pass over other matters, I say that this fact alone is sufficient reason for sending forth a single prayer, whose fulfilment is to the advantage of all.[47] And this is, not that Mesopotamia be recovered, or the Further Scythians come to their senses, or the Germans restore the cities they have pillaged.[48] For if we succeed in the first case, the Syrians alone shall be aware of it, if in the second, only the Thracians, if in the third, the Galatians, each neighbouring territory with its own triumphal monument. But a light hand in taxation is a boon shared by all who are nurtured by the earth. The enjoyment of plunder and captives falls only to those who have borne arms – nor is it equitable for some to get paid for conquering the enemy while those who pay them receive no share in the prizes.[49] But where all share the benefit equally, some taking more from the **[115]** enemy, others giving less from their own pockets, one could say that this was a triumph for the common happiness, this the true victory by which we shall gain the ascendancy over both the Scythians and the tax-collectors. And so the tax-gatherers[50] **[173]** shall not terrify

---

[45]Rivalry between military and financial officials could be fierce. As part of the price he had to pay for their support after Constantius' death, Julian seems to have allowed the eastern military to assert themselves over Constantius' civilian and financial officers: Amm. Marc. 22.3, esp. 7ff. Aristides the Athenian was a by-word for justice; cf. Plutarch's *Life*, chaps. 4, 6-7, 22, 24, etc.

[46]τῶν μόνον τοῦτο ἔργον πεποιημένων. The contrast in this allusive phrase is apparently between Valens, who has mastered the τέχνη, in the sense of 'skilled understanding', of the office of emperor, and other emperors who have performed it on a much lower level, as a routine task, or ἔργον.

[47]We now come to why the speech is important for Romano-Gothic relations. Financial good sense is offered as a justification for not pursuing further the war against the Goths.

[48]There were good reasons why warfare might have been pursued on any of these fronts. The Goths had supported Procopius against Valens, Mesopotamia had been lost to the Persians in 363 after Julian's disastrous campaign and death (Amm. Marc. 25.7.5ff.), and the Alamanni had taken advantage of the succession crises after Julian's death to raid across the Rhine (26.5.7f.).

[49]Though major victories over 'barbarians' were sometimes followed either by the selling off of captives as cheap slaves (Sozomen, *Hist. Eccl.* 9.5; Orosius, 7.37) or by their distribution away from the frontier as *coloni* to those who wished to claim them (*CTh* 5.6.3; *Pan. Lat.* 4[8].9.1-4).

[50]Themistius uses two words for tax-collectors (δασμολόγοι and πράκτορες) in close proximity; it is not clear whether they reflect different Latin administrative titles, or whether Themistius is merely varying his vocabulary.

me more than the barbarians nor shall the farmers' harvest be emptied out before it is gathered in, the money-lenders shall not stand beside those who bring in the vintage nor winter pass without festivals, the storehouses fallen into decay;[51] but rather there shall be good things in overflowing abundance: then shall I see the spoils of the Scythians, when no-one takes what is mine as spoil.

Know that these words now go abroad over every land and sea, or, rather, come together in one utterance – my own. We bring you this levy, receiving no small share of profit from the common fund but contributing goodwill from a store of unanimous sentiment: a contribution most honourable for a king to receive, thank-offerings for his goodness. And in return for the fruits of the earth which you have given up to us, it falls to you to garner fruits everlasting. For nothing that springs from the earth flourishes eternally or extends through time in the same way as a good and everlasting reputation.[52] This is what continually renews the reign of Augustus, keeps Trajan from growing old, and revives Marcus Aurelius each day; among whom I would like our king to be numbered. However their triumphs would bring no profit to the reputation of any of these remarkable men if, while being hard on the barbarians, they were not most beneficent to their subjects. It is of no importance to one who is ill treated whether it is a Scythian or a Roman who wrongs him; whosoever causes him to suffer wrong, that man he considers his enemy. Many of royal birth who receive the sceptre from three generations make their subjects **[174]** long for the barbarians.[53] But not now: domestic and foreign affairs keep step with the nature of your family; men at home rejoice while those abroad tremble.

So as a result of this conscientiousness you are not unaware how much must be spent, but daily reduce it where it is not necessary, so that you can be bountiful where it is. Now no one of those reputed

---

[51] Cf. Jones, *LRE*, 463ff. Agricultural production was the main source of tax revenue; hence Themistius' picture of the benefits of a tax reduction concentrates on the rural scene.

[52] Tax reductions were popular, and, in linking them causally to a cessation of the Gothic war, Themistius attempts to defuse any criticism that the war has not been fully won.

[53] A further disparaging reference to the dynasty of Constantine, and particularly to Julian, its fourth generation after Constantius I, Constantine, the sons of Constantine – particularly Constantius II – and Julian himself, Constantius' cousin.

to serve in the army has his name enrolled **[116]** fraudulently,[54] nor is he a soldier, merely to the point of wearing a uniform. Either he provides the reality of the service into which he has enrolled himself or he is rejected. While once there was a muster of grand titles in the ranks, now the soldier actually is a soldier, the horseman truly that, the javelin thrower not merely so in name. Only yesterday I saw an army, better trained than any chorus. Homer is obviously quite outdated in admiring Menesthenes as one fit to handle infantry and cavalry. The poet did not know the ordered movement of your phalanx, the instinctive understanding of your cavalry or those trained to live with their weapons, nor was he ever struck with joyful amazement at such a sight. He would, I believe, mock the story of the line and the dove, having seen the mobile archers who, leaving the reins to their steeds, shoot more accurately than those with their feet on the ground.[55]

It is not surprising that Priam called Agamemnon blessed for bringing so many Phrygian soldiers from Greece [*Iliad* 3.164ff.]. Now in your case, there is a man who, rejecting his ancestral **[175]** throne – and that of no obscure kingdom – comes as a wanderer to bear arms: a good omen of victories in the East.[56] What at least is clear from all this is that the sum and essence of all that I have said relates to you. For he who instils in each man the desire to accomplish his own particular part is responsible for the success of the whole venture. Each man is enthusiastic, firstly when he knows that he does not go unnoticed, then when he receives the reward for

---

[54] Roman military commanders filed regular returns on the number of troops in their commands, and received the appropriate amount of pay from the office of the praetorian prefect. A commander could reduce actual numbers while keeping the registers full of bogus names, and pocket the extra pay. See Jones, *LRE*, 623ff. According to Ammianus (31.14.2), Valens was very harsh with corrupt officials, a feature of Valens' rule noted again in *Or.* 10.

[55] I.e. Homer would mock his own story, which is told at *Iliad* 23.850ff. In the archery competition which figured among the funeral games for Patroclus, a bird was tethered by a line. Teucer missed the bird and cut through the line with his arrow, but Meriones won the greater prize for bringing down the bird in untethered flight. Valens' mounted archers were even more accurate than Homeric heroes standing on the ground.

[56] This must be the Iberian prince Bacurius, known from other sources to have served in the Roman army from the 370s onwards until his death at the battle of the Frigidus in 394 (*PLRE* I, p. 144). This reference has not, as far as we know, previously been identified, and suggests that it was precisely at this juncture (i.e. in 367/8) that he entered Roman service. Themistius uses Bacurius' arrival to look forward to future success in the east (i.e. against Persia), but it proved elusive (Amm. Marc. 29.1; 30.2); Valens was still embroiled there when the Goths arrived on the Danube in 376 (*ibid.* 31.7.1f.).

his virtue. With you, the successful man can neither be overlooked nor, once noticed, remain unrewarded.[57]

But now, while you scrutinise the commanders and captains and your two generals are above suspicion,[58] do you overlook the civilian officers? Is it possible for one of them to escape detection in taking bribes or in enforcing exactions beyond what is laid down, **[117]** or in perverting justice or in some other way abusing those in his power? Not so: you oversee and overhear all things as if standing close by – almost like a personal witness of everything each man says or does. You cast your eyes over all things – as Homer says that Zeus turned his two eyes from Ida far over the horse-rearing Thracians and the Mysians who fight at close quarters [*Iliad* 13.3-5]. You look out from Mysia over the Phoenicians and are much vexed at the wrongs they suffer.[59] It is for this reason that you have brought about a dearth of office-seekers; now no market for offices is open, nor are governorships announced for sale like market goods, but the **[176]** ancient dignity has returned to justice and experience. And if anyone is found to possess these qualities, he will have no need to petition for tablets of appointment[60] but will serve the common good, even against his inclination. When Satibarzanes petitioned Artaxerxes for a satrapy to which he was unsuited, with an offer of three thousand darics, Artaxerxes gave him back the money and refused him the office. For in giving such a sum of gold, he said, 'I shall be none the poorer, but to entrust office to a bad man would be quite unjust'.[61] Nothing must be of greater

[57]This passage recalls Zosimus' story (4.11.2f.) that Valens offered his troops a monetary bonus for every Gothic head they produced during the war of 367-9.

[58]The two generals are Valens' senior commanders: the *magister equitum* Victor and *magister peditum* Arintheus. They were sent to negotiate with the Goths in 369; Amm. Marc. 27.5.9.

[59]Possibly a reference to the revolt of the 'Saracen Queen' Mavia, which troubled Phoenicia and Palestine until 373/4. If so, this dates the outbreak of trouble more closely than the other sources; cf. *PLRE* I, p. 569.

[60]πινακίδες are writing tablets, here the formal letters of appointment given by emperors to their officials; they are described as 'tabulae' by Claudian (*Carm. Min.* XXV, 85), otherwise as δέλτοι or 'codicilli', and, at least in the case of higher officials, were made of ivory trimmed with gold (cf. Themistius, *Or.* 18, 224b). They are among the objects shown in the illustrations to the *Notitia Dignitatum*, cf. the full discussion of Robert Grigg, 'Portrait-bearing codicils in the illustrations of the *Notitia Dignitatum*', *JRS* 69 (1979), 107-24.

[61]A version of this story, with the same participants, is told by Plutarch, *Sayings of Kings and Commanders*, 173E (*Moralia*, ed. Loeb, Vol. III, p. 18). Plutarch gives a figure of 30,000 for 3,000 darics (these are gold coins, first struck by Darius I) and describes a slightly different situation. It may be that Themistius has deliberately adapted the story to his context, opposition to the sale of office. Like the emphasis

importance to the king than the body of his kingdom. For it would be no mistake to call the land under his rule the body of the kingdom. As with our bodies, when, if any part of it is in distress, it transmits the pain to the whole, so it is with the whole kingdom: if a single city fares ill, it does not allow the empire as a whole to be in good health.

Now I hear that many emperors of the past were most concerned that their hair should not appear to be growing thin yet looked on while entire cities fell into ruin, and spent their time making up their eyes but were not troubled at allowing the land to go untended. They would not use horses that had not been extensively schooled yet would employ men for the most responsible positions without scrutiny. When spectators in the arena, they would not countenance charioteers who did not drive to perfection but thought it of no importance to entrust the reins of the cities to anyone at all, ignorant of the fact that everyone who takes office assumes the likeness in miniature of **[177/118]** the kingdom.[62] Men judge the appearance of the original from its image. They cast down a statue as absurd if it is not entirely lifelike, and at once erase the picture if it bears no resemblance to what is being copied. But when it comes to living likenesses, they care not if they are done carelessly. And yet a bronze image that does not preserve the likeness of the king does no harm to those who look on it, but a governor who does not bear your stamp spells doom and disaster for those bidden to submit to him, and transforms the power that had fallen to him for good, to its opposite. You do not bestow their swords and javelins upon the soldiers to use against us if they should so choose, but to be employed on our behalf against the barbarians. If anyone thinks that he should enjoy ill-gotten gains from a nobly given weapon, he undergoes punishment as a plain murderer, not a soldier. A man who has been ordered by you to guard the flock but turns out to be a wolf rather than a shepherd, you allow to reap the reward that is due to him.

---

on tax reduction, this part of Themistius' speech finds its echo in Ammianus, who reports that Valens took particular care over official appointments and the conduct of his officers (31.14.2).

[62]It is unlikely that Themistius is referring in more than general terms to these archetypal failings of emperors of former times; however, Caligula and Domitian are said by Suetonius to have been worried by their baldness, Nero, L. Verus and Commodus were notorious lovers of horses and chariot-racing, and Elagabalus made up his face and eyes. The shortcomings in government connected with these failings in imperial conduct are chosen for their relevance to fourth-century conditions and to Themistius' argument, rather than for their historical accuracy.

So, taking such great pleasure in your rule as I do, I am overjoyed at this above all else, that you have set in place this long disregarded law and know to demand of your friends as gifts, **[178]** not horses or hounds, by Zeus – for it is for kings to give rather than receive these – but good men fit for authority, without whom your subjects would have no inkling of your care for them. Even if you exact just one choenix or a single kotule,[63] all the respect you gain from this bears no fruit and passes unremarked if the exaction is badly administered. There is nothing so onerous in the tax assessments that, taken in itself, it cannot easily be met: it is in the particularities – the 'when' and 'how', the 'not there but here', 'not tomorrow but at once' – these are what make the small matter large, the easy difficult, the two obols' into a talent's worth. These are questions which cannot be determined in law, for their nature is not such as to admit a fixed form.[64] What is needed is an embodiment of the law[65] which accommodates itself to each particular case, and justice at a more everyday level which is always sympathetic to the people's present circumstances. Such men are needed who shall administer the parts for him upon whom the whole depends – **[119]** a fitting name for this totality would be the universe – whose most important aspect, salvation, is the province of God, with each man guiding whatever part he has been assigned by Him. This is the order that you consider that the world which you govern must enjoy.

Now this speech, moving in its quiet progression from one topic

---

[63] Cf. n. 43 above; these are proverbially small measures.

[64] The Greek in this passage is slightly expanded for clarity. The imperial government calculated a lump sum exaction from each city (and surrounding territory), based on its assessed number of tax units. There was considerable discretion, however, in how this lump sum was allocated and when it was to be collected, and in this discretion resided much scope for corruption. Themistius is perfectly correct to focus attention on the specific details of tax collection, as much as on the centrally set overall tax rate. Valentinian and Valens attemped to cut down on such corruption at the very start of their reigns by shifting the responsibility for allocation and collection away from the city councils towards retired officials from the office of the provincial governor, explicitly because the former were too corrupt (*CTh* 12.6.9 – of 365 – quoted by Jones, *LRE*, at p. 146; other laws relevant to the campaign are *CTh* 12.6.5-8; 8.3.1; 8.6.23; 8.7.8).

[65] The idea of the virtuous king as the living embodiment of law (νόμος ἔμψυχος) is central to Hellenistic discussions of kingship; cf. Erwin R. Goodenough, *Yale Classical Studies* 1 (1928), 55-102; Aristotle expresses in passing a similar conception of the good judge as 'a sort of living justice' (οἷον δίκαιον ἔμψυχον, *Nicomachean Ethics* V, 1132a; Goodenough, 63). Themistius compresses the idea, writing not of the law as incarnate in someone else (king, judge, emperor), but as possessing a living soul in itself, able to rise by wisdom above the inflexible restrictions of written law.

to another, has somehow surpassed in its many marks of **[179]** distinction the total given by Plato.[66] For the king should not only be generous, but must also be a strict examiner of the <revenue> . . . . overseeing both the lesser and greater affairs of his subjects. In short, he has done what not even Plato dared bring together in his discourse, and revealed himself to possess all these qualities in reality. At this point (our speech) takes a stand and circles round, <testing> easy hypothesis against the truth in practice, both with regard to the king's valour and his disposition in face of dangers,[67] to see if in any way the king possesses these qualities in lesser measure than Plato prescribed. What I shall say will in the first instance concern both emperors. They assumed command of the empire when it was like a ship assailed from all sides;[68] events in the East had hewn it at the edges, and what the enemy did not expect to gain by arms they bought with treaties. The Germans were disturbing the West and, checking its course slightly, did not so much alarm as irritate; the Scythians loomed threateningly over the middle territories and exacted tribute for staying their hand. Taking on such a circle of war and peace, all vying with each other in wrongdoing, you suffered the opposite of what one might have guessed; those who stayed their hand gave you more trouble than those who went to war.[69]

And so: what remains of our marks of distinction? Have we forgotten any? Come; I shall consult the words of Plato. He seeks a king who is young, learned, mindful, kind, brave, self-controlled and great-hearted.[70] Now concerning self-control, what need is there of words when we see him subjecting his **[180]** body with thirst, hunger, living the outdoor life each and **[120]** every day,

---

[66]Themistius now picks up an allusion to Book 5 of Plato's *Republic* (473c-d, described by Jowett and Campbell as 'the keystone of the Republic') from the earlier part of his speech, not translated here (162/107c). For the 'marks of distinction', see n. 70 below.

[67]The text has suffered damage at various points in this passage. Our translation is not an attempt to restore it, but to indicate what seems to be its logic. This advances in the first lacuna (shown at lines 3-4 of this page) from what the good king *should* do to what Valens has in fact done.

[68]Cf. above, note 48; Amm. Marc. 26.4.5-6 takes a similar view of the problems facing the two emperors (the passage is in part an anticipation of future events, rather than an account of what was happening at the exact moment of Valens' coronation).

[69]I.e. the Goths were a greater problem than the Germans (Alamanni) or Persians; as we have seen, they first threatened the Danube and then sent aid to Procopius. On the significance of Themistius' emphasis on tribute, see our Introduction.

[70]See *Republic* VI, 503c-d.

delighting in a single wife with whom he is joined in marriage – and that at the prime of manhood, when the promptings of nature are hard to resist even for men in private life? Moreover, from this sacred and holy match there comes a most divine shoot, much beloved and prayed for, whom I would fashion into Alexander, and philosophy once again would boast of having such a one as her charge.[71] He offers me even now proofs of his royal identity, a thoughtful countenance. No jester leads him beyond the measure, no miracle man awes him,[72] as is right for one who in future will take delight in philosophy and have other things to admire. May God bring this prayer to pass for us.

2. *ORATIO* 10; 'ON THE PEACE'.

[196/129] I did think that you had already had more than your fill of me, so often have I held forth in times gone by, and it was for this reason that I was reluctant to come forward to speak again now, so as to avoid seeming unnecessarily wearisome to you. Yet since you do not allow to remain in retirement even one who most earnestly desires to do so, but consider that a contribution should also come to you from oratory just like an annual payment of tax, I must yield, and from this take, if I may, my opening remarks. For, of all the blessings that oratory receives from you, there is none that should take precedence over its own high place in your regard.

Indeed, this is the first of my praises of you, Your Majesty, that while eager to relieve the farmers of their financial duties to the state,[73] you offer no such accommodation to philosophers; you would cheerfully see the former paying over in each successive year a decreasing proportion of what they produce while exacting an ever increasing levy from oratory. And what is still more surprising than this, is that of these same words you hold ours in greater esteem

[71]Valens' wife was Domnica, from a military family; her father Petronius 3 commanded a legion of the *comitatenses* (*PLRE* I, p. 690); the son referred to is Valentinian Galates, born on January 18 366; he died young, probably in 370 (*PLRE* I, p. 381). In expressing the hope that he will be able to fashion Valens' son into a new Alexander, Themistius by extension casts himself as Aristotle; he re-used this conceit in January 383 of Theodosius' son Arcadius (*Or*. 16, 293f./204).

[72]A final disparaging reference to the Emperor Julian: this time to his admiration for Maximus, the Neo-Platonist philosopher and theurgist, generally considered a trickster by our sources (Maximus 21: *PLRE* I, p. 583f.).

[73]See *Or*. 8, nn. 38-9, 41.

than those of men who share your tongue.[74] There is, however, a reason for this. For since you are not dependent on the form of the words but seek after their informing thought, you succumb not to the beauty of the spoken word but to the order of the argument. This is why, as is right, philosophy holds a more honoured station at **[197]** your court than rhetoric. For what you hold in the highest esteem is exactly what this art has pursued most assiduously – to render the thought and not the utterance noble, and to study the means whereby a man might speak not for the greatest pleasure of his audience but for their greatest benefit. It is this, I observe, that gives you most pleasure. For while you are suspicious of flatterers, you render yourself compliant and amenable to your advisors.[75] It was Callisthenes whom Alexander, unable to bear his forthright speech in enjoining him to abide by **[130]** Macedonian customs, cast down.[76] You in contrast summon philosophers to your side even if they demur, and for however long a period you are detained in the field, keep winter quarters with philosophy. Philosophers and generals share the place of honour, and the bodyguard of counsel and might, serving you together, weaves around you a web of utmost beauty.[77] This is why the poets also bring Athena to birth from the head of Zeus, revealing in a most pleasing fashion that neither reason without action nor action without reason are fitting accompaniments for kings, but that thought brings about action and activity has its complement of thought.

Past history bears this out: for, if you bring to mind Alexander or Augustus or Marcus Aurelius, you will discover that they advanced to the height of their reputations for no other reason **[198]** than that the soldiers' and the philosophers' cloaks kept close quarters. Aristotle was honoured no less than Parmenion, Arius no less than

---

[74]Born at Cibalae in Pannonia (Lib. *Or.* 19.15, 20.25 cf. *PLRE* I, p. 930f.) Valens was from the Latin-speaking half of the empire, and spoke no Greek; cf. Themistius, *Or.* 6, 106/71c-d. Ammianus calls him 'something of a boor, with little skill in the arts of either war or peace' (31.14.5). In the same passage of *Or.* 6, Themistius himself disavows knowledge of Latin.

[75]Themistius here attempts to convince his audience that the subsequent praises of Valens are those of an independent philosopher.

[76]Callisthenes of Olynthus accompanied Alexander's expedition as its historian. His refusal to prostrate himself lost him favour; he was executed after being implicated in the plot of Hermolaus (Arrian, *Anabasis*, 4.10.1-4).

[77]An unusually picturesque reference to the consistory, made up of the emperor and senior military and civilian officials. It had no constitution or fixed membership, but provided a forum where emperors and their chief advisors could agree and publicise their regime's policies; Jones, *LRE*, 333-41.

Agrippa.[78] But, in the case of those who have become more devoted either to philosophy or to war, even that part of their achievement which they thought worthy of effort has vanished along with what they disregarded. There can be no tales of glory without the deeds to substantiate them, nor can these deeds pass into the future without report to escort their remembrance. Now while it may be that the words of the poets and the orators do perhaps possess some edifying content or other, they overlook what should have been taken especially to heart. For they are seeking after action on the grand scale, not virtue, and so dwell in their stories on battle orders, wars and the tally of the dead, the major part of their panegyrics consisting of death and destruction. No one ever considers an opportune and properly disposed peace more estimable than a multitude of trophies, but this is not the way things are: contempt for conquest often brings more honour than its accomplishment.

This will stand as the gist of what I now have to say.[79] For I am not so ignorant of the divinely inspired Plato as **[131]** not to know his precept – that both king and legislator are deficient if ready for war but unable to make peace [cf. *Laws*, 628D-E]. It was on this point, I think, that he censured Lycurgus **[199]** the Spartan: for establishing a state suitable for men going to war but difficult to manage once they had laid aside their weapons. This is the act of one who had overlooked the better of the two aspects, for which the other is a necessary condition. The prize of war is peace and when men have to go on campaign, they do so not to remain under arms for ever but in order to live a safe and quiet life. Whoever, therefore, is ready to train for ceaseless activity but cannot organise leisure does a disservice to the more noble aspect.

I have yet greater admiration for Plato for this, when he teaches us that the seeds of war and peace exist first within each and every soul and that whoever can live at peace with himself can do so with his external foes [*Laws*, 628E]; but the man for whom a truce with himself is impossible, would scarcely welcome peace with others. There is in each of us a barbarian tribe, extremely overbearing and intractable – I mean the temper and the insatiate desires, which stand opposed to the rational elements as the Scythians and

---

[78] Aristotle and Arius were the teachers of Alexander and Augustus respectively. Parmenion served as general of both Philip II and Alexander, Marcus Vipsanius Agrippa was a trusted advisor and general of Augustus.

[79] Cf. *Or*. 8; n. 37 above.

Germans do to the Romans.[80] And so, just as it is neither possible nor expedient to wipe out entirely these passions when they rise up against the better element – passions which nature has implanted in the soul for a purpose – since it is virtue's task to render them submissive and amenable to the dictates of the intelligence; **[200]** so it is the task of kings – those who have a right to that title – rather than rooting out completely this surfeit of the human temperament whenever they restrain the insurgent barbarians, to safeguard and protect them as an integral part of the empire.

For this is how things are: he who harries the barbarians to no good purpose when they grow reckless, sets himself up as **[132]** king of the Romans alone, while he who shows compassion in his triumph knows himself to be king of all men, especially over those whom he protected and watched over when he had the chance to destroy them utterly.[81] So I would deny that even proud Agamemnon spoke like a king when he criticised his brother's relenting towards the suppliant, sending up this bitter and unnatural prayer that no Trojan should escape –

> not even one carried in its mother's womb, if a boy
> (*Iliad* 6.58-9] –

that not even he should escape, but those as yet unborn should die before they come into being. But he was not, it seems, a ruler of truly wide dominion, but was king of the Argives and Myceneans alone and not of mankind. And yet, whenever Homer himself calls Zeus 'father', he does not say 'father of the Greeks', leaving out the barbarians, but simply, **[201]** 'father of gods and men'. Whoever then of the kings here on earth has acted like a father, not only towards Romans but now also towards Scythians, that man is the emulator of Zeus; that man truly loves mankind. As for others, I would say that Cyrus loved the Persians but not mankind, that Alexander loved the Macedonians but not all the Greeks, that Augustus loved the Romans, that someone else was devoted to any

[80] Late antique inheritors of Graeco-Roman culture were convinced that its achievements put them on a higher intellectual and moral plane than peoples ('barbarians') who stood outside the tradition and lacked the qualities that it encouraged and developed. Themistius here echoes one standard element of this chauvinism; i.e. that 'barbarians' were less rational than Romans. See further Y. A. Dauge, *Le Barbare: Recherches sur la conception romaine de la barbarie et de la civilisation* (1981), esp. 307-78 and 413ff.

[81] As explained in our Introduction, this is an important claim made by the speech; that Valens' war had been very successful and that any concessions in the peace treaty were made from a position of strength.

other tribe or people over whom he was held to rule: but he who truly loves mankind and is a true king is one who considers no man to be entirely beyond the pale of his consideration.

It was a fine thing to cross the Ister in warlike array and to lay waste the enemy territory twice in succession[82] and we had the confidence to make advances for greater distances than ever before, even as ambassadors.[83] But even though those actions were glorious and noble, and such as have fallen to hardly any of the emperors of other ages, yet whenever I call to mind that day which I witnessed with my own eyes, then the single ship on which the king made peace shall appear superior to Xerxes' raft on which he crossed with his army over the Hellespont: better the barque that bestowed peace than the bridge that conveyed war. I have not seen the Scythians in battle order, but I have seen their congregation of fear, their assembly of panic and a **[133]** Roman general dictating terms to Scythian kings. **[202]** I have not heard the barbarian war shout but I have heard their keening, their wailing, their entreaties, utterances more appropriate to prisoners than peacemakers, by which one harder than adamant would be moved to tears.[84] But while the king sent back many barbarian embassies with their purpose unfulfilled,[85] he bowed to our own and, as is right, you [the senate] gave your vote on behalf of the Scythians to Philosophy, who alone is able to assuage even a just temper.[86]

---

[82] According to the reliable Ammianus, Valens' army crossed the river twice in three years, 367 and 369, not 'twice in succession'. Themistius' meaning might just be construed as 'twice in quick succession'.

[83] Ammianus 27.5.6 agrees that in 369, at least, the Roman army advanced a long way from the Danube, attacking the Greuthungi.

[84] Ammianus confirms that the Goths did not try to resist Valens by giving battle: cf. our Introduction. When Valens eventually agreed to make peace, he sent the *magister equitum* Victor and *magister peditum* Arintheus to the Goths to arrange terms (27.5.9); the use of the first person here would indicate that Themistius accompanied them.

[85] Ammianus again agrees with Themistius that Valens turned away a number of Gothic embassies before eventually listening to their entreaties. The Goths were keen to make peace because they were short of supplies, commerce having been cut off (27.5.8f.; see further, Chapter 3).

[86] We translate the reading φιλοσοφίαν, τὴν μόνην οἷαν τε οὖσαν καὶ δίκαιον θυμὸν καταπραΰνειν, reported as an early correction by Dindorf and Downey. This seems both clearer and more pointed than their printed text, φιλοσοφίαν, τὴν μόνην θείαν τε οὖσαν, κτλ; philosophy may be 'divine' (θείαν) but fails in this instance to produce intelligible syntax (the infinitive καταπραΰνειν is not governed). Better would be φιλοσοφίαν, τὴν μόνην θείαν τε οὖσαν καὶ δίκαιαν, θυμὸν καταπραΰν-

It was then my special task to rehearse words on love of mankind and to show the king that those who preserve are closer to God than those who destroy. It was a difficult and hardly-won endeavour but he was brought round, relented and with a more benevolent aspect brought his ship to anchor close in. The river at Troy stood in Achilles' path when he was provoked to rage against the Trojans, harrying the youth with its foaming waves [*Iliad* 21.233ff.], but the Ister, which bore its yoke unwillingly as the king passed over on the way to war,[87] shared his purpose as he went to end hostilities and of its own accord spread a calm beneath the ships on their mission of peace. They rode in midstream as if moored and one might have thought that they had taken root by their anchors. He made it clear from the preliminaries that he allowed them to enjoy what was theirs, putting in close to but showing no inclination to disembark. They were dispersed in groups along the bank in docile and amenable mood, **[203]** a horde defying enumeration. That indeed was the first time that such vast numbers of Scythians had been viewed by the Romans with equanimity.

> O blessed son of Atreus, favoured at birth, of
> blessed lot [*Iliad* 3.182],

might one have said looking then at both banks of the river, the one glittering with soldiers who in good order looked on with tranquil pride at what was being done, the other burdened with a disordered rabble of suppliants cast down upon the earth.[88] Rather one could have said that you were even more fortunate than Agamemnon, since he was called blessed only by those under his command, while you are called so both by your own men and those with whom you were

---

ειν; philosophy is now 'both divine and just (δίκαιαν)', but again the syntax is incomplete. Themistius again seeks to distance himself from Valens' regime, emphasising that he rather acted as the independent head of the senate. Amongst other benefits, this allows him to claim, as here, that Valens was persuaded by his own people (*sc.* the senate) to change his mind – granting peace instead of pursuing war – rather than by 'barbarians'. Ammianus agrees that Valens' decision to grant peace followed careful consultation (27.5.8).

[87]Themistius may here be alluding to the events of 368, when the river's unwillingness to support war was shown by the floods which prevented the crossing of the Roman army into barbarian country (cf. Amm. Marc. 27.5.5).

[88]Emperors consistently fed their subjects the expectation that they would be victorious; as a corollary, 'barbarians' could not be portrayed in official propaganda (whether verbal or pictorial) as anything other than submissive. See for instance Dauge, *Le barbare* (n. 80 above), 681-715 and 742-72 or F. Millar, 'Government and diplomacy in the Roman Empire during the first three centuries', *International History Review* 10 (1988), 345-77, at 374-6 (with refs.).

treating.
[134] Xerxes was not a courageous spectator of the naval battle against the Greeks but sat in a tent shaded by a golden awning, an indication of his effeminacy more than his wealth.[89] The king on the other hand showed his endurance in the negotiations to be such as the Scythians could not have borne in battle, standing on deck under the sun at a time when it was especially and unwontedly fiery, and keeping the same position from dawn to late afternoon. And having taken his stand against the barbarians in a contest on behalf of what is just, he singlehandedly won a more glorious victory, and one in which no other shared, neither general nor officer nor soldier. Now for long I had only admired the sagacity **[204]** which I observed him employ in affairs and thought it a success of nature, which fashions a king into a born orator.[90] But not even in an orator performing this task would I expect to observe such great ingenuity that, harnessed with such depth of thought and verbal felicity, combined the capacity to disconcert and reassure. This is why I set no great store by Pericles or the man who admired Pericles for being able by his words both to strike terror into confident Athenians and to restore them, when frightened, once more to confidence.

And so I see that the barbarians had the same experience faced with the king's words as one might expect of Greeks, above all of Athenians, before the most skilful of the orators of those times; and this even though the man who was addressing them was beyond their comprehension in two respects, being a barbarian no more in speech than he was in thought, but one wiser in conciliation than under arms. Thus indeed he rejects the title of king and embraces that of judge, since one denotes power but the other wisdom.[91] Then it

---

[89] In a story that gains in the telling, Xerxes watched the battle of Salamis from the slopes of Mt. Aigaleos, seated on a gilded throne and surrounded by secretaries to record the names of heroes on the day: Herodotus 8.90; Aeschylus, *Persae* 465ff.; Plutarch, *Themistocles* 13.1.

[90] We translate the text καὶ φύσεως ᾤμην κατόρθωμα εἶναι αὐτοφυῆ <ῥήτορα> βασιλέα δημιουργούσης; 'a success of nature, which makes a born orator of a king'; ῥήτορα is added as a correction in the best MS and in another from the same hand (Downey, pref., p. x). The omission of ῥήτορα, as in Dindorf's and Downey's printed text, would give the meaning 'nature, which fashions a born king'. This is intelligible, but lacks point, and misses the contrast with οὐδὲ ἐν ῥήτορι in the following sentence. The allusion just below to 'the man who admired Pericles' is to Thucydides, who expresses the view referred to by Themistius at 2.65.9.

[91] The Tervingi were led by a 'judge' (*iudex*, δικαστής): Amm. Marc. 27.5.6; 31.3.4; Ambrose, *de Spiritu Sancto*, prol. 17 (*PL* 16.736); Auxentius §36[58] (cf. below Chapter 5). This passage has often been cited as a further reference to the Gothic

was shown just how much more hazardous it is to be judged than to sit in judgement, the orator being proved a laughing stock, the judge confident of his excellence. **[205]** For he was so much cleverer than the man who spoke for the barbarians that he undermined their confidence in him and rendered the verbal contest more hazardous than the armed.[92] All the same, having thrown his opponent he then set him on his feet once more, **[135]** stretched out his hand to him in his confusion and made him a friend before witnesses who had firmly believed that they were being wronged. In this way he released him from the turmoil into which he had cast him. And so he [the barbarian] went away highly contented, in the grip of contrary emotions at once confident and fearful, both contemptuous and wary of his subjects, cast down in spirit by those aspects of the treaty in which he had lost his case but exulting in those in which success had fallen to him.[93] And so it was possible to see an unbelievable spectacle coming to pass at long last, that of the Romans bestowing and not buying peace. No one saw gold coin counted out for the barbarians, countless talents of silver, ships freighted with fabrics or any of the things we were in the habit of tolerating before, enjoying the fruits of the peace and quiet that was more burdensome than the incursions, and paying yearly tribute, which we were not ashamed to do, although we refused to call it by that name.[94] Yet although the king is most generous, nevertheless he did not scruple at that time to be considered of the greatest frugality, removing from them even their accustomed source of provision and, in place of the extensive supplies that were formerly

---

leader (e.g. Thompson, *Visigoths*, 45 n. 1), but there is no doubt that the 'judge' here is Valens. It may be that Themistius is punning, developing the metaphor of the oratorical competition with Valens as judge, precisely because he knew that to be Athanaric's title. Portraying Valens as a superior 'judge' emphasises the Gothic leader's inferiority.

[92]Athanaric negotiated for the Tervingi (Amm. Marc. 27.5.9). Themistius depicts a verbal contest between the two, which would imply that Athanaric spoke Latin. Valens for his part spoke no Greek (n. 74 above), and is very unlikely to have been fluent in Gothic. Interpreters could have been used, cf. Millar, 'Government and Diplomacy' (n. 88 above), 361ff., but the scene is probably not to be taken literally. Ammianus and Themistius agree that the conditions were agreed beforehand (27.5.9), and the Danube meeting was probably not concerned with substantive negotiations, but (however prolonged, cf. 204/134 above) was essentially ceremonial.

[93]A clear statement that the 369 peace was a compromise. The surrounding material tries to conceal this by portraying Valens as completely dominant in the negotiations.

[94]On the question of gifts portrayed as 'tribute', see the discussion in our Introduction, with n. 30.

handed over, conceding on one single point, that was a compromise in name only, on the grounds that this was no less convenient to Romans than Scythians. And he was at such pains to make it completely clear that he was not eager **[206]** himself for peace but rather showing mercy to the barbarians, that he now did not even allow them unlimited control over the commercial activities and markets which during the previous peace they were able to conduct with impunity wherever they wished.

Although the profit that comes from the give and take of business transactions was enjoyed by both races in common, he established only two of the cities which had been founded along the river as trading posts. This was both a sign of his absolute imposition of peace terms on the barbarians and an act of forethought that made it less likely that their transgressors would escape notice, since their contacts with others were restricted to defined areas.[95] For, in my opinion, he recognises that while he is able to keep the barbarians from power, he is unable to change their nature and so deprives them of the facility to break faith.[96] It was for this reason that he built some **[136]** completely new border forts, restored others that had fallen into disrepair and furnished others with what they required - height where this was too low, thickness where this was needed, an abundant water supply where before this was sorely lacking, hoards of provisions everywhere and ports on the neighbouring coastline,[97] soldiers from the lists and garrisons whose numbers were not fraudulent, weapons and missiles and war engines - everything was calculated down to the last detail. For hitherto as a result of the neglect of the garrisons, the enemy had believed **[207]** that war and peace lay entirely in their hands, seeing on the one hand the soldiers not only without weapons but the majority without clothing, cast down both in body and spirit, and on the other the commandants and officers acting as merchants, even slave traders, this being their sole employment - to buy and sell as much as possible.[98] They reduced the numbers of those on guard

---

[95]The preceding passage shows free trade to have existed between the Roman empire and the Goths before 367, which is very exceptional; cf. Thompson, *Visigoths*, 14ff.

[96]Cf. n. 80.

[97]For an assessment, including archaeological evidence, of Valens' building on the Danube frontier, see Scorpan, *Limes Scythiae*, 120f.

[98]The lands north of the Danube were an important source of slaves, cf. Julian's comment at Amm. Marc. 22.7.8, and Symmachus, *Ep*. 2.78. Ammianus reports that the desire of Roman officers to make money by procuring cheap slaves from hungry

duty so that the pay of those missing would fall to them.[99] In this way the border forts fell into disrepair, denuded of men and arms, so that when the barbarians saw this, they not unnaturally thought themselves to be better than those making forays against them,[100] and that, if open warfare did not seem for the moment to be regarded with favour, at least the opportunity for piracy with impunity was theirs. They dispersed in all directions along the bank, not only in ones and twos but in organised companies of horse and foot, not soldiers but brigands who called theft the spoils of war. But no longer: from the hinterland to the coast you would think that a wall of adamant had been marked out, with such a defensive bulwark of forts, arms and soldiers has it been consolidated.

Passing over other details, it is sufficient to consider one indication of the care taken in these matters. I speak not from hearsay but of things which I myself have witnessed. All of you who have been to that area surely know that although it is the most beautiful part **[208]** of Scythia within our dominion, it is also the least secure as regards the barbarians. The river does not flow through it in a clear stream, **[137]** but has been churned up with soil, creating a semicircular lagoon which extends a considerable way into the mainland, neither navigable by boat nor passable on foot.[101] Now it was this area that for a while afforded a base for the skirmishing parties of the enemy who, lacking the confidence for an open and concerted force while the façade of peace existed, perpetrated acts of pillage and malefaction in single craft, lying up among the islets and then falling suddenly upon those settled along the river. Then, while the widely separated garrisons were communicating the intelligence to each other, they would make inroads as far as they could and then vanish into the river, pursuit thenceforth being impossible, the lagoon allowing the pursuing parties neither to sail nor to go on foot. This was an insufferable state of affairs – to endure acts of piracy before one's very eyes, but to lack the means to take vengeance. The king was not, however, unequal to the

---

Goths was a major cause of the revolt which led to Hadrianople: 31.4.9-11.

[99]Cf. *Or.* 8, note 54.

[100]I.e. Roman border troops; cf. the listings in the *Notitia Dignitatum* for the middle and lower Danubian areas: *Not. Dig., Or.* 39-42. These were backed up by regional field armies for both Thrace and Illyricum: *ibid.* 8-9.

[101]Themistius is describing the Danube in the area of the Dobrudja. The river runs north and then east before reaching the Black Sea. Before modern interference, the river had a marshy flood-plain over 10 miles wide. As Themistius indicates, this offered many suitable hide-outs for raiders.

demands of the terrain. He discovered in that land a narrow peninsula which extended into the lagoon and terminated in a high mound from which the whole surrounding area could be observed.[102] There he raised anew a fort, following a trace of walls which a previous emperor had laid down because of its **[209]** advantages but had discontinued because of the difficulty involved. In a place where there was no stone near at hand nor easily available supplies of brick and mortar, but where everything had to be transported over however many miles on countless pack teams, who would not excuse those who had abandoned the venture as impracticable? But the emperor surpassed the skill which Amphion showed in the fortification of Thebes.[103] You would have declared that the stones moved of their own accord, the bricks likewise and that the wall went up without masons or carpenters, so great was the soldiers' compliance and such their ability to cope with the difficulties. For he assigned responsibility to everyone and allowed no part of the force to be burdened beyond its capabilities, dividing the task into small portions as if it were a piece of freight and allowing no one at all to be aware of the load **[138]** by making everyone share it, himself first and foremost. Can you believe me, that not even the chamberlains or the guards of the royal chamber were exempt, but that even they joined in carrying their allotted share of mortar? I used to admire Demosthenes son of Alkiphron for his fortification of Sphacteria because he treated his willing troops in such a way that, because of a dearth of containers, they transported mud by locking their hands behind their backs, men numbering no more than a thousand - and these oarsmen rather than infantry soldiers, stranded by a storm, who built a mere parapet **[210]** rather than a wall.[104] But where neither officers nor generals sought to take up the burden, how can one consider either the man who issued such instructions, or those who accepted them, to be worthy of respect?

And now while peace is extended over virtually the whole border

[102] This cannot be identified.

[103] Amphion, son of Zeus and Antiope, was given a lyre by Hermes with which he charmed rocks to arrange themselves into the walls of Thebes.

[104] Demosthenes was actually the son of Alkisthenes; the episode described is his fortification of Pylos, the headland opposite the island of Sphacteria: Thucydides 4.3-5. Safeguarding the frontier through military building was one of the activities expected of an emperor, and a prop to civilian morale, cf. M. Whitby, 'Procopius and the Development of Roman Defences in Upper Mesopotamia,' in P. Freeman and D. Kennedy (edd.), *The Defence of the Roman and Byzantine East* (1986), at 722ff.

area, so also is the readiness for war. For the king knows that they who best prosper are they who are are best prepared for war.[105] The river bank bears its burden of forts, the forts their burden of soldiers, the soldiers their weapons, the weapons their splendour and protection. Luxury has been banished from the lists and in its place has been restored an abundance of the necessities, so that those on garrison duty are not forced to war against the subject population instead of the barbarians, and to hold off from the latter because of the truce while they harass and harry the farmers through dire need. Fear and daring have somehow reversed their normal stations for the soldiers. They despise the barbarians but are terrified of the farmers; the censure of the latter is much more frightening to them than ten thousand attacking Scythians. Thus does peace keep hold of us, both within and without the borders, fear of arms the enemy, fear of the law our soldiers.[106] It is not river, lagoon or parapet that keeps apart Scythians from Romans – for these can be broken down, sailed across and **[211]** surmounted – but fear, an obstacle which no man has ever surmounted, once he is convinced that he is inferior. And he has set up a trophy of that victory that has not been fashioned out of stone, nor fixed in one particular place in bronze **[139]** or gold, but which is part of the daily lives of all the barbarians and all the Romans. And the king raised it not by masses of dead and wounded nor by the tombs of countless corpses, but by parley alone and by endurance.

There was a man who lived in the time of our forefathers, a boxer called Melankomas, who was extremely handsome, of enormous stature and extremely renowned in his art and whose lover was, so they say, the emperor Titus.[107] This man never wounded or struck any man but wore all his opponents down just by his stance and the raising of his fists. And so they retired happy to have been

---

[105]We translate Helmreich's suggestion εὐθαλοῦσι, 'flourish, are prosperous', for the MSS and Downey's ἀληθεύουσιν, 'speak truth', 'are/prove true'; we find this hard to understand. Another possibility is εὐθηνοῦσιν, 'thrive, flourish'.

[106]Roman troops were largely supplied by the farmers of the area in which they were stationed; this left the latter open to various types of exploitation, eg. *CTh* 7.4.12; 20-3; 26; 28; 31; and Jones, *LRE*, 623ff. for commentary.

[107]The legendary (not to say eccentric) boxer Melankomas, who won all his contests without hitting anyone or being hit, is the subject of *Orations* 28 and 29 of Dio Chrysostom (ed. Loeb, Vol. II, pp. 360ff.). Themistius may owe something to Dio, but is the only writer to claim that the Emperor Titus was a lover of Melankomas. See *PIR*² M 448 and C. P. Jones, *The Roman World of Dio Chrysostom* (1978), 15ff.

spared but defeated by his training. And this is exactly what the enemy have now experienced at the hands of the king. They have been beaten without taking the field, have fallen without taking a stand, worsted not in physical or armed encounter, in which the better side is often beaten by the inferior, but by judgement, intelligence and by having been persuaded of their great inferiority. Nor can they blame generals' trickery, ambush, an unfavourable position or unexpected attack, which offer the vanquished the hope of renewing the fight once more on equal terms; even **[212]** having spent time on their preparation and in fighting an open and declared war, they were unable to come to grips with the king's defence which he brought forward in three entire years and so forced the cowards to yield – three years in which they dared neither march against him in winter nor stand against him in summer, and so were beaten twice a year.[108]

Now it remains for us to count, not the corpses over which we have made ourselves masters, but the living, and we have not gained conquest only to lose those whom we conquered. In one way men master other men, in the other way bears, boars and leopards. Yet even when hunting we let their offspring be, and he who destroys them utterly is considered to violate the spirit of the chase. While we spare the most savage beasts from which we are separated not by the Ister or Rhine but by **[140]** nature herself, so that their species might survive and endure, and feel pain when elephants are wiped out from Libya, lions from Thessaly and hippopotami from the Nile marshes, in the case of a race of men – even if one could by all means say barbarian, yet still men – impoverished, downtrodden and consenting to submit to our rule, shall we not admire him who does not wipe them out completely but cares for and spares them?
[213] I recall that one of the supreme commanders of the past was called Achaicus because he laid waste Greece, another Macedonicus because he turned Macedonia into an uninhabited desert[109] and the great Scipio, grandson of the famous Scipio, acquired the title Africanus from the people and senate because he razed Carthage to her foundations and obliterated her when she had surrendered and

---

[108]Themistius returns to a main theme of the speech, emphasising Valens' military achievement; even though he had not managed to defeat them in a full-scale battle, that the Goths had refused to stand against him was tantamount to a Roman victory on each occasion on which they *might* have done.

[109]Quintus Caecilius Metellus Macedonicus campaigned against the Achaean Confederacy in 146 B.C., and his task was continued by Lucius Mummius Achaicus who crushed it.

was completely spent. If these men could with justice acquire their titles from those whom they destroyed, should you not with more justice take your name from those for whom you have cared? For this is how, it seems to me, we name the gods - Pelasgian Zeus, Amyclaean Apollo, Cyllenean Hermes - from those places for which they have special care and closely watch over. Whom, then, is it most fitting to call Gothicus:[110] him through whom the Goths exist and are preserved, or him at whose hands they would have ceased to exist, if he were given his choice? Pyrrhus was king of Epirus and gave many problems to the Macedonians, and in turn to the Greeks, and finally made life difficult for the Romans too. Although he conquered widely and often, he was never satisfied with the present state of affairs but looked only to what he had not yet mastered. So it was that he wasted his strength in victory, exchanging one war for another, and Kineas had no success in rebuking him from afar for his insatiability, saying that, since the culmination of those many countless dangers he endured whenever he met with success **[214]** was the drinking party, this he could enjoy in safety even now, while sitting at home and preserving the empire he had acquired.[111]

But no limit or boundary, even should you name the Atlantic Ocean, **[141]** checks those who always reach out for more. For those in whose soul no bound is fixed, neither is there one here on earth. These men go to war to satisfy their own desire and not out of consideration for the common good. But this is not how a king acts who is intractable and inflexible only for so long as the common good is in doubt, but when it has been well disposed, considers the rest superfluous ambition. Our situation with regard to the barbarians is and will be in good order, while it is for you, I say, to make the peace fruitful for your subjects and productive; may she journey forth, so to speak, to every corner of the realm.[112] Listen to the divinely-inspired Plato: Cyrus was no king, nor was Darius;

---

[110]*Gothicus* was one of a number of victory titles, by which emperors had from the earliest times marked military and/or diplomatic successes over different peoples living beyond the frontier. Claudius was the first to take this particular title after defeating a Gothic army at Naissus in 269 (Wolfram, *History of the Goths*, 54ff.). The whole practice became increasingly formalised as time went on, cf. T. D. Barnes, 'Imperial Campaigns, A.D. 285-311', *Phoenix* 30 (1976), 174-93.

[111]Cf. Plutarch, *Pyrrhus* 14.6.

[112]It is striking that Ammianus (27.5.8f.) and Eunapius (as preserved in Zosimus 4.11.4) both consider that the peace of 369 was a reasonable solution to the Gothic problem, and echo Themistius' line that a well-judged peace is better than stubbornly continuing with war. They may have had access, if not to the speech itself, then to other imperial propaganda presenting a similar view of events.

still less would he have said that Alexander was. For it seems that all these men took care that their empire, like a body, should appear beautiful in outer form, while taking no thought for its inner wellbeing. And so it follows that they were generals, but not kings. For generals are praised for the overthrow of enemies, but kings for the happiness of their subjects.

CHAPTER THREE

THE SÎNTANA DE MUREŞ-ČERNJACHOV CULTURE

In 1900/1901, Russian archaeologists excavated a cemetery at Černjachov not far from Kiev in the Ukraine. The gravegoods they unearthed proved to bear a marked similarity to material discovered shortly afterwards by Romanian archaeologists at a cemetery in central Transylvania, Sîntana de Mureş (Mureş is the nearby river). These two cemeteries were the first identified finds of a relatively rich and homogeneous archaeological culture, which, in the late Roman period, spread across large tracts of south eastern Europe (comprising essentially the eastern half of modern Romania, the Moldavian Republic of the USSR, and the southern Ukraine). Over 2,000 finds have been made within the Soviet Union, and Romanian finds are comparable in number. Map 2 (overleaf) shows the larger finds of sites and cemeteries, of which over sixty have been identified in Romania; in the USSR, some ninety sites and seventy cemeteries have been investigated.[1] Findspots extend from the Danube to the Don, and somewhat beyond to Poltava and Kharkov, and from the Black Sea as far north as Lvov, Rovno, Kiev and Sumy.

No large-scale study of the Culture has appeared in English, and what follows makes no claim to be based on detailed knowledge of the original artefacts. It is rather intended as a critical distillation of what has so far been published – a user's guide to the physical culture of the world which generated, in contact with the Roman empire, the texts translated in this volume. Much of the material has been published in French and German as well as Russian and Romanian, and so is reasonably accessible to those who might wish to pursue further any of the points raised. The picture which emerges from this material will no doubt be revised substantially as more finds are published, but there is already more than enough to justify an attempt to bring the Sîntana de Mureş/Černjachov Culture before a wider audience.

---

[1] Cf. Häusler (1979), 23. The map is a collation of Ioniţă (1966), fig. 1, *MIA* 82 plate 1 (opposite p. 10), *MIA* 89, 317 (for Russian Moldavia), and *MIA* 116 plate 1 (opposite p. 8).

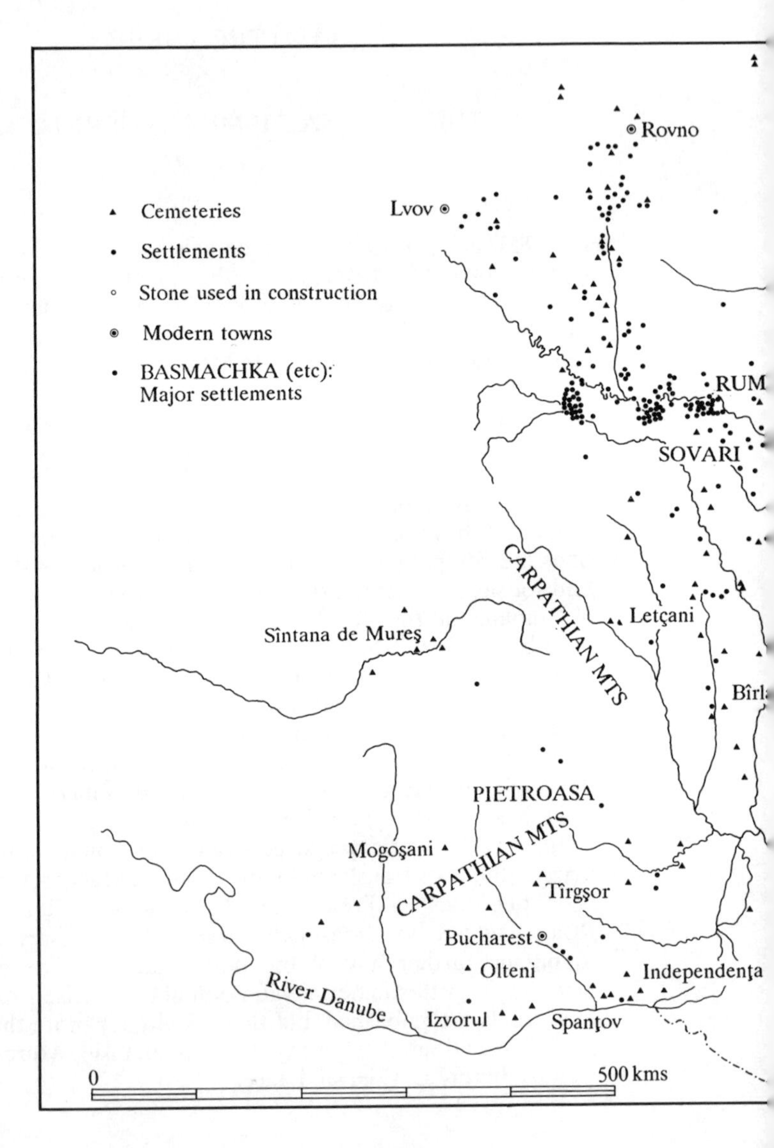

Map 2 Sites and Cemeteries of t

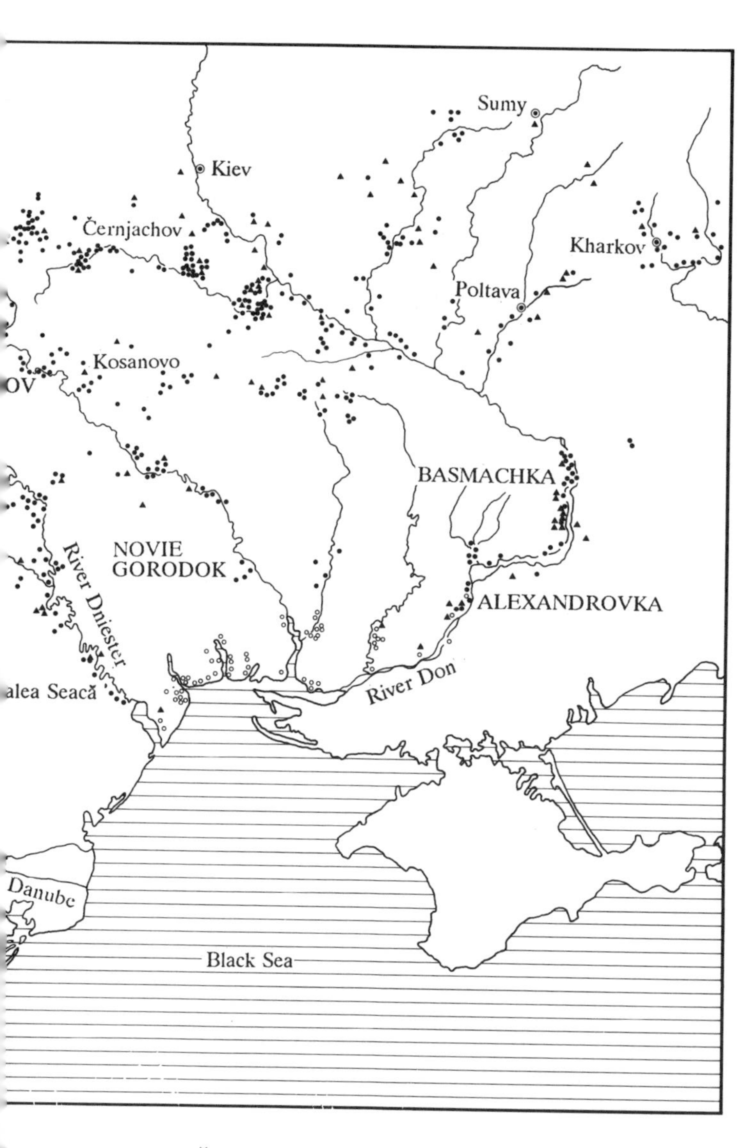

întana de Mureş-Černjachov Culture

1. DATING AND ATTRIBUTION

The identification of this widespread Culture has not been without controversy. Events of the twentieth century have made the spread of a possibly Germanic Culture across large areas of the Balkans and southern Russia at times a sensitive issue. Up to their first major conference on the subject in 1957, Russian archaeologists tended to propose a Slavic origin,[2] but in the past thirty years it has become clear that the so-called Sîntana de Mureş/Černjachov Culture can be associated with the spread of Gothic power in the period before Hunnic nomads forced the Goths into the Roman empire. The Culture dates from the later third and fourth centuries A.D. (see below), and from a wide variety of literary sources we know that Gothic power was dominant at this time north of the Danube frontier of the Roman empire. Ammianus Marcellinus also reports that a group of Alans bordering the Goths were known as the 'Tanaites' or 'Don People' (31.3.1), suggesting that Gothic power, like the Culture, extended no further east than this river. These chronological and geographical coincidences support the basic association of this material culture with the later third- and fourth-century Gothic kingdoms. The extent to which the physical remains are those of the Goths themselves is a separate question, which we will consider below.

The principles by which the Sîntana de Mureş/Černjachov Culture has been dated are those established for central and northern European remains of the Late Roman and Early Migration Periods. Many of the finds in these separate cultural areas are similar to those with which we are concerned, and all pose the same basic problem, in that few precise chronological indicators turn up among the remains. The only specifically datable objects are Roman coins and *terra sigillata* pottery in closed finds (i.e. burials), but with pottery, allowance must be made for a time lag between production and deposition. Coins are even more problematic; large numbers of Roman *denarii*, minted at any time between Nero and Septimius Severus, were circulating beyond the Roman frontier in the third century. Dating thus largely revolves around a number of widely-found objects, most commonly weapons, *fibulae* (brooches), buckles, pottery, combs, glass, and personal ornaments. Each has a

[2] Shchukin (1975), 25ff.

reasonably well-defined pattern of development, so that the appearance of later types can establish at least a relative chronology. The greater the number of objects showing later features in any one find of material, the more secure the chronology, and this kind of relative dating depends not so much on the features of single objects, but on associations. A delineated chronological phase would typically consist of the association (for instance) of particular weapons with certain forms of *fibulae*, buckles, pots, and combs.

Using this kind of approach, the Polish archaeologist Godlowski provisionally defined a series of phases, modifying the efforts of previous scholars. Using closed finds of Roman coins and pottery, he also attached provisional dates to these phases: C1 = late second- and early third-century, C2 = mid third-century, C3 = late third- and perhaps early fourth-century, and D = fourth century. As Godlowski stresses, the absolute dates can only be provisional, and there is no clear dividing line between each phase. In some areas, certain phases are much less clearly marked than others, as one might expect. There is no reason for the material culture of this large and politically disunited area to have followed a uniform pattern of development. Allowance must also be made for the speed at which new forms of weapon, buckle, comb, etc. might be adopted, so that any given association of forms of objects will have become current in different areas at different times.[3] Nevertheless, Godlowski's study has provided the basis for all future work, and a general chronological guide which is fully adequate for our purpose here.

Looked at against this central European material, the Sîntana de Mureş/Černjachov Culture can be dated firmly to the later third and fourth centuries. Few finds belong to the C1 phase, except perhaps in the regions of Volhynia and the upper Dniester, and most can be placed in phases C3 and D.[4] The chronologically diagnostic 'monstrous' *fibulae* (Fig. 8), reasonably common in the Culture's early phases, for instance, tend to place associated finds at and after the transition between phases C2 and C3. There is some evidence that developments occurred first in south-eastern Europe and were then adopted further north, so that the absolute date attached to these phases in the Sîntana de Mureş/Černjachov Culture might be

---

[3] Godlowski (1970), esp. chapters 3 & 4, pp. 101ff.

[4] E.g. Godlowski (1970), 109f.; Shchukin (1975), 32f.; Werner (1988), 244ff. We have been unable to consult J. Kmiecinski (ed.), *Peregrinatio Gothica*, Arch. Baltica Łódź 7 (1986), which is likely to shed light on the early phases of the Culture.

a little earlier than their equivalents in central Europe.[5] Nevertheless, there is a broad chronological coincidence between the remains of the Sîntana de Mureş/Černjachov Culture and the Goths' domination of lands north of the Danube and the Black Sea.

Other equally important chronological questions cannot be answered, unfortunately, because no thorough study has yet been made of all the remains. It is unclear, for instance, when the Culture may have spread to all the areas in which it can be traced. As we noted, early remains might suggest that it occurred first in Volhynia and the upper Dniester, and it probably spread into Transylvania only at a relatively late date, perhaps after *c.* 350. Otherwise, little is known, although in both Moldavia and Muntenia, the preceding archaeological cultures seem to have been present up to the late third century.[6] Analysis of the archaeological evidence for the end of the Culture has also been far from secure. Excavators have often reported that a site or cemetery quickly fell into disuse in the late fourth century. This, however, is not an archaeological date, but one drawn from the literary evidence, which has been taken to show that the Goths all fled from the Huns in the 370s. In the last decade or so, later phases of the Culture have been identified, using methods similar to those which provided the initial date, suggesting strongly that some kind of continuity prevailed, on certain sites at least, into the early fifth century.[7] The full history of the Sîntana de Mureş/Černjachov Culture is thus far from clear, but we can proceed on the basis that the remains reflect the level of material culture prevalent in Gothic realms in the period before the Hunnic invasions.

2. SETTLEMENTS

Settlements tend to be found along main river valleys and secondary valleys leading off from them, a pattern apparent even in the small scale of our map. Sites were generally on unwooded land, protected from the wind, and, naturally enough, close to a source of water. The map also suggests that particular concentrations of population

---

[5] Godlowski (1970), 110.

[6] Transylvania: Horedt (1986), 8ff. Only inhumations are found in there, suggesting a late date (see below), as do late forms of brooches, combs, etc. Moldavia: Bichir (1976), 137ff.

[7] Bierbrauer (1980), 131ff.

were to be found along the Lower Danube, the Prut, the Upper Dniester and the Upper Don, but this, of course, is dependent on what sites have happened to be identified. Even along the Middle Dniester, settlements were usually separated by no more than 2 or 3 kilometres, so that certain areas, at least, were host to a fairly concentrated population.

In general, sites were quite large. Between the rivers Prut and Dniester, the settlement of Delakeu covers an area of 10 hectares, Zagajkany, Kobuska, Veke, Rusjany, Solonečeny, and Koşnica around 20 hectares, Sobaŕ and Lukaşevka I 25 hectares, and the largest of all, Budeşty, 35 hectares. At the other end of the scale, Petrikany is only 2 hectares and Komrat 4.5 hectares. Houses were often organised roughly in parallel lines. At Lepeskovka, 12 large houses, 19 animal shelters, and two potteries were found in lines either side of a main avenue.[8] No Sîntana de Mureş/Černjachov site with any fortification has yet been discovered, but excavators have begun to identify more complex centres. These may well have been aristocratic or royal courts rather than normal villages which, as we shall see, were largely concerned with agricultural production. Within Romania, Pietroasa, findspot of a famous treasure, may have been one such centre, and other larger than average sites have been found along the Danube. Within the USSR, similarly, Kropotkin has highlighted 5 large settlements which would seem to be political centres;[9] these are plotted on the map.

Actual houses are of two types. More numerous are sunken huts (in German, *Grubenhäuser*). These are usually rectangular, occasionally oval or half-oval, and cut into the ground to varying degrees; some would have had little more than their roof showing above ground, most were about half-submerged. They were small in size, the average floor area varying from 5-16 square metres. The floor was generally of beaten earth, walls of wattle and daub, and rushes were used for roofing; each house was also provided with a hearth. Near the Black Sea, stone was often used for the floors and lower parts of houses; this variation is shown on the map. Often side by side with sunken huts in the same settlement, excavators have also found surface dwellings, which are found in two sizes. The largest are 6-8 by 11-16 metres (66-128 square metres), of the type known in German as *Wohnstallhäuser*. As this name implies, these houses

[8] Häusler (1979), 42f. with refs.

[9] Diaconu (1975), 73f.; Kropotkin (1984), 87.

were divided in two, with living quarters in one part and animals in the other, which, to provide extra protection, generally faced the prevailing wind (*Wohn* means dwelling, and *Stall* a stable). Smaller surface dwellings have also been found with a floor size of 10-30 square metres. Both kinds of surface dwelling were timber-framed with plastered walls, rushes once again being used for roofing, and with beaten earth floors and hearths. Not all these house types are found throughout the Culture. In Romania, no *Wohnstallhäuser* have been uncovered, and on some sites house-types are not mixed. Only sunken huts have been found at Alexandria and Dancu, and only surface dwellings at Botoşani, Jassy, and Ionăşeni.[10]

In part, the different house-types must reflect socio-economic differences. *Wohnstallhäuser* are usually associated with extended family groups, and larger surface dwellings probably also betoken greater wealth than the smaller sunken huts. Some of the variation in building style may also derive from the fact that the Culture was the product of a population of disparate ethnic origins. *Wohnstallhäuser* are typical of the Germanic cultures of central Europe, and have not been found in earlier archaeological cultures of either Romania or the southern USSR. They can thus possibly be associated with the Gothic immigrants who dominated this area militarily in the late third and fourth centuries.[11] Sunken huts are well-attested in earlier Dacian cultures of the Carpathians.[12] In their use of stone, similarly, Sîntana de Mureş/Černjachov houses of the North Pontic region are similar to those of previous cultures of the area, and it seems likely that at least some of these sites continued to be occupied by the indigenous population.[13] Simply to attribute *Wohnstallhäuser* to Goths, and sunken huts to an indigenous population would, however, be rash. Within the Culture, sunken huts are found well away from the Carpathians in southern Russia, where they were not previously common, and Ammianus' evidence makes it clear that there were Goths north of the Danube in what is now Romania,[14] even though *Wohnstallhäuser* are

---

[10]Häusler (1979), 43ff; Ioniţă (1966), 252f.; Diaconu (1975), 69f.

[11]Cf. Häusler (1979), 48f. Surface dwellings are found among the second- and third-century Carpi of the eastern Carpathians (Bichir (1976), 7ff.), but are much smaller (3-5 by 3-6 metres).

[12]Cf. Bichir (1976), 11ff.

[13]Gey (1980), 51.

[14]Valens' campaigns between 367 and 369 are clearly directed at a population living between the lower Danube and the Carpathians; cf. Heather (1991), chap. 3.

absent. Variation in house types may well reflect different ethnic origins, but skills and styles belonging originally to one group seem to have been adopted more generally by all the peoples contributing to the Culture.

3. CEMETERIES AND FUNERARY PRACTICE

Cemeteries have so far been published in more detail than settlements, and both halves of the Culture are even named after cemeteries - Sîntana de Mureş and Černjachov - whose plans provide us with a convenient starting point (Figs. 1a & b).[15] In what follows, we will concentrate on the Romanian cemeteries of Independenţa, Spanţov, Izvorul, Olteni, Tîrgşor, and Mogoşani (cf. Map 2), with cross-reference to Russian finds at, in particular, the cemetery of Kosanovo, in order to emphasise that this was a uniform Culture stretching from the Danube to the Don.[16]

The plan of Černjachov displays one general characteristic of the cemeteries. There are some exceptions (including, so it happens, Sîntana de Mureş), but, in general, cemeteries contain both inhumation and cremation burials. At Independenţa, 8 cremations and 27 inhumations have been uncovered, at Spanţov 10 and 59 respectively, Izvorul 1 and 31, Olteni 34 and 5, Tîrgşor 110 and 176, Mogoşani 51 and 34, and at Kosanovo 82 and 39. As these numbers suggest, inhumation tends to predominate on Romanian territory, but the picture is much less clear for the USSR.[17] A few graves do not contain human remains at all (e.g. Spanţov grave numbers 12, 13, 46, and 69), and would seem to be cenotaphs for people whose bodies could not be secured for burial.

It was usual for the dead to be buried with a wide variety of grave goods, whether the basic rite was inhumation or cremation. Pottery

---

[15] The plan of Sîntana de Mureş is after Bierbrauer (1980), figures 8-10; that of Černjachov after Petrov in *MIA* 116, 65 figure 1.

[16] The evidence from Independenţa, Spanţov, Izorul, and Olteni was published by Mitrea and Preda (1966); on Tîrgşor, see Diaconu (1965); Mogoşani: Diaconu (1969); the material from Kosanovo was published by Kravchenko in *MIA* 139, 77-135. Since Mitrea and Preda, Independenţa has received a fuller treatment in Ioniţă (1971). Other published cemeteries from Romania include Miorcani: Ioniţă (1977), and Letçani: Bloşiu (1975). The huge cemetery of Bîrlad-Valea Seacă has been partly published by Palade (1986). From the USSR, Dančeny has recently been published: Rafalović (1986); other cemeteries are discussed in the pages of *MIA* 82, 116, and 139.

[17] Compare Ioniţă (1966), 255 and Werner (1988), 241f.

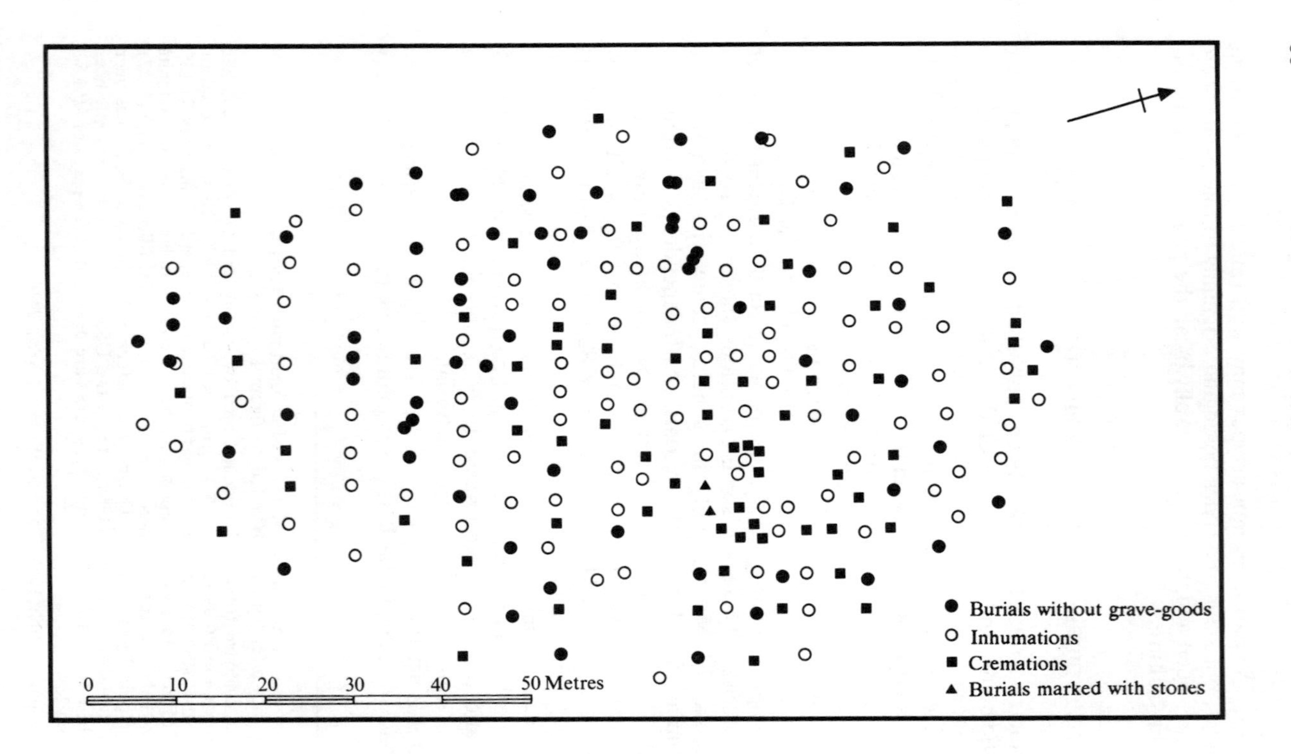

Figure 1a: The Cemetery of Černjachov

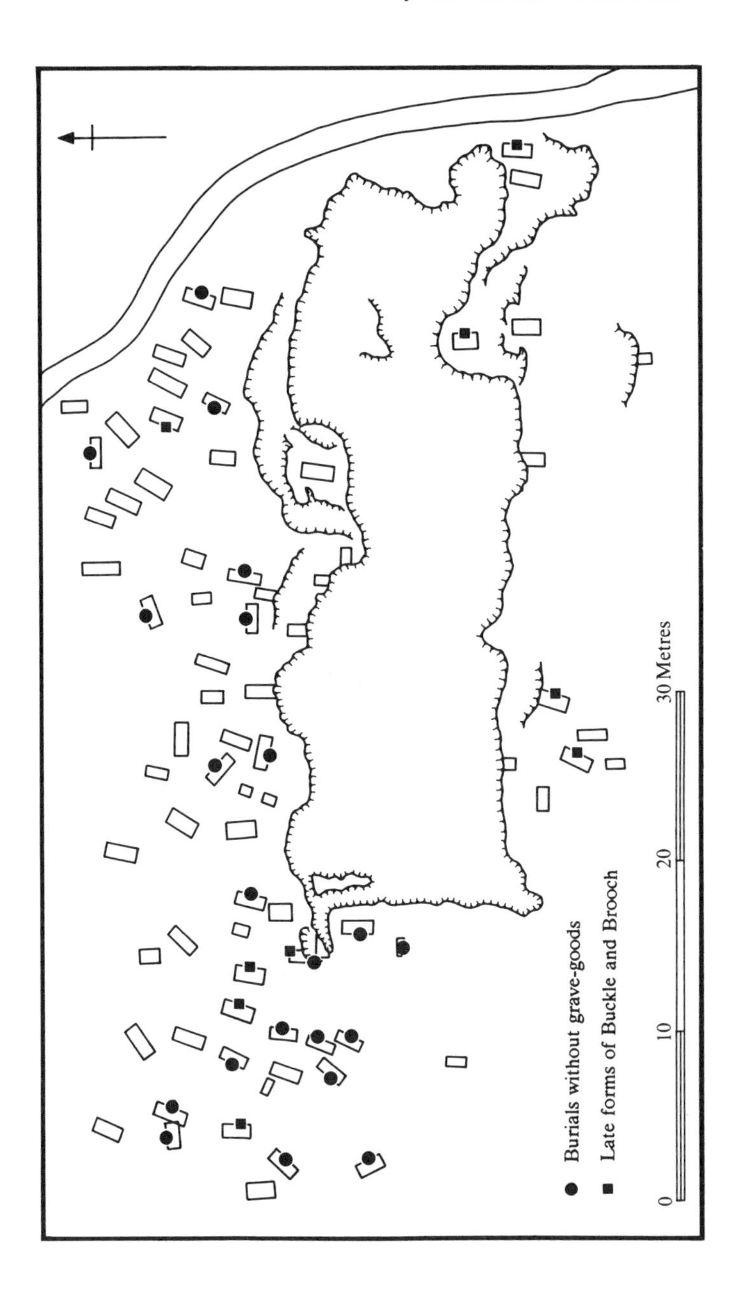

Figure 1b: The Cemetery of Sîntana de Mureş

(often both hand- and wheel-made) is very common, as are bone combs and iron implements (though not weapons), and items of personal ornamentation (see below). In an important minority of burials, however, no grave goods at all accompanied the corpse; the figures which follow are approximate because some burials have been disturbed. At Kosanovo, perhaps 6 inhumations and 7 cremations lacked them, at Independenţa 8 and 3 respectively, Izvorul 6 inhumations, Spanţov 11 inhumations, and Mogoşani 1 cremation (all burials at Olteni had some goods).

A number of other variations in funerary practice are worth noting. The major variation among inhumations is the orientation of the corpse. In most cases, the dead were buried on broadly a north-south axis, with the head towards the north. In a significant minority of cases, however, graves were dug to face east-west. At Kosanovo, 7 out of 39 inhumations are so oriented, at Spanţov 2 out of 59, at Tîrgşor 4 out of 286, and at Independenţa 5 out of 27; at Izvorul, Olteni, and Mogoşani, no east/west burials were discovered.[18] Apart from this, Diaconu's detailed publication of the excavations at Tîrgşor illustrates a number of smaller-scale variations in practice.[19]

In the case of cremations, the detailed publication of Tîrgşor has again allowed Diaconu to distinguish nine different types. Many are rather small-scale differences, however, and there seem to be only two of general importance. The most striking distinction is between those cremations where the remains were collected together and buried in some kind of urn, and those where they were placed directly into a hole in the ground. The cemetery at Kosanovo, for instance, produced 4 burials in urns and 78 without, Independenţa 5 in urns and 3 without, Spanţov 8 and 2 respectively, Mogoşani 18 and 33, Olteni 11 and 23, and the one cremation found at Izvorul involved the use of an urn. The second major variation is the fact that, in a few cremations, the grave goods (particularly the pottery) show no signs of having been burnt along with the corpse, whereas, in the vast majority of cases, corpse and goods were clearly burned on the same pyre. Both urn and urnless burials are found with and without grave goods bearing such burning marks.[20]

It is a striking feature of the Culture as a whole that weapons were

---

[18]See also Bloşiu (1966), 219 for the cemetery at Letçani, and Fedorov on the Černjachov Culture in Moldavia: *MIA* 89, 89f.

[19]Diaconu (1965), 137-9.

[20]Diaconu (1965), 136-9.

not included in burials. In just a few cases, however, weapons have been found in cremations; one such burial turned up at Tîrgşor (number 147), another at Mogoşani (number 15), and Soviet excavators have found nine examples in Moldavia.[21] On a slightly larger scale, the cemeteries of Cozia-Iaşi, Todireni, and Braniste have produced burials which differ strikingly from the norm. At Cozia-Iaşi, a small number of cremations contained pottery of types usually found further to the north and west among the Germanic cultures of central Europe. The inventory of cremations at Todireni suggested a similar Germanic group who were some way towards adopting local pottery, and at Braniste the cremations were incorporated into a mound.[22]

Some of these variations in practice, and particularly the major distinction between cremation and inhumation, suggest very strongly that the same cemeteries (and hence probably the same settlements) were used by groups of people who believed quite different things about the afterlife, and how to prepare an individual for it. In this highly important way, the Sîntana de Mureş/Černjachov Culture differs markedly from cultures previously dominant in and around the Carpathians. The vast majority of burials in the cemeteries of the Carpic cultures of the second and third centuries, for instance, were cremations.[23]

Some have argued that the differences in funerary practice are the result of different ethnic groups having used the same cemeteries, and this may well explain some of the variations. Cranial deformation, for instance, seems to be diagnostic of Sarmatian tribes, and inhumation graves where the skeletons betray this characteristic can be associated with such groups.[24] At Tîrgşor, the small number of cremations containing goods with no marks of secondary burning perhaps also indicates that the cemetery was used for a short period by local so-called Daco-Getans before the arrival of the

[21] Diaconu (1963), 302ff. with refs. For an illustration of a spearhead and shield boss, see Fig. 13a.

[22] Ioniţă (1980), 126f. and idem (1975), 79f.

[23] Cf. Bichir (1976), 18ff. A high proportion of the few inhumations which have been found also bear the marks of the cranial deformation characteristic of nomadic Sarmatians. In these cemeteries, one is probably dealing with just a few outsiders buried according to their own rites, rather than genuinely bi-ritual burial grounds.

[24] Sulimirski (1970), 142ff.; Bichir (1976), 24ff.; Diaconu (1965), 135f. At Tîrgşor, however, the stratigraphy suggests that the 20 such Sarmatian graves (10 of which display cranial deformation) are older than the Sîntana de Mureş/Černjachov levels, 9 of them having been disturbed: Diaconu (1965), 134.

bearers of the Sîntana de Mureş/Černjachov Culture. The lack of burning marks, and the associated grave goods, it has been argued, are distinctive, and these burials come from a lower stratigraphic level.[25]

The small-scale local variants at Cozia-Iaşi, Todireni, and Braniste, likewise, can probably be explained as small groups of Germanic outsiders, who maintained their separate customs for a brief period. None of these individual groups is very numerous, however, and they probably represent Germanic immigrants who quickly adopted the practices followed throughout the Sîntana de Mureş/Černjachov cultural area.[26] The same seems true of the few cremations containing weapons. They are otherwise indistinguishable from the mass of others found in Sîntana de Mureş/Černjachov cemeteries; they contain, for instance, identical inventories of pottery with secondary burning marks and personal ornaments. The weapons, however, are similar to those found in cremation burials of the probably Germanic Przeworsk Culture of central Europe, and it seems reasonable to suppose that relatively small population groups from this area (to judge from the rarity of such burials) at some point made their way south and east into the lands of the Sîntana de Mureş/Černjachov Culture. The large-scale but confused population movements of the third century provide a plausible context for such events.[27]

Attempts to argue from these few cremation burials with weapons that all the cremations within Sîntana de Mureş/Černjachov cemeteries belong to this separate strand of population are much less convincing. Apart from the very few with weapons (and the few other variants we have noted), cremations and inhumations have produced identical types of grave goods. Against this mass of evidence, weapon burials seem to be a departure from the norm, and an insufficient basis on which to build an interpretation of the mass of cremations which do not share this distinguishing feature.[28] The

[25]Diaconu (1965), 136f.; cf. idem (1964), 197ff. But Palade (1980), 250f. has questioned whether secondary burning marks really are a distinctive feature.

[26]Ioniţă (1980), 126f., and (1975), 79f.

[27]Diaconu (1963), 302ff.; cf. Shchukin (1989), 300f.

[28]Contra Diaconu (1963), 302ff. Diaconu also attempted to identify the cremators as the Taifali, whom he envisages as living in mixed settlements with Gothic inhumators. Taifali did occupy lands above the Danube in this period, and occasionally operated with the Goths (*Pan. Lat.* 3[11].17.1 and Amm. Marc. 31.9.3ff.), but they were a separate people. In the 370s, for instance, the Taifali crossed the Danube separately from the Goths, and only later chose to join up with some of

bi-ritual nature of the cemeteries requires some other explanation, therefore, and a consensus seems to be emerging that there was a steady, though neither uniform nor total, shift from cremation towards inhumation during the period that the cemeteries were in use.

Russian scholars, it is reported, tend to think that this was the case, and, although we have found no such strong statement in the literature, some of the Romanian evidence would tend to support such a conclusion. At Mogoşani, 6 of the inhumations were found to have disturbed cremations (numbers 12, 14, 40, 50, 52, and 59), but in no case did a cremation impinge upon an inhumation. This might suggest that, in this case, inhumations generally postdated the cremations. Again, certain Romanian cemeteries contain only inhumations. These include Sîntana de Mureş itself (cf. Fig. 1b), and all are in Transylvania or the uplands of the Carpathians, areas to which the Culture seems to have spread at only a relatively late date; the others are Tîrgu Mureş, Palatca, and Izvoare.[29]

The evidence awaits a comprehensive discussion, but Bierbrauer has made some convincing observations about certain Sîntana de Mureş/Černjachov cemeteries (Kosanovo, Tîrgşor, Independenţa, Gavrilovka, Sîntana de Mureş itself, and Ranzevoje: cf. Map 2), which tend to confirm that there was a general chronological progression towards inhumation. His main concern was to identify and date later phases of the Culture on the basis of particular forms of glass, brooches, buckles, and combs (cf. Figs. 8, 9, and 11). From this he was able to show that his chosen sites, at least, provided evidence that the Culture continued throughout the second half of the fourth century and even into the fifth. It also emerged that cremation burials and inhumations containing earlier forms of these goods were generally found towards the middle of cemeteries, and that later types were not only found solely in inhumations, but also that these burials were generally towards the periphery of cemeteries. This indicates that cemeteries developed in a radiating pattern,

---

them (Amm. Marc. 31.9.3). Other literary evidence confirms that, unless in alliance with the Goths, they were quite separate: Zosimus 2.31; Amm. Marc. 17.13.19f. and 31.3.7 (the latter clearly distinguishing 'Taifalorum terras'); Ambrose *Expositio Evangelii Lucae* 10.10 (contra Wolfram, *History of the Goths*, 91, etc.). Cf. Mitrea and Preda (1964), 227f.; no convincing means of identifying the Taifali has yet been established.

[29] Häusler (1979), 56.; Diaconu (1965), 144. It is not certain that Sîntana de Mureş never contained cremations because the central part of the cemetery was damaged by a gravel pit.

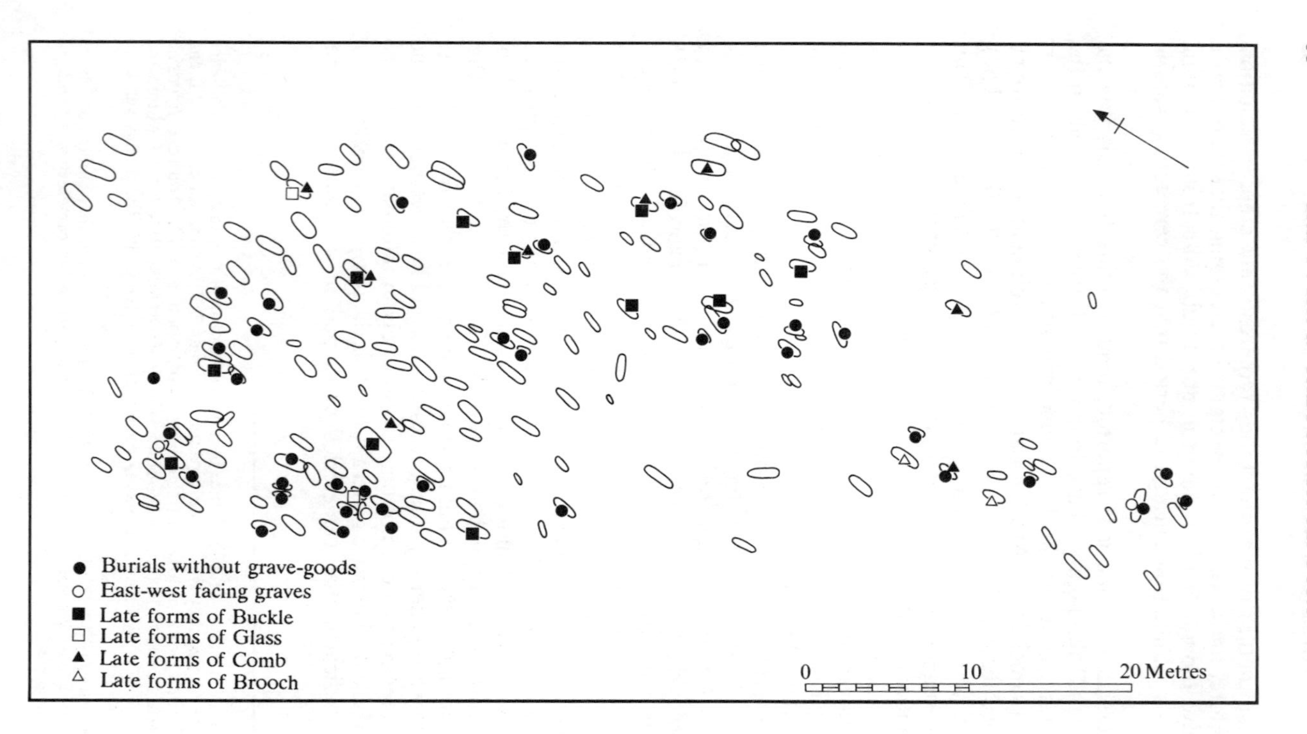

Figure 2: The Cemetery at Tîrgşor

starting from the centre and working outwards, and implies that cremations, clustering in the centre, belong generally to earlier phases of the Culture. As one would expect, there is no simple dividing line between earlier and later burials in cemeteries that were in continuous use, but the observations and the implications drawn from them are convincing. As an illustration, Fig. 2 marks graves containing late goods at Tîrgşor.[30]

We are still left with the problem of identifying what change in belief prompted this general change in funerary practice. Part of the explanation may lie in the fact that Christianity was spreading through these lands at this time (see Chapters 4 and 5). A trend towards inhumation might well be at least partly explicable in these terms, as might the occasional east-west orientation of graves. It has also been suggested that the burials lacking grave goods may likewise be evidence of Christianity. There may well be something in these arguments, especially where more than one possibly Christian custom are found together. Thus, both broadly east-west graves at Spanţov lack any goods (numbers 11 and 51), as do 4 out of the 5 east-west graves at Independenţa (numbers 15, 27, 28, and 29; 31 contained just a few a pearl beads), and all 3 east-west graves at Letçani.[31] Bierbrauer has also pointed out that most of the east-west graves, like those without grave goods, tend to be situated in the periphery of cemeteries, alongside the graves containing later varieties of grave-goods. Christianity does not seem to have achieved preeminence in Gothic lands beyond the Roman frontier before the arrival of the Huns, so that the relatively late date of these customs might well strengthen their association with this new religion.[32]

It would be rash, however, to ascribe all of these later variations to the influence of Christianity. Cremations without inventory are known, and these are unlikely to have belonged to Christians.[33] At least in part, a shortage of grave goods may reflect differences in wealth; as we have seen, goods vary significantly in number and

[30]Bierbrauer (1980), 132ff.; cf. Horedt (1986), 8ff. with refs. Figure 2 is based on Bierbrauer's Figures 3-5. The evidence from Tîrgşor also confirms that there was no linear development. The earliest phase consists of cremation burials impinged upon in 14 cases by inhumations, which should, therefore, be later. But these inhumations are themselves cut into in 4 cases by more cremations, and then there would seem to have been a further level of inhumations: Diaconu (1965), 134f.

[31]See, for instance, Mitrea and Preda (1964), 232f.; Federov in *MIA* 89, 89f.; Ioniţă (1975), 80.

[32]Bierbrauer (1980), 134f. See also Chapters 4 & 5.

[33]E.g. Kosanovo cremation burials 71, 77, 80, 88, 94, 103, and 110.

quality. Bi-ritual cemeteries are also known from the Germanic cultures of central Europe. Cremation seems to have been the rite originally practised by all Germanic peoples, but inhumation burials dating back to the period before the birth of Christ are known. And of later Germanic cultures chronologically coincident with Sîntana de Mureş/Černjachov groups, at least one, the so-called Wielbark (or East Pomeranian-Mazovian) Culture, is itself distinguished by bi-ritual cemeteries. At least in some cases, the choice of cremation or inhumation may thus have revolved around different non-Christian views of the afterlife.[34]

Conclusions can thus only be tentative. Bierbrauer's arguments in favour of a trend towards inhumation are persuasive, but need fuller confirmation. It is, however, a further point in favour of his analysis, that the rites generally practised in later phases of the Culture (an inference from the peripheral areas of his chosen cemeteries), correspond to what became the norm in the increasingly Christian Germanic cultures of the fifth century. These cultures typically produce cemeteries composed entirely of inhumation burials, of which the vast majority lack any inventory, but where a few are richly endowed. The peripheral areas of Sîntana de Mureş/Černjachov cemeteries, where inhumation increasingly became the norm and where some burials without grave goods have been found, thus provide a bridge between such a pattern and the old norm of cremations with plentiful grave-goods.[35]

Christianity was probably also involved to some extent in the later phases of this transformation, but other explanatory factors must also be taken into account. Earlier cremation and inhumation burials strongly suggest that economic circumstance and ethnic origin affected funerary rites, and there is no reason to suppose that they did not continue to have some influence (as we shall see, the Culture was fundamentally multi-ethnic). Above all, the trend towards inhumation among Germanic cultures of the north and west, at a time when they could not have been substantially affected by Christianity, means that even the most basic transformation we have observed in funerary practice may have originally had little to do with the spread of the new religion. There is no reason, of course

---

[34]Hachmann (1971), 138ff., conjectures that cremation may be associated with the cult of Tiu, and inhumation with that of Woden. On the Wielbark Culture, see Shchukin (1989), 293-301 and Godlowski (1970), 31ff. (Godlowski calls it the East Pomeranian-Mazovian Culture).

[35]Bierbrauer (1980), 135f.

(and it is impossible to tell archaeologically), why a progression towards inhumation might not mean different things in different contexts: in one community, the spread of Christian belief, in another, the spread of a different non-Christian cult.

4. CERAMIC WARES

Pottery is much the commonest artefact in both settlements and cemeteries of the Culture. In general, both manufacturing techniques and the range of forms employed are notably homogeneous. Much of the pottery, it would seem, was made locally, since kilns have been found in many villages. These were efficient, if not highly sophisticated.[36] Both wheel- and hand-made pottery occur in sites and cemeteries (and both are often found in the same burial: e.g. Spanţov graves 4 and 26), although the wheel-made variety would seem to predominate. The latter accounts for over 80% of pots found on the territory of the Moldavian Republic of the USSR, and for about two-thirds of the pottery found within the settlement and cemetery of Bîrlad-Valea Seacă in Romania, where 2102 wheel-made pots have been discovered compared to 1086 made by hand.[37] Beyond this most basic of distinctions, the ceramic ware can be further subdivided by type of clay used, the forms employed, and to a lesser extent geographical origin.

If we look first at the wheel-turned pottery, the majority of pots within this category were made using a good quality, fine clay. At Bîrlad-Valea Seacă, for instance, 1463 out of 2102 wheel-made pots were produced from such clays.[38] The characteristic colour of these fine wares is grey, but other colours – particularly red and black – were occasionally, and no doubt deliberately, achieved by manipulating the conditions of firing. These fine wares were also on occasion decorated with linear designs.[39]

The most common type of pot made with this material was a wide, shallow (drinking?) bowl. This form of pot is characteristic of the whole Culture, and occurs in numerous variants throughout. The

---

[36] Ioniţă (1965), 253; Häusler (1979), 37ff.; Palade (1980), 237.

[37] Häusler (1979), 37f.; Palade (1980), 229. We have been unable to consult an important paper by I. Ioniţă on the chronology of the pottery in *Peregrinatio Gothica* (n. 4 above).

[38] Palade (1980), 229.

[39] Ioniţă (1966), 253f.; Mitrea and Preda (1966), 185; Palade (1980), 237-49; Symonovic, *MIA* 116, 270-361.

examples we have chosen for illustration are taken from a number of different sites in the USSR and Romania, and represent but a fraction of the range of forms (Fig. 3).[40] Also made of fine grey clay was a less shallow bowl, generally with steeper sides (Fig. 4).[41] Again, this comes in a various shapes and sizes, and sometimes with two, or more rarely, three handles. It is not totally dissimilar to our first type of pot, and it is a matter of convenience whether they are classified together or separately.[42] Within the sites and cemeteries of both Romania and the USSR, jugs, in a number of variant forms, provide a third major type of fine ware. These range from the tall and slender to others which resemble mugs or cups. Again, our chosen examples can illustrate only a fraction of the forms (Fig. 5).[43] The final category of wheel-turned pots made from fine grey clay comprises a range of what would seem to be storage jars (Fig. 6).[44]

A second category of wheel-turned pots comprises those made out of much less good quality clay: rougher wares incorporating sand and grit. Perhaps not surprisingly, clay of this quality was used to make a more limited variety of object, seemingly just storage jars and cooking pots of different sizes and shapes. Palade, the excavator of Bîrlad-Valea Seacă, suggests that these pots, in some cases at least, were imitating hand-made pottery.[45] Both perhaps had the same workaday functions, with the richer or more ambitious substituting wheel-turned, even if relatively coarse, varieties for their hand-made pots.

Hand-made pots, the other main category of vessel, occur less frequently than wheel-turned varieties. They remain, however, a substantial minority, and have been found in any number of shapes and sizes, with much greater variety of form than in the wheel-turned pottery. Most of these pots would probably have been used for storage or cooking. Despite such mundane purposes, they were

---

[40] **1** & **3**: Mitrea and Preda (1964), 385; **2** & **4**: Diaconu (1969), 337; **5**: Blosiu (1975), 268; **6**: Diaconu (1965), 232; **7** & **8**: *MIA* 139, 118.

[41] **1** & **3**: Mitrea and Preda (1964), 386; **2** & **4**: Blosiu (1975), 268; **5** & **7**: *MIA* 139, 120; **6**: Diaconu (1969), 376; **8** & **9**: Diaconu (1965), 232, 260.

[42] Hence some Russian scholars would divide the wheel-turned pottery into seven types and sub-types, rather than the five defined here: Häusler (1979), 37f. with refs.

[43] **1** & **2**: Mitrea and Preda (1964), 392, 391; **3**: Blosiu (1975), 268; **4**, **5**, & **6**: *MIA* 139, 130; **7**: Diaconu (1965), 282; **8**: Diaconu (1969), 378; **9**: *MIA* 82, 229.

[44] **1** & **2**: Mitrea and Preda (1964), 389; **3** & **4**: *MIA* 139, 122; **5**: Diaconu (1965), 231; **6**: Diaconu (1969), 374; **7**: Blosiu (1975), 273.

[45] Palade (1980), 249f.

often decorated, mostly with incised linear motifs.[46] One interesting exception to this pattern, found reasonably often on Romanian soil, is the so-called 'Daco-Getan cup'. This comes with or without a handle, and would seem, in fact, to have been used as a lamp. Such vessels were common among second- and third-century cultures in and around the Carpathians, and clearly continued in use into the fourth century (Fig. 7).[47]

Pottery of quite different kinds from the common types we have so far discussed does occasionally turn up in excavations. Two of these have particular importance: Roman amphorae, and pottery from the Germanic cultures of central Europe. At Bîrlad-Valea Seacă, Roman amphorae account for only 70 out of a total of 3186 pots, but point to a not inconsiderable trade with the Roman world. We do not illustrate these amphorae, as they await a comprehensive study, but they probably contained wine, and have been found throughout the area covered by the Culture (see further below).[48] Pottery from the Germanic north and west occurs in even smaller quantities but is of some historical significance. It is always hand-made, and quite distinctive, even compared to the types of hand-made pottery found more commonly in Sîntana de Mureş/Černjachov cultural levels. As we have seen, it is associated with some distinctive burials on sites such as Cozia-Iaşi, and is otherwise found regularly, if in small quantities. It is probably a secure indication of the physical presence of Germanic peoples.[49]

It is worth reflecting briefly on the origins of this pottery, since cultural areas tend to be defined largely on the basis of pottery types (on the principle that humbler goods such as ceramics are unlikely to move as far from their place of manufacture as luxury items such as metalwork). Apart from the few exceptions noted in the last paragraph, its origins do not lie in the Germanic cultures of central Europe. Good quality wheel-made pottery only begins to appear in these lands in the period *c.* 275-300, and scholars have long been clear that some other origin must be sought.[50] In the past, Russian

---

[46]Häusler (1979), 37f.; Mitrea and Preda (1964), 185; Ioniţă (1966), 254; Palade (1980), 230-4.

[47]Palade (1980), 233f.; Bichir (1976), 50ff. Figure 7: **1**: Mitrea and Preda (1964), 383; **2**: Diaconu (1965), 215; **3** & **4**: Mitrea and Preda (1964), 283.

[48]E.g. Palade (1980), 229; Ioniţă (1966), 254; Häusler (1979), 37f.

[49]Palade (1980), 227; Ioniţă (1966), 206; Mitrea and Preda (1964), 233.

[50]Todd (1975), 56ff.; cf. Werner (1988), 258; Mitrea and Preda (1964), 233f.; Palade (1980), esp. 250f.

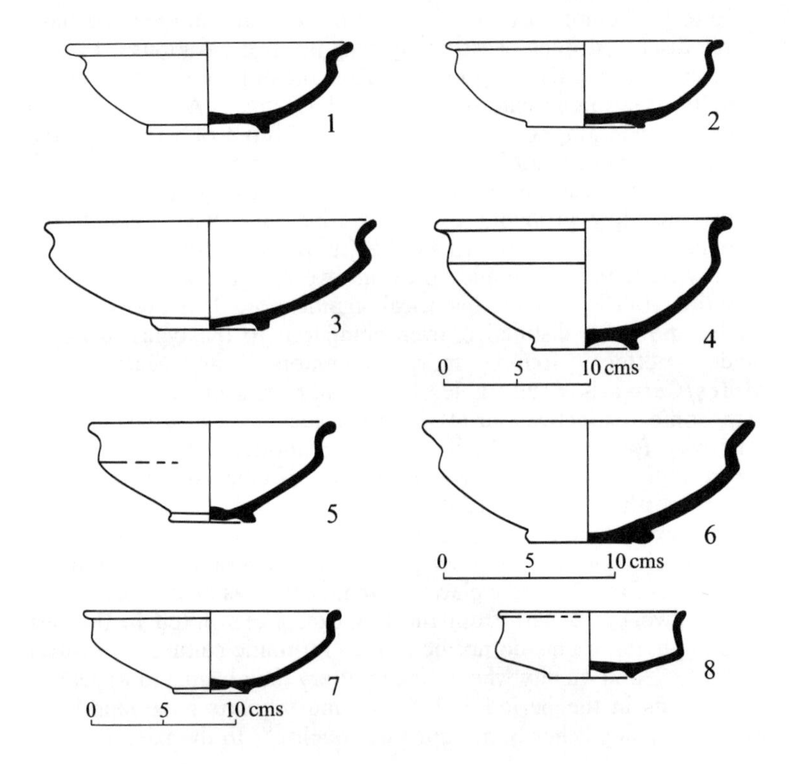

Figure 3: Wide, Shallow (Drinking?) Bowls

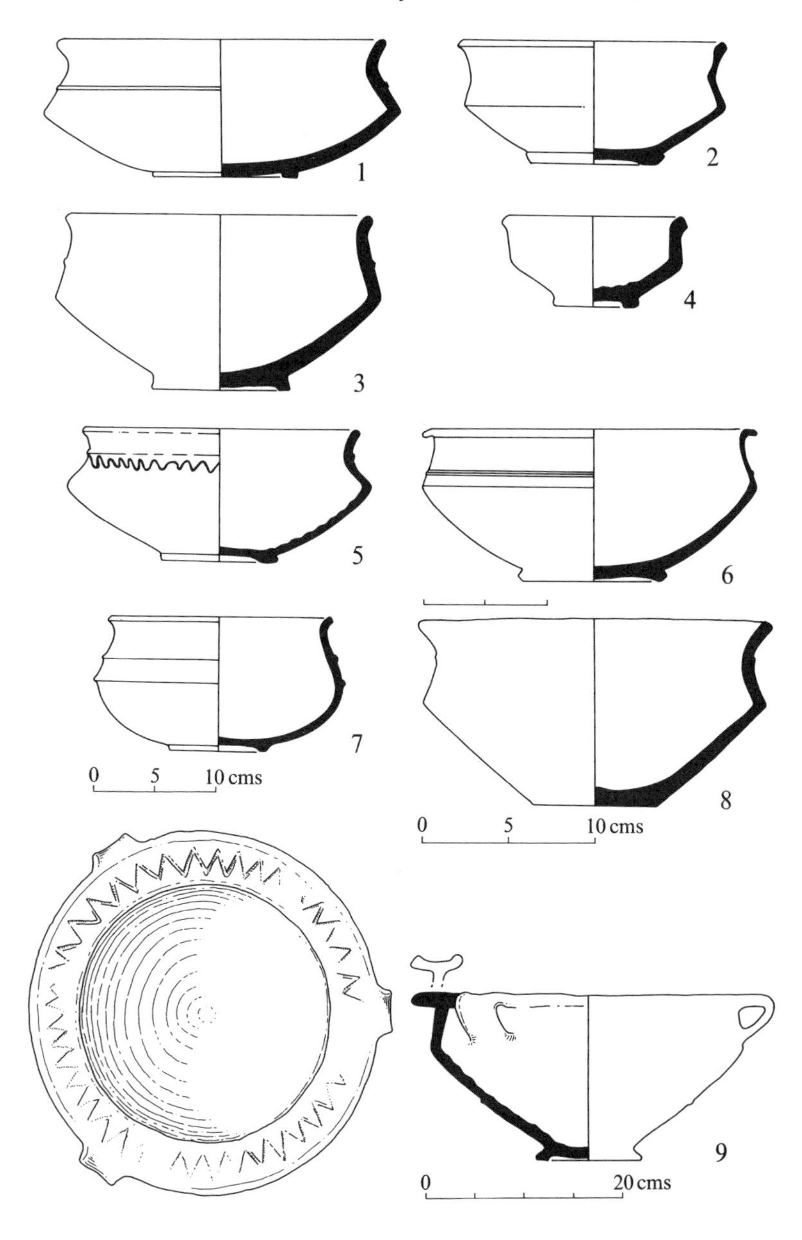

Figure 4: Bowls

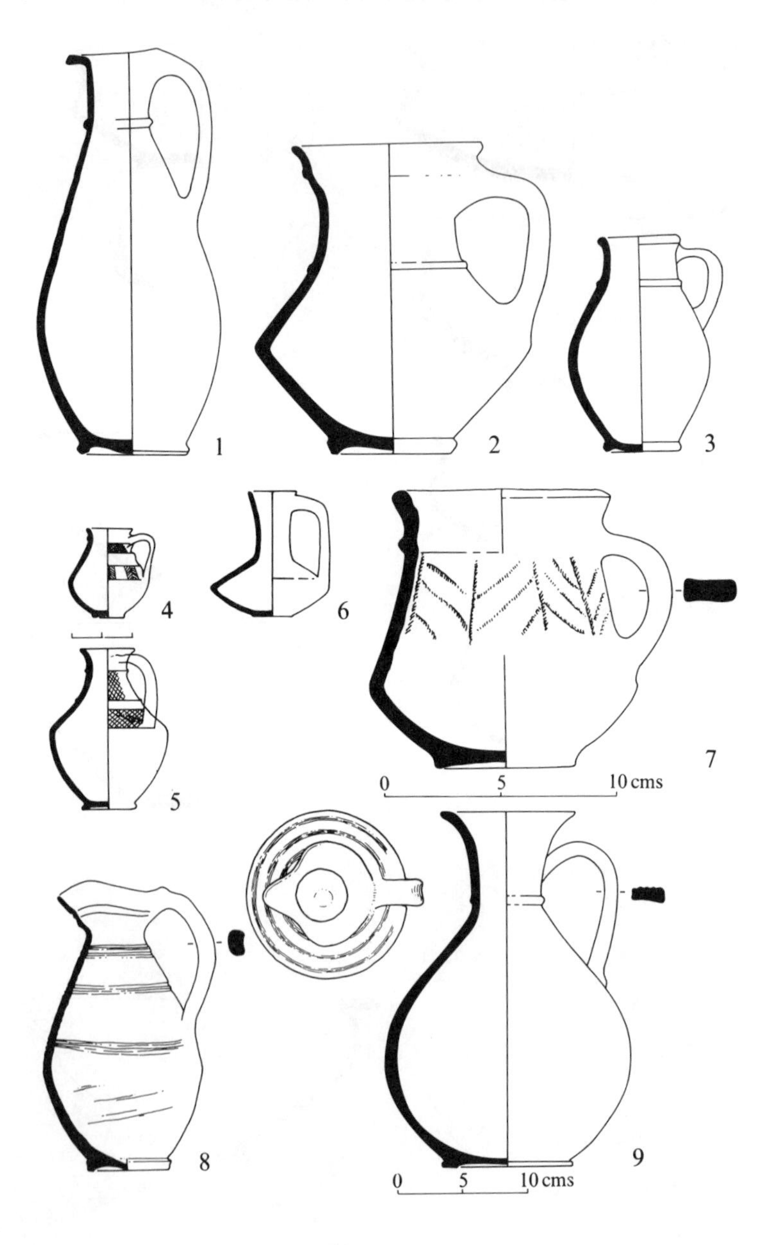

Figure 5: Jugs

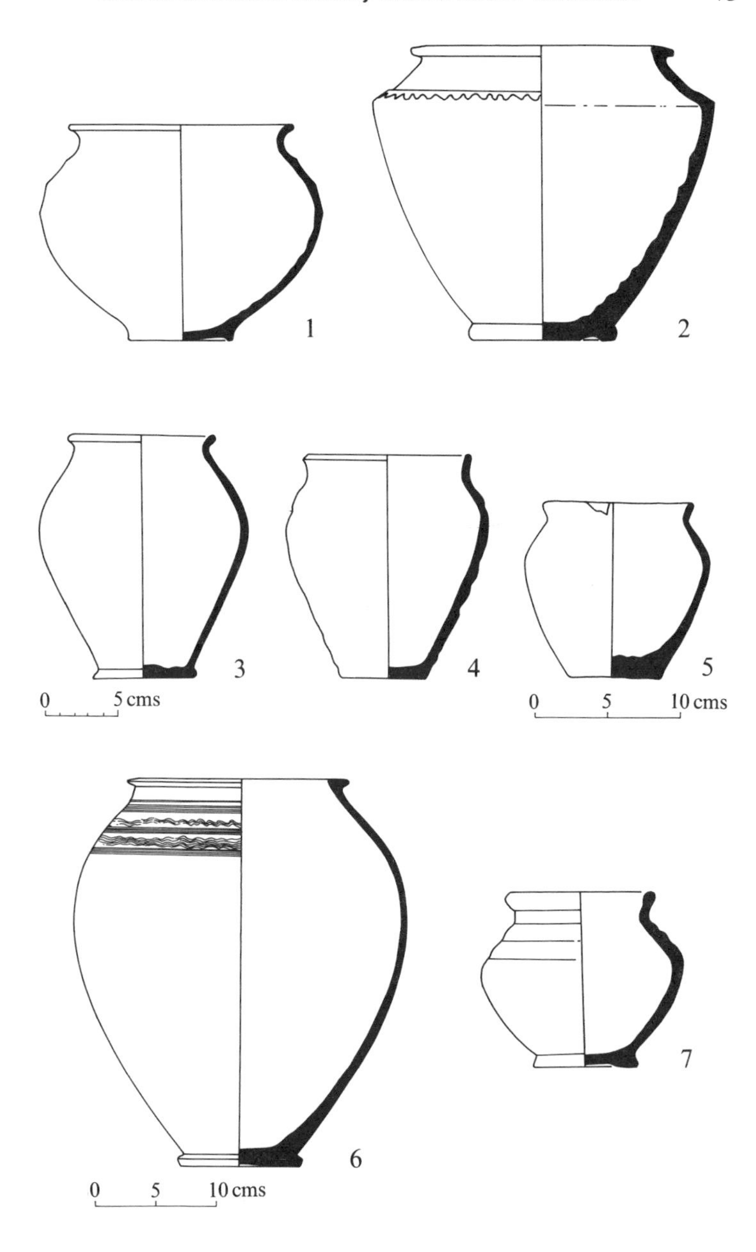

Figure 6: Storage Jars

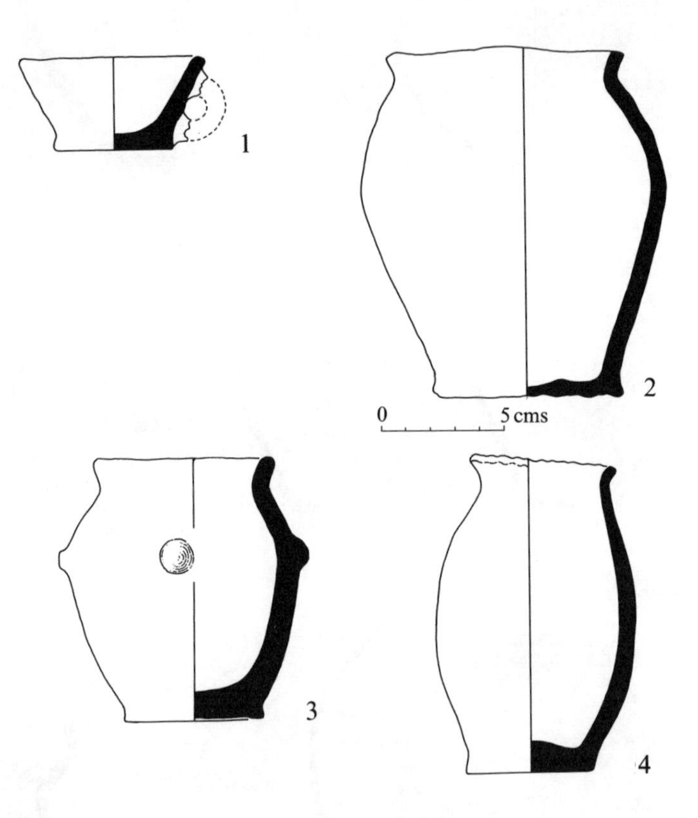

Figure 7: Hand-made Pots

investigators tended to view Sîntana de Mureş/Černjachov pottery as essentially provincial Roman in character, and even sought to explain it on the basis of Roman prisoners known to have been brought to these lands in the third century.[51] Romanian scholars have been able to show, at least in part, however, that the pottery types and techniques employed bear a strong resemblance to those used by previous cultures in and around the Carpathian mountains. There was, indeed, a continuous tradition of producing good quality wheel-made pottery in these areas from the late Iron Age La Tène period onwards.[52] Comparable studies for the different areas of the USSR are lacking, but similar wares are known from the Pontic cities of Olbia and Tyras, so that indigenous traditions (including the Carpathian one) were surely strengthened by contact with the technologically advanced world of the Roman Mediterranean. One of the Pontic pots, for instance, has a Greek inscription, perhaps suggesting that a Greek craftsman was responsible for its manufacture.[53] At this point, conclusions can only be tentative, but the Culture with which we are concerned was probably able to draw on continuous, if perhaps localised traditions of ceramic manufacture, and, at the same time, even if Roman prisoners were not the medium, skills common to the Mediterranean world were probably also imported.

5. PERSONAL POSSESSIONS

A wide range of personal possessions has been found among the remains of the Culture. Apart from pottery, brooches (*fibulae*) and belt buckles are among the most common. These were in the first place functional items, proving, incidentally, that the dead were sent to the next world fully clothed, but they also had ornamental value and could express social distinction. Both brooches and buckles were usually made of bronze, but silver ones were clearly a status symbol, and turn up regularly in both cremations and inhumations. These items also have an known sequence of development, giving them, as

[51]Häusler (1979), 40f; on the prisoners, see Chapter 5.

[52]Palade (1980), 230ff.; Bichir (1976), 47 & 50ff., cross-referencing Carpic and the Sîntana de Mureş/Černjachov Cultures.

[53]Werner (1988), 258ff. As cited by Häusler (1979), 40f., Shchukin, takes a view, similar to that of the Romanians, that there was a continuous tradition of ceramic manufacture to draw upon throughout the area of the Culture.

we have seen, an important role in establishing archaeological dates.

In the case of both objects, we have attempted to illustrate some of the more important types. Our first four brooches are examples of the so-called 'crossbow' *fibula*, which was a standard item of dress for peoples living beyond both the Rhine and Danube frontiers of the Roman empire, affected by Germanic and non-Germanic groups alike (Fig. 8).[54] Usually of bronze, though occasionally of iron, it occurs in many variants, and is by far the most common type of brooch to be found in Sîntana de Mureş/Černjachov cultural levels. For dating purposes, however, the rarer varieties, often made of silver, tend to be more valuable. Of these, we have illustrated here the so-called 'monstrous' *fibula* (*monströsen Fibeln*), and variants of the 'plate *fibulae*' (*Blechfibeln*). 'Monstrous' *fibulae* are characteristic of the transition between periods C1 and C2 (the mid-third century: see above), while silver-plate *fibulae* belong to the late fourth and early fifth centuries.[55] Of buckles, we illustrate here the 'D-shaped' type, along with a variant incorporating a stamped backing-plate (*Gürtelschnallen mit ausgeprägter Beschlagplatte*). The latter again helps to date later phases of the Culture (Fig. 9).[56]

Personal ornaments of a wide variety of types are just as common as the more functional brooches and buckles: rings, earrings, bracelets, necklaces, etc. These come in so many shapes and sizes that comprehensive categorisation is impossible, and we have merely included a few illustrative examples (Fig. 10).[57] Of all this material, the pendants and amulets have perhaps been most studied, and these emphasise that the Sîntana de Mureş/Černjachov Culture incorporated elements from many preexisting cultures. Many axe-shaped pendants, for instance, have been found, and they were also common in the Germanic cultures of the north and west. Finds of bucket-shaped pendants are even more widespread, and were clearly

---

[54]Compare, for instance, Godlowski (1970), plate 7 with Bichir (1976), 90ff. and illustrations.

[55]Werner (1988), 247ff.; Bierbrauer (1980), 134ff. Figure 8: **1** & **2**: Diaconu (1965), 285; **3** & **4**: *MIA* 139, 124; **5**: Werner (1988), fig. 3; **6** & **7**: Diaconu (1969), 384; **8** & **9**: *MIA* 82, 233.

[56]Bierbrauer (1980), 134ff. Figure 9: **1** & **2**: Diaconu (1965), 284; **3** & **4**: *MIA* 82, 234; **5** & **6**: Mitrea and Preda (1964), 357; **7** & **8**: Diaconu (1969), 385; **9**: Blosiu (1975), 266; **10**, **11**, & **12**: *MIA* 139, 125; **13**: Diaconu (1969), 385.

[57]**1**: Werner (1988), fig. 14; **2**: *MIA* 89, 343; **3** & **4**: *MIA* 139, 131; **5**: Diaconu (1969), 388; **6**: *MIA* 89, 343; **7**: *MIA* 139, 131; **8**: *MIA* 82, 235; **9**: Mitrea and Preda (1964), 280; **10**: Diaconu (1969), 391; **11**: *MIA* 139, 129; **12** & **13**: *MIA* 139, 131; **14**: Werner (1988), fig. 15; **15**: *MIA* 89, 343.

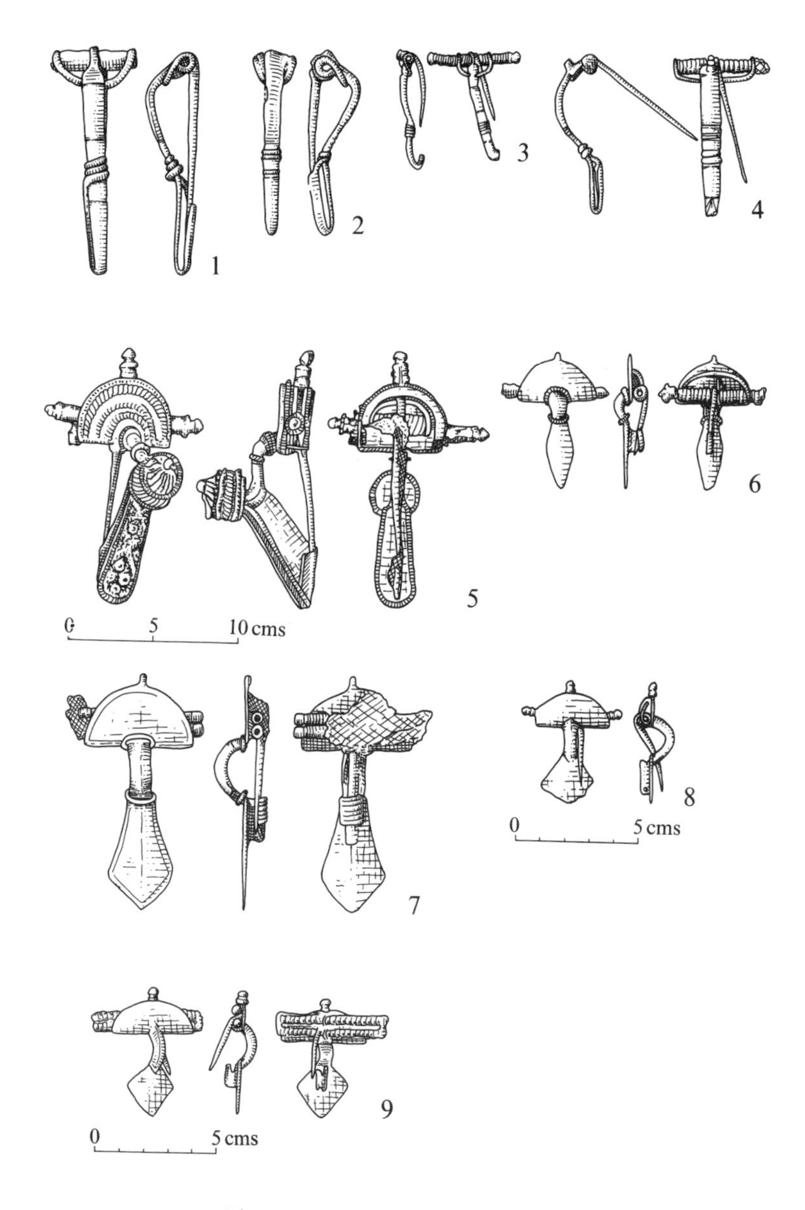

Figure 8: Brooches (*Fibulae*)

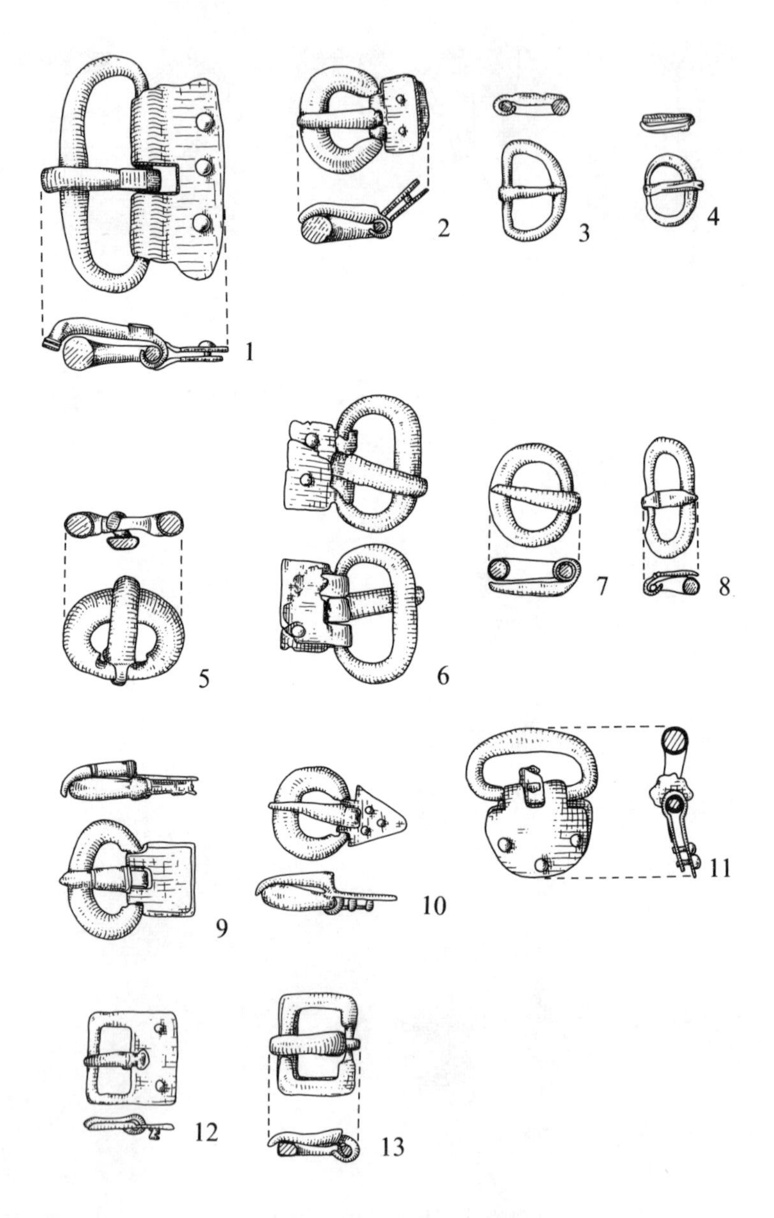

Figure 9: Belt Buckles

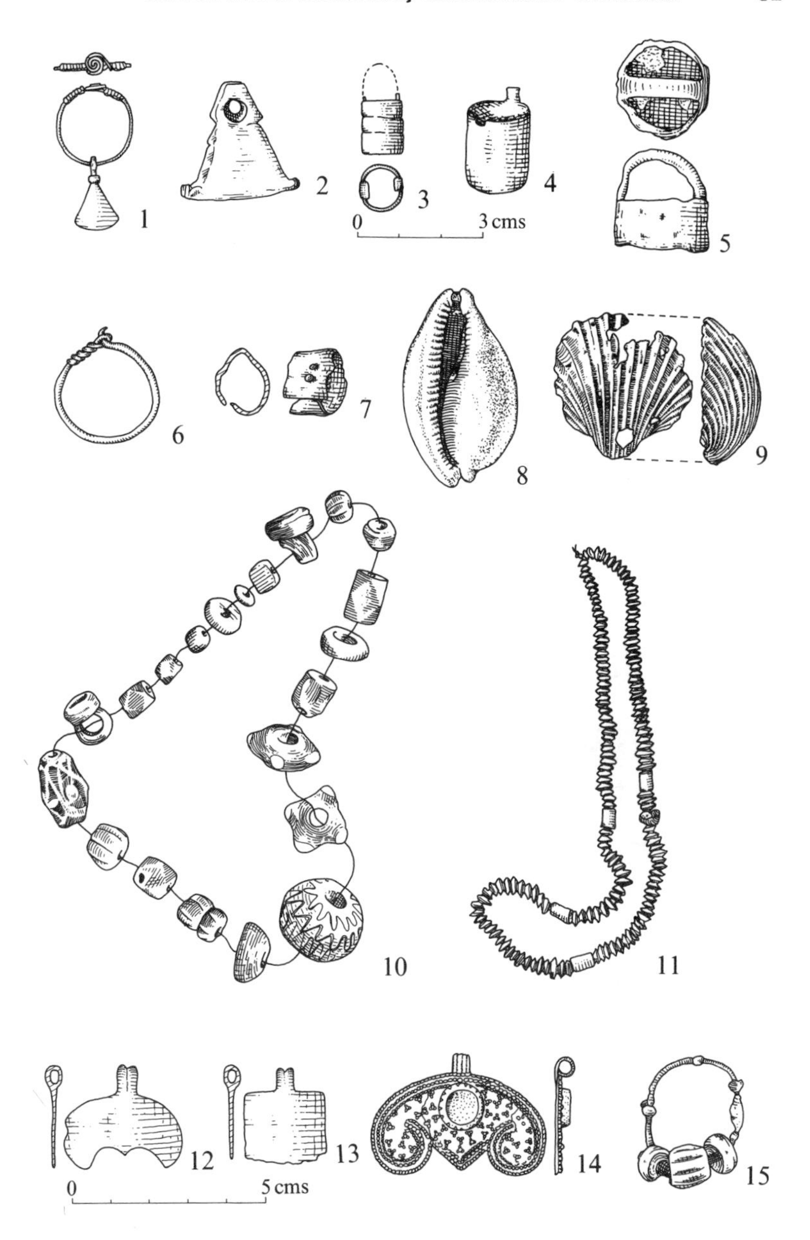

Figure 10: Personal Ornaments

a) Find raw material

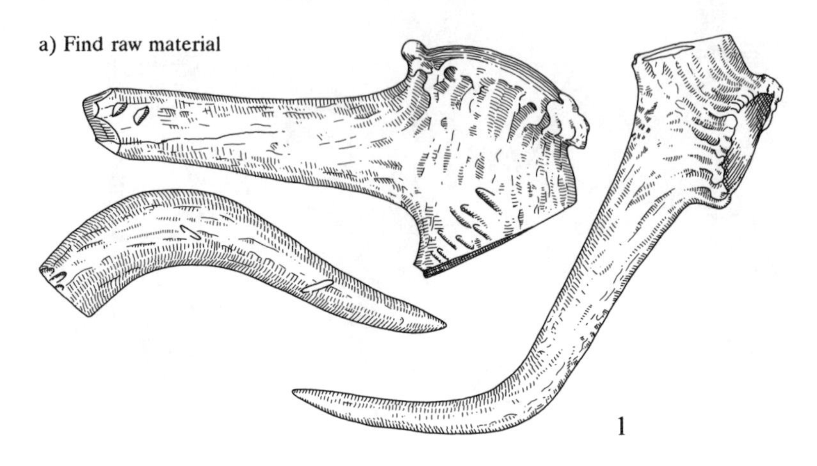

b) Cut horn extensions into short sections and split

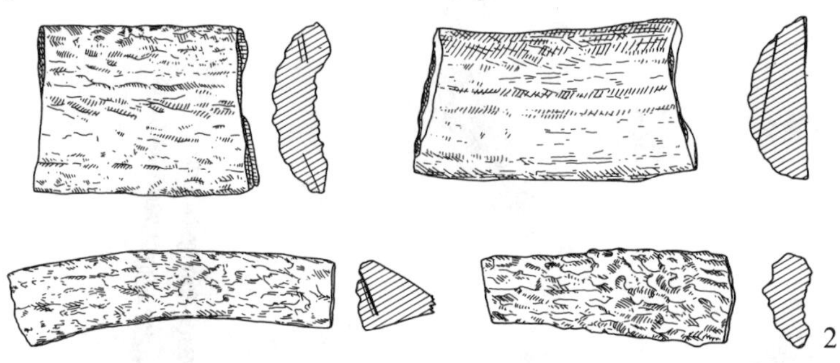

c) Cut away curved surface and trim to create thin, flat, rectangular plates.

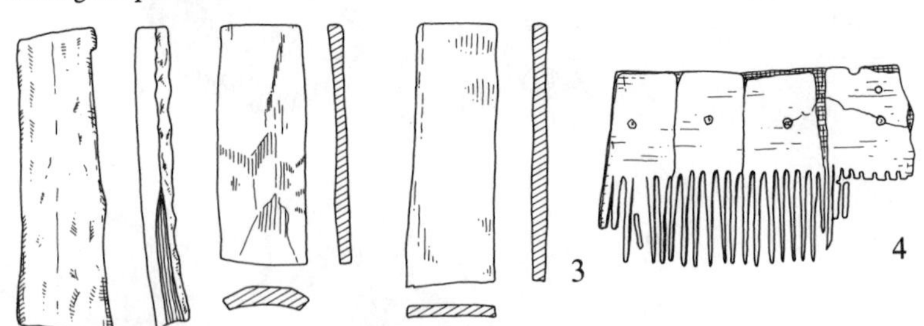

N.B. Those shown are in varying stages of completion; *do not* cut teeth until very end of process

Figure 11: How to make your own Bone Comb

d) Take remaining part of horn, split and work into flat, semi-circular shape

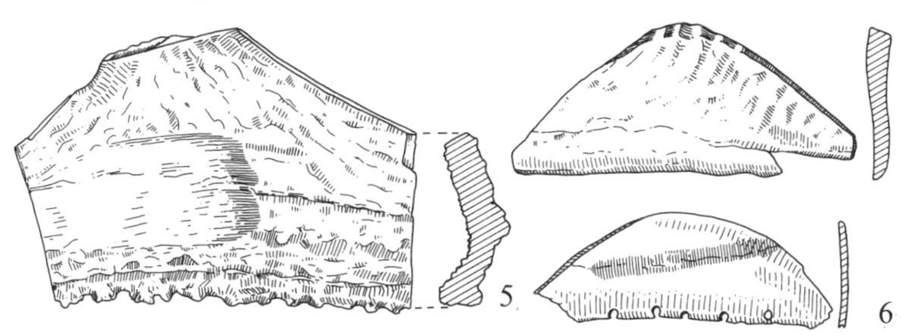

e) Take a series of plates, place semi-circular piece either side and rivet together (copper)

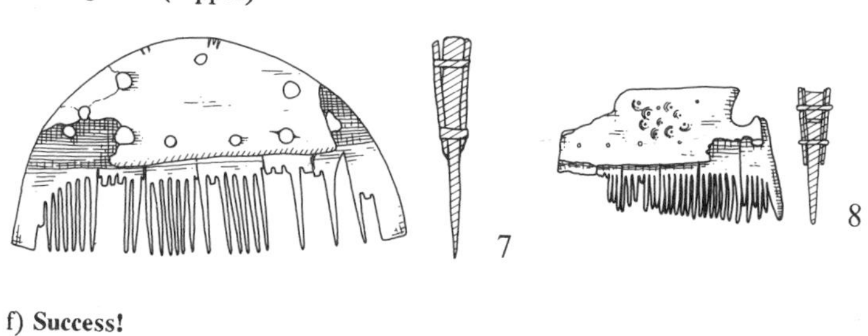

f) **Success!**

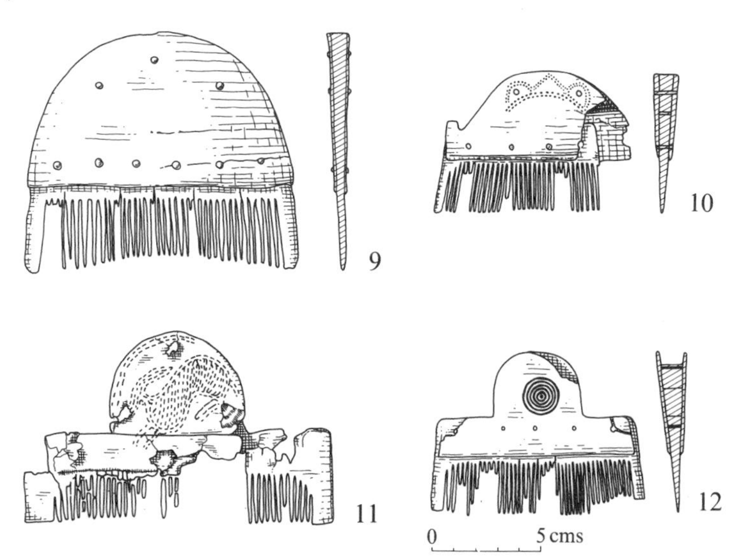

worn throughout non-Roman Europe.[58] Such objects were usually made of copper or bronze, but, once again, occasional silver examples mark out richer individuals.

The dead were also often interred with necklaces made of coloured glass or amber beads, so that this kind of material has survived in great quantities. Individual pieces of amber were also sometimes made into amulets or pendants, as, on occasion, were pearls and carved fragments of bones. Without colour, there is little point in illustrating such finds, but it is worth emphasising that they do turn up in large quantities. We unfortunately lack the detailed information which would allow us to establish the significance of individual items, but many of these objects, while obviously decorative, must also have had a religious significance.[59]

The comb, finally, was a commonly owned object. Both iron and bone combs have been found, but the latter is much more common. Combs would appear to be a characteristically Germanic item. The famous long hair of the Franks comes immediately to mind, and, while common in central Europe, combs do not seem to have been found in the cultures which flourished around the Carpathian mountains before the arrival of the Goths.[60] Considerable light has been shed on the manufacture of the bone variety by discoveries made at Bîrlad-Valea Seacă in Romania. The team led by Palade had, by 1975 (the last report we have been able to find), unearthed a total of 16 workshops dedicated to the manufacture of such combs, the basic raw material being deer antlers. Within these workshops were combs at all stages of manufacture, enabling us to provide a fully illustrated guide to the making of bone combs (Fig. 11).[61] While fewer in number, iron combs are good evidence for dating the earlier phases of the Culture, and also provide another link with the Baltic region. They were common there in the transition period between Godlowski's phases C1 and C2.[62] Bone combs are similarly useful. The simple semi-circular comb and its variants belong to earlier phases of the Culture, while those with handles

---

[58] Werner (1988), 262ff.

[59] Ioniţă (1966), 255ff. with illustrations.

[60] Compare, for instance, the illustrations of Godlowski (1970), with those of Bichir (1976), where no examples of combs are given.

[61] **1**: Palade (1966), 216; **2**: Palade (1966), 269; **3**: Palade (1966), 272; **4**: Mitrea and Preda (1964), 315; **5** & **6**: Palade (1966), 270-1; **7**: Palade (1966), 274; **8**: *MIA* 139, 126; **9** & **11**: Ioniţă (1966), 214; **10** & **12**: *MIA* 139, 126.

[62] Werner (1988), 254ff.

shaped like a semi-circle upon a rectangle are characteristic of later phases.

Apart from pottery, then, individuals tended to own clothing and its fastenings (brooches and belt-buckles), personal ornaments of a number of kinds, and very often a comb. While functional, all these items were at the same time decorative – even the design of comb handles became more complicated over time – and different grave good collections give a powerful impression of social differentiation, through variations in both the number and quality of objects. We have chosen to illustrate one quite well-endowed example: grave 36 from the cemetery of Letçani (Fig. 12). This fourth-century woman took with her to the next world four pots, a brooch, two spindle-whorls, an uncut bone comb, an iron knife, a necklace, and some pendants. One of the richest burials so far uncovered, grave 8 from Izvoare in Romania (cf. Map 2), contained a total of no less than sixty-two objects, including seventeen pots, a glass beaker, two silver brooches, a bone comb, a bronze buckle, glass and amber beads, together with a range of other items culminating in two goose eggs.[63]

Rich burials, in fact, are not too uncommon. Using the presence of silver as a distinguishing mark, 5 out of the 69 burials at Spanţov might be considered rich, 1 out of 39 at Olteni, 1 of 35 at Independenţa, 4 of 32 at Izvorul, and 7 out of 84 at Mogoşani (no silver seems to have been found in graves at Kosanovo). At the same time, the inventory of just as many burials consists of no more more than a small amount of pottery or a few beads. Putting the mark at three or less pots and no bronze or silver ornaments, at least 14 out of 121 burials at Kosanovo might be classed as very poor, 5 out of 35 at Independenţa, 14 out of 69 at Spanţov, 6 out of 8 at Mogoşani, 3 out of 32 at Izvorul, and 3 out of 39 at Olteni. These figures are very conservative, not counting cremations where excavators often report that fragments of pottery were found without estimating the original number of pots involved. We must envisage, therefore, a world of considerable diversity in wealth.

---

[63]Letçani: Bloşiu (1975), figure 30, 267; Izvoare: Ioniţă (1966), 255.

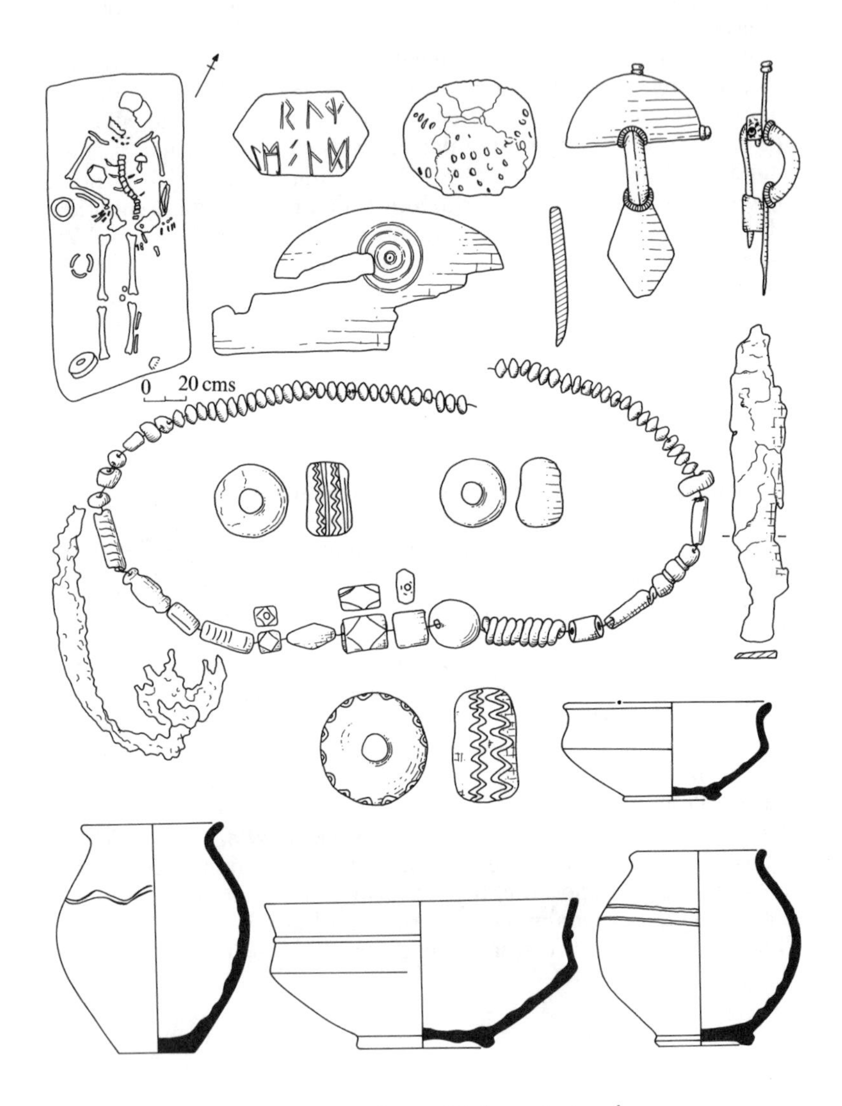

Figure 12: Grave 36 from Letçani

6. ECONOMIC LIFE

We do not propose to give an exhaustive analysis of economic activity within the Sîntana de Mureş/Černjachov Culture, but it is worthwhile to gather the main evidence for the basic pattern of life in these lands. From the archaeological evidence, it is very clear that we are dealing with an essentially sedentary population, living in not too widely-dispersed villages, whose primary occupation was the pursuit of agriculture, a high priority being given to the production of cereals. To judge from deposits in storage pits, the most important crops were wheat, barley, and millet; rye, oats, peas, acorns, and hemp were also harvested.[64] Millstones from small, hand-powered grinders have also been excavated from a number of sites.

Similarly, many of the metal tools discovered in graves and sites were produced for agricultural purposes; Fig. 13 gives some idea of the range of equipment that has been unearthed. Finds of iron ploughshares, sickles and scythes have been quite common. Wood-working tools, such as iron axe-heads, have also been discovered in substantial quantities, and in one house at Luka-Vrubleveckaja on the Dniester a complete tool-kit was recovered: hand saws, two chisels, borers, and specialist knives. The more usual domestic utensils of the villagers have also come to light: knives, scissors, pincers, needles.[65] There is a basic correspondence between this physical evidence and the *Passion of St. Saba*, whose vignettes of village life indicate some of the social structure that would have prevailed in these settlements (see Chapter 4).

Considerable effort was also put into animal husbandry. Among domesticated animal bones, those of cattle are the most common, pointing to the importance of cattle herding. Sheep and goats were also kept, along with pigs, and some horses. According to the opportunities offered by the terrain, the relative proportion of these animals varied. In Moldavia, in the foothills of the Carpathians, the countryside was more suitable for sheep and goats, and such animals

---

[64] Häusler (1979), 24; Ioniţă, 91 (1966), 253ff., or (1975), 77f.

[65] See generally, Ioniţă (1966), 252ff. with illustrations, and Häusler (1979) 35. Cf. Ioniţă (1975), 77f., more recent evidence suggests that Thompson (1966), 25f. underestimated the use of iron. Figure 13: **1**: *MIA* 89, 322; **2**: Ioniţă (1966), 218; **3**: Ioniţă (1976), 78; **4**: Diaconu (1965), 167; **5**: Ioniţă (1966), 218; **6**: *MIA* 116, 218; **7**: *MIA* 139, 127; **8-13**: *MIA* 116, 218; **14**: Ioniţă (1976), 78; **15 & 16**: Diaconu (1969), 373.

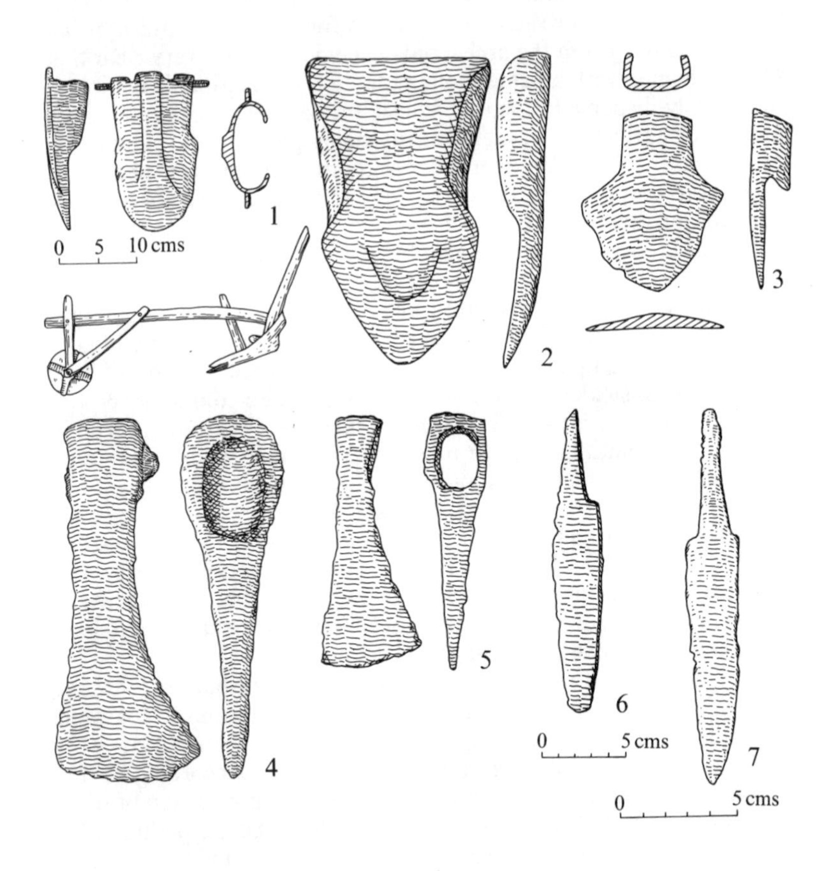

Figure 13: Iron Tools and Weapons

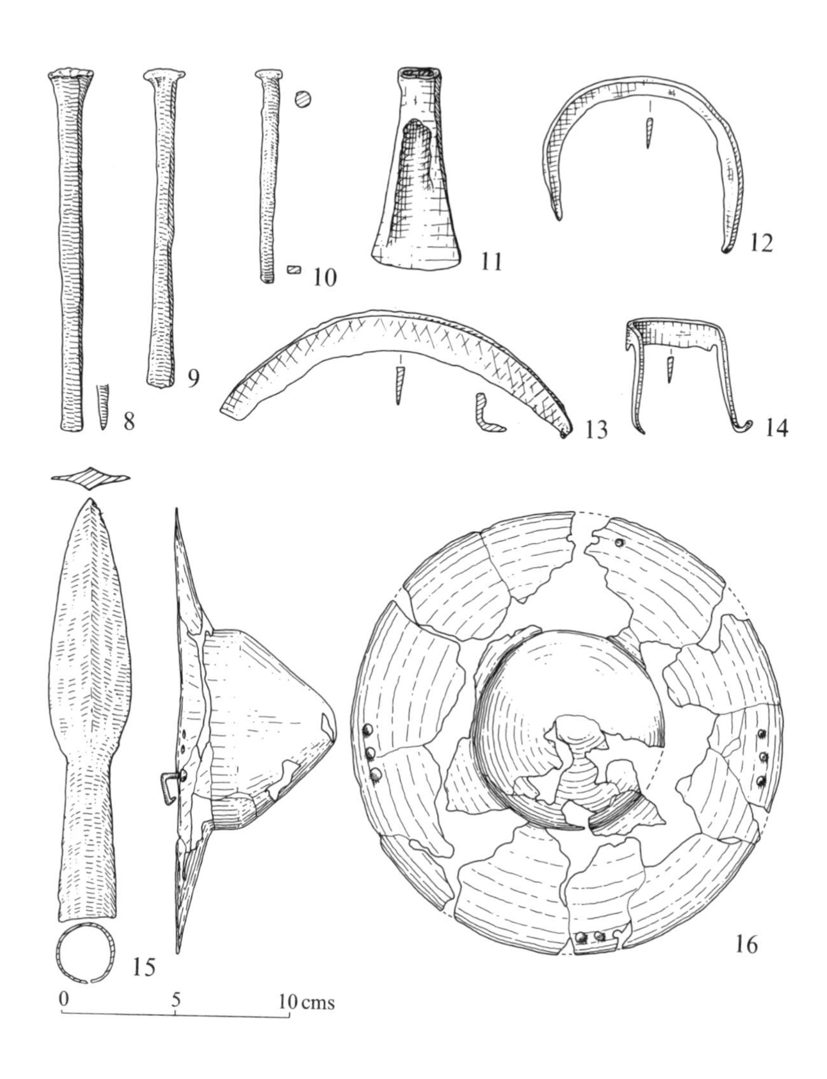
8
9
10
11
12
13
14
15
16
0
5
10 cms

were nearly as common here as cattle. In the Ukraine proper, pigs took second place, and it was only right out in the Steppe that horses seem to have played a prominent role.[66] Hunting seems to have been no more than a subsidiary part of the economy. The bones of deer and other such animals appear on Sîntana de Mureş/Černjachov sites in much smaller percentages than on those of the cultures which had previously occupied the same areas.[67]

With regard to manufacture, local craftsmen, not to say domestic production, rather than large-scale trading networks, seem to have been the norm. As we have seen, many villages would seem to have had their own potters. Likewise, spinning and weaving were probably undertaken largely in the home; spindle-whorls are a common item of grave furniture.[68] That said, other crafts suggest a slightly more developed economic structure.

Metal-working skills, for instance, were clearly widespread within the Culture. As we have seen, everyday iron objects and tools are quite common, as are those of bronze. Precious metals are less in evidence, but the upper strata in society did at least possess silver brooches and belt fittings. Little work has so far been done of the origins of the metals used for these items. Iron ore workings have yet to be discovered, and it is no more than a guess that silver may have been obtained from melting down Roman *denarii*. Centres of iron and bronze production, however, have been found in the USSR; at Sinicy, for instance, 15 or so smithies were found clustered on the bank of the nearby river. This suggests some economic specialisation, even if it should not be exaggerated. Sinicy is quite small, compared even to Iron Age La Tène complexes of the same area, and most villages would seem to have had their own blacksmith.[69]

A second example of craft specialisation is provided by the workshops at Bîrlad-Valea Seacă devoted to comb-making. Neither comb nor iron production was in any sense an industry, but the economy would seem to have been at a stage of development at least one remove from local self-sufficiency. And if those who worked in

---

[66]Häusler (1979), 27ff.; Ioniţă (1966), 254; Diaconu (1975), 69f. The Gothic version of the parable of the Prodigal Son offers different words for enclosed (arable) land, and for open land on which pigs were herded; below, Chapter 7, Passage I, v. 25 with note.

[67]Häusler (1979), 28f.

[68]Ioniţă (1966), 253f.; Häusler (1979), 36.

[69]Häusler (1979), 29-33.

these crafts really did make a living from their activities, then some system of exchange must have evolved by which they could trade the fruits of their labour for the necessities of life. This could well have been via barter, of course, but large numbers of Roman coins were circulating in the Goths' lands, at least within the territory of modern Romania.

The evidence for this is presented in Fig. 14; we could find no comprehensive study of Roman coins from the relevant areas of the USSR. The huge number of coins from the mid-fourth century, particularly from the reign of Constantius II, is immediately striking. Of Roman bronze coins issued in the 225 years between 275 and 500 A.D. and found in Romania, some 65% of those in hoards (4078 out of 6272) and about 70% from single finds (1038 out of 1496) were minted in the forty or so years between *c.* 320 and 360.[70] Silver coins of the period have been found in similarly disproportionate numbers: *c.* 70% of those from hoards (189 out of 272) and *c.* 55% of single finds. Of an earlier era, Tacitus reports that in the first century A.D. the Germanic tribes closest to the Rhine frontier quickly learned to use Roman coins for commercial purposes (*Germania* 5), and it is hard to see why a similar situation should not have prevailed north of the Danube in the mid-fourth century.[71]

As such a coin circulation suggests, economic relations with the Roman empire were an important fact of life. Similarly, Roman amphorae, which would not have been empty when they crossed the frontier, are a substantial presence in the archaeological evidence. Roman glassware and other luxury items also made their way across the frontier in greater quantities than in previous centuries.[72] Of items flowing in the opposite direction, we know only that slave traders operated in Gothic lands. By the late empire, slaves were expensive and hard to come by, and this alone would have generated Roman interest in commercial links.[73]

The treaty of 332 between the empire and primarily the Tervingi, the Gothic people closest to the Danube, greatly extended these

---

[70]Based on Preda (1975), 444 (cf. his figure 1 opposite 446). We have consolidated the figures, so that coins of Crispus and Fausta, for instance, appear under Constantine I.

[71]Down to the 340s, the Bosporan kingdoms also issued coins in substantial numbers: e.g. Anokhin (1980) and Frolova (1983).

[72]Häusler (1979), 54ff.

[73]Amm. Marc. 22.7.8 refers to Galatian slave traders preying on the Goths, and the practice was continued south of the Danube (id. 31.4.10f.); cf., for a slightly later period, Synesius, *De Regno*, 21. On the slave trade, see de Ste Croix (1981), 226ff.

	Hoards			Chance Finds			
	AV	AR	AE	AV	AR	AE	Total
274-285	-	-	3	5	1	45	54
1st Tetrarchy	-	-	1	3	4	73	81
2nd Tetrarchy	-	-	14	-	-	59	73
Constantine I	2	-	44	2	6	398	452
Constantine II	1	-	13	1	-	72	87
Constantius II	1	185	3795	2	34	526	4543
Julian	-	1	226	-	1	36	264
Jovian	-	3	-	1	1	6	11
Valentinian & Valens	2	82	75	3	28	123	314
Theodosius I	14	1	297	4	1	47	364
Arcadius	8	-	264	11	-	30	313
Theodosius II	24	-	197	14	-	7	242
Marcian	2	-	-	-	-	-	2
Leo I	2	-	-	1	-	-	3
Zeno	1	-	-	-	-	1	2
Unidentified finds, 4-5 Cent.	20	-	1343	1	-	73	1437
Total	77	272	6272	48	77	1496	8242

Table 14: Roman Coins North of the Danube, 275-491

Coins p.a. averaged over the period 275-491; 38.2
Coins p.a. averaged over the period 332-369; 153.3
Proportion of coins falling in the period 332-369; 68.8%

cross-border links. It authorised, most unusually, that trade could take place at any point along the shared frontier. It also involved diplomatic presents of various kinds to Gothic leaders, and, under its terms, Gothic soldiers were paid on occasion to serve with the Roman army (see Chapter 2). All of these measures must have both increased the Goths' desire for Roman goods, and, at the same time, provided them with the wherewithal - i.e. Roman money - for purchasing them. Indeed, it is very hard not to associate the extraordinarily high numbers of Roman coins of the mid-fourth century with the workings of the treaty of 332. The close relations it established encouraged trading contacts, in which Goths were able to build up reserves of Roman cash to spend on Roman luxury goods. A sizeable majority of these coins has also been discovered in hoards, so that these figures may well reflect the fierce campaigns of the years 367-9. The treaty of 369 introduced much greater supervision, but even so, commercial contacts continued through two designated centres (cf. Chapter 2, p. 20). Themistius records that trade was mutually beneficial (*Or.* 10, 205/135); Roman slave traders and merchants of luxury goods did not want to lose access to Gothic lands.[74]

To summarise, the physical remains of the Sîntana de Mureş/Černjachov Culture suggest an economy devoted largely to subsistence agriculture, but with some craft specialisation and considerable trade with the Roman empire. There were some differences of wealth; at one end of the spectrum were those buried with silver ornaments, and at the other those buried with little or nothing. It is also possible that the top strand of society has not been unearthed in the main cemeteries we have discussed. In the *Passion of St. Saba*, Atharid, who has ultimate authority over the village, comes from outside it, and does not live alongside the Gothic rank and file (see Chapter 4), and debate continues about the treasures found at Pietroasa. If even part of this is fourth-century,[75] the real rulers of these lands ornamented themselves not in silver, but in gold.

---

[74]Thompson (1966), 19f. has even suggested that the Goths were dependent on Roman supplies, since, in 369, 'the interruption of trade had reduced the [Goths] to such want that they sent a number of delegations to beg for peace' (Amm. Marc. 27.5.7). But the Goths' distress followed three years of Roman campaigns, during which they could not have planted a harvest. The interruption to trade must be seen against this background: as a reinforcement of distress, but not its only cause.

[75]For different views and references to the literature, compare Harhoiu (1977), 3ff. with Diaconu (1975), 73f., esp. n. 39.

7. ETHNIC IDENTITIES

There is no longer any real doubt that the Sîntana de Mureş/Černjachov Culture reflects in some way the Goths' domination of lands north of the Danube and the Black Sea. Uncertainty does remain, however, over the precise mixture of races contributing to the Culture. It is not our purpose to resolve this difficult question, but it is important to gather the main pieces of evidence, and to highlight some of the problems.

The single most striking feature of the whole Culture is its uniformity. Apart from a few short-lived local variants, more or less the same physical culture has been found in sites and cemeteries all the way from the Danube to the Ukraine, and even out on the Steppe. The constituent elements of this uniformity, however, have differing origins. Certain elements either clearly attest the presence of a Germanic population, or are strongly reminiscent of Germanic cultures to the north and west. A spindle-whorl inscribed with runes was discovered in Letçani grave 36 (Fig. 12), and other runes have been found on pottery.[76] Similarly, as we have seen, certain types of hand-made pot are paralleled only in Germanic cultures, and combs are not found in earlier indigenous cultures of the region, although they are common in Germanic ones. The builders of *Wohnstallhäuser* seem, likewise, to have come from the north, and the habit of wearing two brooches (*fibulae*), rather than one, would seem to have originally been Germanic. Some types of pendant and amulet are also paralleled only in the north.[77]

Other characteristic features of the Culture have different antecedents. Many of the styles and, above all, the basic techniques used in the wheel-made pottery, the single most common artefact in sites and cemeteries, are indigenous to the Carpathian and perhaps also to the North Pontic region. Descending from La Tène Iron Age cultures, and strongly affected by Roman influence, the ceramic wares have little to do with the Germanic north. *Grubenhäuser*, similarly, are strongly attested in earlier cultures of the Carpathian region. Some elements of the Culture were also inherited somehow from Sarmatian Steppe nomads. Apart from incidences of cranial

[76] Bloşiu (1975), 219; cf. Diaconu (1976), 269ff.; Diaconu and Anghelescu (1963), 167ff. Runes are also inscribed on one of the torques of the Pietroasa treasure: below, p. 154 and Harhoiu (1977), 13f.

[77] *Fibulae*: Bichir (1976), 91; amulets: Werner (1988), 262f.

deformation, a few burials are similar to the mass of Sarmatian graves, for instance, in making use of a platform, and some items of jewellery and ornamentation have as their models items from these earlier Steppe cultures.[78] Despite the homogeneity of the end result, the diverse origins of different elements of the Culture raise the question how to measure the contribution to the end result of the different ethnic groups from whom these elements originally came.

The literary sources, except where deliberately archaising, are unanimous that Germanic Goths were the main focus of fourth-century Roman policy north of the Lower Danube. This is indicative of an important truth. It was the military power of the Goths which was the prime determinant of the political geography of this region at the time. It seems likely, therefore, that the dominant Goths exploited the agricultural surplus of any indigenous groups who lived alongside them.[79] The Huns certainly exploited the Goths in their turn at a later date when they were dominant (Priscus, fr. 39 Müller/49 Blockley), and we also have a little evidence that Gothic hegemony had to be established by force. Archaeologists have uncovered levels of burning, perhaps an indication that both Sarmatian cultures in southern Russia, and indigenous Daco-Getan in western Romania were displaced forcibly by the bearers of the Sîntana de Mureş/Černjachov Culture.[80]

If the political and military dominance of the Goths seems clear enough, other matters are more perplexing. In particular, what was the basic pattern of life? Did the Goths and other peoples live side by side in the same villages, using the same cemeteries, or did their settlements remain separate? Romanian scholars have tackled this problem from two quite different directions – through funerary rites and methods of production – suggesting from both that the different ethnic elements of the population lived cheek by jowl. The argument from funerary rites is based on the bi-ritual nature of the cemeteries, with further attempts to isolate other elements of funerary ritual which might also be diagnostic of ethnic identity.[81] As we have seen, however, it now seems probable that behind the bi-ritual

---

[78]Werner (1988), 262; Diaconu (1965), 137-9.

[79]Cf. Ioniţă (1975), 86ff. for a different view, emphasising economic rather than ethnic ties, and suggesting that the aristocracy exploited all, regardless of race. We are unconvinced that locals and Goths mixed so freely (cf. below).

[80]Gey (1986), 87; Bichir (1984), 107ff. A late example of such displacement is provided by Amm. Marc. 31.4.13, where Athanaric takes refuge in the so-called 'locus Caucalandensis', driving out its Sarmatian inhabitants; 'Sarmatis inde extrusis'.

[81]E.g. Ioniţă (1975), 83f.

pattern of the cemeteries, there is a chronological development which has little to do with race; none of the other rituals supposedly diagnostic of ethnic identity has won much support either.[82]

As for methods of production, great stress has been placed on the evidence of the pottery, with its heavy dependence on indigenous forms and techniques, to argue that it shows the local Daco-Getans to have played a leading role in the creation of the Culture, and to have been present on most sites (the pottery is found everywhere).[83] But while there is no doubting the origins of the pottery, it was certainly used by Germanic Goths. The usual pottery was discovered, for instance, alongside the rune-inscribed spindle-whorl of Letçani grave 36, which must surely be that of a Goth. It is also hard to see why potters among the Gothic immigrants should not have been able to learn the superior techniques practised by the people with whom they had now come into contact. In any case, it is perhaps dangerous to be too insistent on the non-Germanic nature of pottery forms. A wide and shallow (drinking?) bowl, similar to the wheel-made one so common in Sîntana de Mureş/Černjachov Culture, but made by hand, is a common element of the Wielbark Culture.[84]

Such observations are inconclusive, but do emphasise the difficulties of deciding ethnic identities on the basis of material objects. This is more than usually applicable here, where a number of strands with different origins fused to create a homogeneous culture. Whatever the original groups from whom particular cultural elements were taken, the homogeneity indicates that all groups within these lands quickly adopted much the same material culture. As a result, any attempt to detect ethnic identities on the basis of objects is likely to be at best inconclusive, and other approaches might produce better results.

Stepping outside the archaeological evidence for a moment, we know that ethnic groups of the migration period could on occasion absorb outsiders. Priscus, for instance, met a Greek merchant who had become to all intents and purposes a Hun (fr. 8 Müller/11.2 Blockley) and the *Strategicon* of Maurice reports that the Slavs gave released prisoners a chance to stay with them as full members of the

---

[82]Cf., for example, Palade (1980), 250f. arguing against the significance of secondary burning. Likewise, Mitrea and Preda (1964), 236f. are unconvinced by attempts to accredit the adoption of inhumation to the influence of Sarmatians.

[83]Palade (1980), esp. 250-3.

[84]Compare, for instance, Godlowski (1970), plates 8 and 9.

tribal group (11.4).[85] The question to ask of the evidence, then, is whether, and to what degree, this occurred within the Gothic realms of the fourth century.

Again, there is no clear answer, but some observations are worth making. As we have seen, there is a little evidence for small numbers of Germanic outsiders on certain sites, who then quickly disappear from the archaeological record. These, it seems likely, represent heterogeneous Germanic groups who were absorbed into Gothic tribal units. The same process is perhaps also suggested by occasional finds of Sarmatian burials. Important evidence of a different kind, however, has emerged from three sites in the eastern Carpathian area of Romania. Excavations have been able to show that on these sites – Costișa-Mănoaia, Botoșana-Suceava, and Dodești-Vaslui – settlement was continuous from the period of the Sîntana de Mureș/Černjachov Culture (or even before in the case of Dodești-Vaslui) right through the Migration Period into the Middle Ages proper. There are also clear links between these and related sites and others in western Romania (the so-called Bratei Culture). This would suggest that an indigenous Daco-Getan population lived in and around the Carpathians before, during, and after the period of our Culture.[86] This conclusion, should further research maintain it, has obvious relevance for the question that concerns us here. If a distinct local population remained in the area beyond the period of the Sîntana de Mureș/Černjachov Culture, this would suggest strongly that these groups had not become inextricably mixed up with the Goths, most of whom, as we know from literary and archaeological evidence, left for areas further west in the course of the Migration Period.[87] This is what we might expect if the locals were subservient to the militarily dominant Goths; in such a situation, full intermingling is hard to imagine.

The question is far from resolved, and much will no doubt emerge from future excavations. We can conclude, however, that the Sîntana

---

[85] See also *Miracula Sancti Demetrii*, ed. Lemerle, pp. 284-7, for the creation of a new, ethnically-mixed political unit within the Avar Empire of the seventh century.

[86] Teodor (1980), 3ff. On the Bratei Culture, see Zaharia (1971).

[87] The literary evidence is well known; on the archaeology, Bierbrauer (1980), 137ff. This may be the place to mention the the so-called 'Crimean Goths', recorded from the ninth down to the late eighteenth century and described in 1562 by the Flemish scholar-diplomat Ogier Ghislain de Busbecq: cf. MacDonald Stearns, jr., *Crimean Gothic: analysis and etymology of the Corpus* (1978); and P. Scardigli, *Lingua e storia dei Goti* (1964), 288-311. The relevant texts are transcribed and translated at pp. 4-20 of Stearns' book (Busbecq at 9-15). Presumably these Goths were an authentic survival of the original settlement in the region; cf. below, Chapter 4, p. 105.

de Mureş/Černjachov Culture was both homogeneous, and at the same time the product of a number of different ethnic and cultural strands. These strands reflect the involvement of different peoples, but there is no easy correspondence between material objects and ethnic identity in the fully-developed Culture. The Goths were militarily and therefore politically dominant, and may well have absorbed some outsiders. At the same time, the exercise of domination is likely to have kept superior and inferior distinct, and there is evidence of a indigenous population not absorbed by the Goths. The Sîntana de Mureş/Černjachov Culture is a synthesis, but its physical remains do not prove that its constituent groups mingled inextricably, nor even that they lived side by side in the same villages.

BIBLIOGRAPHY FOR CHAPTER THREE

Anokhin, V. A., 1980. *The Coinage of Chersonesus*, BAR International Series 69.

Bichir, Gh., 1976. *Archaeology and History of the Carpi*, BAR International Series 16.

– – , 1984. *Geto-Dacii din Muntenia în epoca romană* (French summary at 107-111).

Bierbrauer, V., 1980. 'Zur chronologischen, soziologischen und regionalen Gliederung des östgermanischen Fundstoffs des 5. Jahrhunderts in Sudösteuropa' in Wolfram and Daim (edd.), *Die Völker*, 131-142.

Bloşiu, C., 1975. 'La nécropole de Letçani (dép. de Jassy) datant du IVe siècle de n.è.', *Arheologia Moldovei* 8, 203-280 (French summary at 239-42).

Constantinescu, M., Pascu, S., and Diaconu, P. (edd.), 1975. *Relations between the Autochthonous Population and the Migratory Populations on the territory of Romania*.

Diaconu, Gh., 1963. 'Archäologische Angaben über die Taifalen', *Dacia* n.s. 7, 301-15.

– – , 1964. 'Einheimische und Wandervölker im 4. Jahrhundert u.Z. auf dem Gebiete Rumäniens (Tîrgşor-Gherăseni-Variante)', *Dacia* n.s. 8, 195-210.

– – , 1965. *Tîrgşor: Necropola din secolele III-IV e.n.*

– – , 1969. 'Das Gräberfeld von Mogoşani (Kreis Dîmboviţa)', *Dacia* n.s. 13, 367-402.

– – , 1975. 'On the Socio-economic Relations between natives and Goths in Dacia', in Constantinescu, Pascu and Diaconu (edd.), *Relations*, 67-75.

– – , 1976. 'Zwei Gefässe aus dem 4. Jh. u.Z. von Pietroasele-Buzău', *Dacia* n.s. 20, 269-71.

– – , and Anghelescu, N., 1963. 'Despre necropola din sec. IV e.n. de la Radu Negru (r. Călăraşi)', *SCIV* 14, 167-174.

Frolova, N. A., 1983. *The Coinage of the Kingdom of Bosporos*, BAR International Series 166.

Gey, O. A., 1980. 'The Cherniakhovo Culture sites of the North Pontic Region', *SA* 1980.2, 45-51 (English summary at 51).

– – , 1986. 'On the date of the Chernyakhovo Culture in the Northern Black Sea area', *SA* 1986.1, 77-87 (English summary at 87).

Godlowski, K., 1970. *The Chronology of the Late Roman and Early Migration Periods in Central Europe*, Prace Archeologiczne 11.

Hachmann, R., 1971. *The Ancient Civilisation of the Germanic Peoples*.

Häusler, A., 1979. 'Zu den sozialökonomischen Verhältnissen in der Černjachov-Kultur', *Zeitschrift fur Archäologie* 13, 23-65.

Harhoiu, R., 1977. *The Treasure from Pietroasa, Romania*, BAR International Series 24.

Heather, P. J., 1991. *Goths and Romans 332-489*.

Horedt, K., 1986. *Siebenbürgen im Frühmittelalter*.

Ioniţă, I., 1966. 'Contributii cu privire la cultura Sîntana de Mureş-Černeahov pe teritoriul Republicii Socialiste România', *Arheologia Moldovei* 4, 189-259 (French summary at 252-7).

– – , 1970. 'Probleme der Sîntana de Mureş-Černjachovkultur auf dem Gebiete Rumäniens', in U.E. Hagberg (ed.), *Studia Gotica*, 95-104.

– – , 1971. *Das Gräberfeld von Independenţa, Walachei: zur relativen Chronologie und zu den Bestattungs-, Beigaben-, und Trachtsitten eines Gräberfeldes der Černjachov-Sîntana de Mureş-Kultur*, Saarbrücker Beiträge z. Altertumskunde 10.

– – , 1975. 'The Social-economic Structure of Society during the Goths' Migration in the Carpatho-Danubian area', in

Constantinescu, Pascu and Diaconu (edd.), *Relations*, 77-89.

– – , 1977. *La nécropole du IVe siècle de n.è. à Miorcani*, Inventaria Arch. Roumanie, fasc. 8.

– – , 1980. 'Die Römer-Daker und die Wandervölker im Donauländischen Karpatenraum im 4. Jahrhundert', in Wolfram and Daim (edd.), *Die Völker*, 123-9.

Kropotkin, A. V., 1984. 'On the Centres of the Černyakhovo Tribes', *SA* 1984.3, 35-47 (English summary at 47).

MIA 82 (1960); 89 (1960); 116 (1964); 139 (1967); various contributors.

Mitrea, B., and Preda, C., 1964. 'Quelques problèmes ayant trait aux nécropoles de type Sîntana-Tcherniakhov découvertes en Valachie', *Dacia* n.s. 8, 211-237.

– – , 1966. *Necropole din secolul al IV lea e.n. in Muntenîa* (French summary at 165-188).

Palade, V., 1966. 'Atelierele pentru lucrat pieptini din os din secolul al IV-lea e.n. de la Bîrlad-Valea Seacă', *Arheologia Moldovei* 4, 261-77.

— — , 1980. 'Éléments géto-daces dans le site Sîntana de Mureş de Bîrlad-Valea Seacă', *Dacia* n.s. 24, 223-253.

– – , 1986. *Nécropole du IVe et commencement du Ve siècle de n.è. à Bîrlad-Valea Seacă*, Inventaria Arch. Roumanie, fasc. 12.

Preda, C., 1975. 'Circulatia monedelor romane postaureliene în Dacia', *SCIV* 26.4, 441-486.

Rafalović, I. A., 1986. *Dančeny. Mogil'nik Černjachovskoj Kul'tury III-IV vv. n.e.* (in Russian).

Ste Croix, G. E. M. de, 1981. *The Class Struggle in the Ancient Greek World*.

Scardigli, P., *Lingua e Storia dei Goti* (Florence, 1964).

Shchukin, M. B., 1975. 'Das Problem der Černjachov-Kultur in der sowjetischen archäologischen Literatur', *Zeitschrift für Archäologie* 9, 25-41.

– – , 1989. *Rome and the Barbarians in Central and Eastern Europe 1st Century B.C. - 1st Century A.D.*, BAR International Series 542 (2 vols.).

Stearns, MacDonald, jr., *Crimean Gothic: analysis and etymology of the Corpus* (Studia Linguistica et Philologica, 6: Saratoga, Calif., 1978).

Sulimirski, T., 1970. *The Sarmatians.*

Teodor, D. Gh., 1980. *The east Carpathian area of Romania V-XI centuries A.D.*, BAR International Series 81.

Thompson, E. A., 1966. *The Visigoths in the time of Ulfila.*

Todd, M., 1987. *The Northern Barbarians 100 BC - AD 300.*

Werner, J., 1988. 'Dančeny und Brangstrup: Untersuchungen zur Černjachov-Kultur zwischen Sereth und Dnestr und zu den "Reichtumszentern" auf Fünen', *Bonner Jahrbuch* 188, 241-286.

Wolfram, H., and Daim, F., edd., 1980. *Die Völker an der mittleren und unteren Donau im fünften und sechsten Jahrhundert*, Österreichische Akademie der Wissenschaften, Phil.-Hist. Kl., Denkschriften 145.

Zaharia, E., 1971. 'Données sur l'archéologie des IV-XI siècles sur le territoire de la Roumanie. La culture Bratei et la culture Dridu', *Dacia* n.s. 15, 269-88.

CHAPTER FOUR

MARTYRS AND MARTYROLOGIES

Two main outbreaks are recorded of persecution by the Gothic authorities of Christians among their people: in 347/8, when Ulfila and his followers were driven from Gothic territory to the Roman empire (see Chapter 5 below), and in the early 370s by the Tervingian 'iudex' Athanaric. The texts translated in this chapter, with the possible exception of Text 4(iii), relate to the second outbreak. The martyrdom of St. Saba is dated precisely to 12 April 372, and the episode described in Text 4(i), which is also mentioned by Sozomen and in the Gothic martyrology presented as Text 4(ii), took place in the reigns of Valentinian, Valens and Gratian (367/75). It is not accidental that the persecution closely follows the peace treaty of 369 between Valens and Athanaric (above, Chapter 2). Whatever the balance of advantage between Goths and Romans achieved by the treaty, the preceding hostilities had exposed the question of the loyalty of individuals and communities among the Goths who seemed to owe allegiance to the religious ideology of a foreign power: the persecutions can be seen as an attempt to reinforce solidarity at a time of stress. The same may be true also of the persecution of 347/8, if Thompson and others are right (Chapter 2, Introduction) in detecting an outbreak of hostilities between Goths and Romans at that time.

1. SOZOMEN, *ECCLESIASTICAL HISTORY* 6.37

INTRODUCTION

The account of the Goths given by the fifth-century church historian Sozomen derives from that of his predecessor Socrates, with the addition of three significant blocks of material from another source, or sources: (i) an account of the manner in which the Goths were supposed to have become known to the neighbours the Huns; we may detect here the influence of the pagan historian Eunapius, probably as mediated by Philostorgius, who can otherwise be shown to have used Eunapius;[1] (ii) a description of the earlier career of Ulfila, an explanation of his adherence to Arian doctrines in the time of Constantius, and the connection of this with the Arianism of the Goths in general: this too may well derive from Philostorgius; and (iii) a fuller account than is found in Socrates of the character of the Gothic persecution of Christians conducted by Athanaric. This includes an allusion to Gothic pagan practice, and a description of the mass martyrdom of Gothic Christians by fire in their church, an episode also commemorated in the Gothic martyrologies translated below.

In adapting his predecessor's narrative, however, Sozomen compounds several errors of Socrates, notably in supposing Ulfila to have been active in Gothia in the time of Fritigern and Athanaric, and he moves from the persecution of the late 340s, as a result of which Ulfila left the Gothic territories, to that of the early 370s without any apparent awareness that different events are in question, or that Ulfila, expelled from Gothia in the first persecution, had no personal connection with the second. Further, his conception of the chronological connection between the Hunnish attack on the Goths, the settlement of the Goths in Thrace, the supposed dissension between Athanaric and Fritigern and the latter's conversion to Christianity is, to put it mildly, confused (nn. 6, 14 below). On the other hand he correctly distinguishes the conversion of Fritigern as an act of 'public policy' among the Goths, from the missionary work of Ulfila which, in time at least - although by much more time than Sozomen thought - preceded it.

In these circumstances it is difficult to judge the value of Sozomen's remark in §6 that the Gothic embassy to Valens requesting permission to settle in Thrace after the Hunnish attack,

[1] Since both Sozomen and Philostorgius were familiar with the *History* of Eunapius, Sozomen's use of the latter in this passage could in principle be direct or indirect. It would however be more economical to assume that Sozomen used a single source which went on from the Huns to discuss Ulfila and the persecutions in Gothia. When Sozomen wrote, at some time between 439 and 450, Philostorgius' *Ecclesiastical History* was only recently published, and might well be known to the later writer. The relationship between Socrates and Sozomen, and the question of Eunapius/Philostorgius, are discussed in detail by Peter Heather, 'The crossing of the Danube and the Gothic conversion', *GRBS* 27 (1986), 289-318, at 293-310. For the date of Philostorgius (late 430s), see F.M. Clover, *HAColl, Bonn 1979-81* (1983), at 136-41; for that of Sozomen, Charlotte Roueché, *JTS* n.s. 37 (1986), 130-2 - 439/50 rather than 443 or soon after, as was previously believed on the basis of §13 of his Preface (ed. Bidez-Hansen, p. 3), and *Nov. Theod.* 23, issued at Aphrodisias on 22 May 443. The Heraclea there mentioned is clearly Heraclea Salbake in Caria, not Heraclea Pontica, mentioned by Sozomen, and the texts should not be connected.

was led by Ulfila; for further discussion of this intriguing possibility, see n. 5 and below, p. 135. In our translation, passages derived or closely adapted from Socrates are introduced by [Soc.], those derived from Philostorgius by [Phil.]. The text translated is that of J. Bidez, *GCS* (2nd ed., rev. by G. C. Hansen, 1960), at pp. 294-7.

TRANSLATION

1. [Soc.] As a result of these arguments of Themistius,[2] the emperor assumed a rather more humane disposition and imposed penalties [on deviant Christians] less severe than they had been before. He would not, however, have refrained completely from his anger against the clergy, had not new anxieties in public affairs conspired to inhibit his urgency. **2.** The Goths, who in former times inhabited the region beyond the Ister and [Phil.] were masters of the other barbarians, were driven from their lands by the people called the Huns and crossed over into Roman territory. **3.** Now this race, so they say, was previously unknown to the Thracians living by the Ister and to the Goths themselves, and lived as their neighbours without either party realising it – the reason for their ignorance being that a huge lake lay between them, each people believing that the country in which they lived was the last dry land to exist, and that beyond lay sea and an infinite expanse of water. It came about, however, that an ox, driven mad by insects,[3] ran through the lake and was followed by its herdsman, who saw the land on the other side and reported it to his fellow-tribesmen. **4.** Others say that a deer, fleeing in the chase, showed its Hunnish pursuers the way, which lay concealed by the surface of the water; and that the hunters, admiring the country with its gentler climate and ease of cultivation, at once turned back and reported what they had seen to the ruler of their race.[4] **5.** The Huns

---

[2]The speech of Themistius does not survive. Its argument, as summarised by Socrates and Sozomen, was that knowledge of God is very difficult to attain, so that it is not surprising that there should be differences of opinion on the matter (such observations are also found in other writers, such as Libanius and Symmachus); indeed, God will actually find it pleasing that the unattainability of knowledge about himself is so reflected in diversities of sentiment.

[3]The word οἰστροπλήξ, used by Aeschylus to describe the wanderings of Io (*Prom. Vinct.* 681) is traced to Eunapius by Thompson, *Attila and the Huns*, 16. Again, Sozomen's knowledge might be direct or indirect.

[4]For the alternative story of the hunted doe, cf. Jordanes, *Getica* 123-5, where it is apparently attributed to Priscus of Panium; this Greek author could easily have got it from Eunapius. Zosimus 4.20.3 gives, undoubtedly from Eunapius, a very abbreviated account of a crossing of the Cimmerian Bosphorus, with no anecdotal details such as we find in Sozomen and Jordanes. A fragment of Philostorgius (9.17; ed.

Huns first tried the strength of the Goths with a small force of men, and later attacked in full force, defeated the Goths in battle and took possession of their entire country. The victims of the attack made to cross the river, and coming over to the Roman frontiers sent envoys to the emperor, promising their services as his allies in the future and asking his agreement to settle whenever he chose. **6.** The leader of this embassy was Ulphilas, the bishop of the Goths;[5] and, negotiations proceeding as they hoped, they were allowed to live in Thrace.

Not long afterwards, however, [Soc.] the Goths fought among themselves and were split into two divisions, one of them led by Athanaric, the other by Fritigern. These two made war on each other and Fritigern, unsuccessful in the battle, asked the Romans to help him. **7.** The emperor ordered the army in Thrace to go to his assistance, and Fritigern, attacking for a second time, was victorious and turned to flight the supporters of Athanaric.[6] Then, as if to return thanks to Valens and as a guarantee that he would be a friend to him in all things, he adopted the emperor's religion and persuaded all the barbarians under his rule to adopt the same belief.[7]

8. In my opinion, however, this is not the only reason why the entire nation of the Goths is still to this day associated with the followers of Arius:[8] there is also [Phil.] the influence of Ulphilas,

---

Bidez-Winkelmann, p. 123) gives 'Nebroi' as the old name of the Huns (cf. Hdt. 4.17, 105; Amm. Marc. 31.2.14); this could well derive from Eunapius' literary speculations on their origin, cf. Thompson, *Attila and the Huns*, 17. For the so-called 'Crimean Goths' attested down to the late eighteenth century, see above, Chapter 3 n. 87.

[5]If true, this is significant. Ulfila lived at this time near Nicopolis in Moesia (Chapter 5, p. 144 with n. 22), and we could envisage him as brought into the negotiations by the Goths as their mediator with Valens. This is plausible, though Sozomen's statement, which does not occur in Socrates, could be an error, or a confusion from some earlier embassy, e.g. that mentioned by Philostorgius under Constantine or Constantius II (Chapter 5, pp. 141ff.). Sozomen shows no awareness (cf. §8) that Ulfila was no longer in Gothia in the time of Fritigern.

[6]The extent, dating and historicity of this 'civil war' between the Gothic leaders are disputed questions; cf. E. A. Thompson, *The Visigoths in the Time of Ulfila*, 87-9; cf. Z. Rubin, *Mus. Helv.* 38 (1981), at 41-9; Peter Heather, 'The crossing of the Danube' (n. 1 above), at 294-8. In any case it would clearly precede, not follow, the crossing of the Danube alluded to in §6.

[7]Peter Heather, at 292-3 so characterises the situation; 'not . . . adherence body and soul to a new set of beliefs, but . . . rather a determination to change public practice'.

[8]This sentence is an adapted transition from Socrates 4.33.5. Socrates attributes the conversion of the Goths entirely to the agreement of Fritigern with Valens. Though he goes on at once to mention him, Socrates does not explicitly connect Ulfila with the adoption by the Goths of Arianism. Sozomen is clearly intent to correct this impression, even though he has no very clear idea of the chronology of Ulfila's life (above, n. 5).

who held the priestly office among them at that time. At first, Ulphilas was in no respect at variance with the Catholic church, but in the reign of Constantius, in my opinion without considering the consequences, he joined the party of Eudoxius and Acacius at the council of Constantinople, while remaining in communion with the clergy of the party who had met at Nicaea.[9] **9.** But when he arrived at Constantinople, it is said that there entered into discussion with him on questions of doctrine the leaders of the Arian heresy, who promised that they would lend their support to his embassy to the emperor if he adopted the same opinions as themselves; and that, compelled by his need - or even genuinely believing it better to think of God in this way - he entered communion with the supporters of Arius and, together with the entire people, split away from the Catholic church. **10.** Under his guidance the Goths were instructed in piety and through him began to participate in a gentler way of life; and so they were readily prepared to obey him in everything, being convinced that there was nothing wrong in anything he said or did, and that everything contributed to the benefit of his supporters. **11.** As a matter of fact, he had given the greatest proof of his courage, resisting many dangers on behalf of the faith at the time when the Goths were still worshipping in pagan fashion. [Soc.] He was also the original inventor of their letters, and translated the holy books into their native language.[10] It is for this reason, then, that the barbarians from over the Danube in general adhere to the doctrines of Arius.

12. At that time, there were many among the subjects of Fritigern who bore witness through Christ and suffered death. Athanaric was annoyed that those under his power also had been persuaded by Ulphilas to become Christians,[11] and subjected many of them to

---

[9] On Ulfila's activities at the council of Constantinople of winter 359/60, see our Introduction to Chapter 5 below. All this of course occurred after Ulfila's departure from Gothia, a fact, to judge by what follows in §10, totally unknown to Sozomen.

[10] This statement also occurs in Socrates and, with more detail, in Philostorgius (below Chapter 5, p. 144). See further Chapters 6-7.

[11] To make Ulfila personally responsible for conversions north of the Danube in the 370s is obviously impossible, and both Socrates and Sozomen write in apparent unawareness that Ulfila had left Gothia in 347/8 (the historians also seem to have conflated the persecutions of the later 340s and early 370s). It is of course likely that Ulfila continued to be concerned with the spread of Christianity among the Goths from his new base at Nicopolis in Moesia. The ease with which the *Passion of St. Saba* envisages the priest Sansalas as moving across the frontier (see below, p. 114) suggests that close links between Gothic Christians north and south of the Danube could have been easily maintained.

many forms of punishment because the ancestral religion was threatened by innovation: [Phil.] some he brought before tribunals and executed when they spoke out bravely for the faith, others he killed without permitting them to speak at all. **13.** It is said that a wooden image was placed on a wagon, and that those instructed by Athanaric to undertake this task wheeled it round to the tent of any of those who were denounced as Christians and ordered them to do homage and sacrifice to it; and the tents of those who refused to do so were burned, with the people inside.[12] **14.** And I have heard that an even more dreadful suffering than this occurred, when a large number of Christians who refused to yield to attempts to compel them to sacrifice by force, took refuge in the tent which formed their church in that place, and all – men and women also, some of whom led their little children by the hand, others with new-born babies feeding at the breast – were destroyed when the pagans set fire to it.[13]

15. [Soc.] Before long the Goths made peace with each other, and, stirred to mindless anger, began to devastate Thrace and to pillage its cities and villages.[14] When he heard this, Valens learned by experience what a great mistake he had made. **16.** In the belief that the Goths would prove useful to himself and those whom he valued, and that, being kept constantly under arms, they would be a source of fear to his enemies, he neglected the Roman armies; while, instead of the customary levies for military service he exacted gold from the cities and villages under Roman government.[15] 17. Now,

[12]The ceremony of the statue is described by Thompson, *The Visigoths in the Time of Ulfila*, 61ff., as a rite to fructify the land; this is of course conjectural. Compare, for similar tests, the *Passion of St. Saba*, III.1-3, translated below. The Greek word ξόανον suggests a primitive cult statue, characteristically made of wood. Some anthropomorphic stone carvings have been found in the Soviet Union in association with Sintana de Mureş/Cernjachov pottery, which perhaps illustrate the type of object we should imagine; see, with illustrations, I. S. Vinoker, in *MIA* 116, 136-43. It is no doubt through confusion or carelessness that Sozomen writes of the 'tents' before which the test of worship was applied; the Goths were not at this time travelling nomads, but lived in settled villages; cf. Chapter 3, §2 (pp. 56-9).

[13]This event is presumably that referred to in the calendar and martyrology translated below, p. 129f.

[14]Sozomen's 'before long' is a vague expression designed to cover up his ignorance of the true chronology. All the events described in §§12-14 had occurred before, not after, the crossing of the Danube mentioned in §$6. Sozomen lacks the independent information necessary to coordinate his different sources satisfactorily. The devastation in Thrace in 376-8 is described by Ammianus, 31.4ff.

[15]Very similar accounts of Valens' reasons for admitting the Goths are given by our other sources: Amm. Marc. 31.4.4; Eunapius, frag. 42 Müller/42 Blockley); Socrates, *Hist. Eccl.* 4.34. It must be doubtful whether Valens was really happy to admit large

deceived of his hopes, he left Antioch and hastened to come to Constantinople; and there ensued also a respite in the persecution of Christians of views other than his own. Upon the death of Euzoius, Dorotheus was put forward as his successor to leadership of the Arian community.[16]

2. *THE PASSION OF ST. SABA THE GOTH*

INTRODUCTION

The trials and execution of the Gothic martyr Saba are narrated in the form of a letter from the Christian church in Gothia to the churches in Cappadocia and elsewhere. Though set in Gothic territory and describing an event there, the text is conceived and written within an established tradition of Greek martyrology. It begins and ends with a conscious evocation of the second-century *Passion of St. Polycarp* (see nn. 17 and 40 below); while the narrative of the actual martyrdom of Saba is followed by an account of the recovery of his relics by Junius Soranus, *dux* of Scythia, and by an exhortation to the churches in the Roman empire to celebrate the day of martyrdom, which is given at the conclusion of the narrative as 12 April (VII.5). The text also contains numerous reminiscences of the Greek New Testament, notably in the introductory sentences (I.1-II.2) and, in the narrative itself, in passages of reported or direct (that is to say, invented) speech, and where the author of the *Passion* is himself attributing motive and sentiment to its central character. The *Passion* is therefore presented in a literary and liturgical, as well as in a historical, dimension. This must be borne in mind by anyone approaching the text as a historical document about Gothic society.

To judge by the reference to the church of Cappadocia, and the part played in the recovery of the relics by the *dux Scythiae* Junius Soranus, the ecclesiastical dignitary addressed in the last paragraph

---

numbers of unsubdued Goths, and it could be that our sources are reflecting imperial propaganda rather than Valens' true motivation (the speeches of Themistius translated above give an idea of what was possible). Valens' freedom of action was severely handicapped by the fact that the bulk of the east Roman army was at this point engaged in operations against the Persians. See further Heather, *Goths and Romans*, Chapter 4.

[16]The name of Dorotheus occurs in the fragment of Gothic calendar translated below, p. 129f.

of the text (VIII.2) was Basil of Caesarea, whose connections with Soranus in this matter are clearly attested in *Ep*. 155, translated below with two companion letters on the same subject. As with other texts of this nature, part of the function of the *Passion* is precisely to authenticate the circumstances of martyrdom in order to validate the cult that ensued from it. The Roman province of Scythia, from which the recovery of the relics was organised, adjoined and was in easy communication with the Gothic territory beyond the Danube; a case is presented below that the *Passion*, and the relics of the martyred saint, were transmitted to Roman Asia Minor not, as often assumed, by Ascholius of Thessalonica, but by a senior cleric in Scythia itself, such as Betranion bishop of Tomi (Constanţa).

The text reveals much about the local nature of a Gothic village community, and in particular about its relations with tribal authorities, who are seen as alien and intrusive, enforcing persecution against the wishes of the villagers themselves. These go to considerable lengths to save Saba from a martyrdom which he is shown as substantially bringing upon himself by his provocative behaviour, and they show annoyance when Saba deliberately circumvents their attempts to save him from persecution (III.2). We find mentioned a village gathering of an unspecified nature (III.2), later a 'sunedrion' or village council (III.4). The agents of persecution, by contrast with this image of humble social status, are connected with the royal families of the Goths (cf. IV.5). At one point we seem to catch a distorted glimpse of the 'Gefolgschaft', or 'following' of a Germanic chief (IV.5, cf. n. 31), and the execution of Saba only comes when he insults Atharidus, the Gothic leader, in the presence of his attendants (VI.3ff.). The 'stage props' found in the narrative are consistent with the scenes of village life enacted in it – axles of wagons, a woman preparing food at night, a house with a wooden roof-beam, a pestle, a skein of wool, woods and thickets round about, a road to a neighbouring village, a nearby river. If this river, the 'Mousaios' (VII.1), is correctly identified as the Buzaŭ, then the Gothic community which is the scene of the *Passion* was situated somewhere on the south-eastern flank of the Carpathian mountains, in the area more recently called Wallachia. In any case, the life of the community may usefully be seen in the light of the Sîntana de Mureş archaeological culture described in the previous chapter. In considering the historicity of the *Passion*, it is worth at least noting that the date attributed to the martyrdom, Thursday 12 April 372, is consistent (below, n. 38).

The text survives in two manuscripts, in the libraries of St. Mark's at Venice (10th-11th cent.) and the Vatican (early 10th cent.). The first publication, from the Vatican manuscript, was in *Acta Sanctorum*, April, II, pp. 966-8 (published 1675), and the first critical edition by H. Delehaye, *Analecta Bollandiana* 31 (1912), 216-21; hence Knopf-Krüger, *Ausgewählte Märtyrerakten* (4th ed., 1965), pp. 119-24. The *Passion* is summarised and discussed by E. A. Thompson, *The Visigoths in the Time of Ulfila*, Chap. 3 (pp. 64-77) and briefly by Wolfram, *History of the Goths*, 104-5. In his article mentioned at n. 43 below, S. C. Alexe refers to one Latin and no less than five Romanian translations of the *Passion*. As far as we know, there is none published in English.

TRANSLATION

The church of God dwelling in Gothia, to the church of God dwelling in Cappadocia and all the other communities of the holy catholic church in any place; may the mercy, peace and love of God the Father and our Lord Jesus Christ be multiplied.[17]

I.1. Now more than ever is the saying of the blessed Peter proved true, that 'in every nation he that feareth God and worketh righteousness is acceptable to him' [*Acts* 10.35]. This is confirmed now in the story of the blessed Saba, who is a witness of God and our Saviour Jesus Christ. **2.** For this man, a Goth by race[18] and living in Gothia, shone out like a light in the firmament, 'in the midst of a crooked and perverse generation' [*Phil.* 2.15], imitating the saints and eminent in their company in upright actions according to Christ. **3.** For from childhood he sought after nothing else but piety to our Saviour and Lord Jesus Christ, thinking this to be perfect virtue, to attain perfect manhood in knowledge of the Son of God [cf. *Eph.* 4.13]. **4.** And since 'to them that love God all things work together

---

[17]The first and last paragraphs of the *Passion* closely imitate the corresponding sections of the *Passion of St. Polycarp*; cf. our Introduction and H. Musurillo, *Acts of the Christian Martyrs* (1972), 2f., 16ff.

[18]It is interesting that this point should be made explicitly, given the fact that many Gothic Christians (including Ulfila) were descended from Roman prisoners taken from Asia Minor by its third-century Gothic invaders. The name of Saba(s) seems more Syriac or Cappadocian than Gothic (cf. *RE* I.A, col. 1537), and, given the likelihood of intermarriage, there could well have been significant numbers of people who, while being full members of Gothic society were nevertheless of mixed Roman-Gothic descent. On the problem of ethnic identities in the Gothic territories, see also Chapter 3, and on the background and name of Ulfila, Chapter 5 with nn. 17-18.

for good' [*Rom*. 8.28], he attained 'the prize of the high calling' [*Phil*. 3.14], which he had desired from his youth; then, striving face to face against the enemy and overcoming the evils of this life and always being peaceable to all, for the sake of his memory and the edification of the worshippers of God after his liberation in the Lord, he bade us not be idle but write of his triumphs.[19]

II.1. Now Saba was orthodox in faith,[20] devout, prepared for every sort of just obedience, a kindly man, 'rude in speech yet not in knowledge' [2 *Cor*. 11.6], speaking peaceably to all on behalf of truth, reproaching the idolaters and not 'exalted overmuch' [cf. *II Cor*. 12.7], but 'condescending to men of low estate' [*Rom*. 12.16] as is fitting, tranquil, not impetuous in speech, most zealous for every good work [cf. *Titus* 1.16]. **2.** He sang God's praise in church and this was his special concern.[21] He took thought neither for money nor for possessions except the bare necessities. He was temperate, self-controlled in all things, uninitiated in woman, abstinent, observed all fasts, was steadfast in prayers without vainglory and subjected all men to his good example. He performed the work required of him and was no busybody in what did not concern him [cf. *II Thess*. 3.11]. In sum he preserved an unblemished 'faith working through love' [*Gal*. 5.6], never hesitating to speak out on all occasions in the Lord.

III.1. Not once but many times before his consummation did he display a pious deed in faith. On the first occasion when the chief men[22] in Gothia began to be moved against the Christians,

---

[19]For the question of the authorship of the *Passion* see our comments below on the letters of Basil of Caesarea.

[20]This claim of orthodoxy is no doubt designed to counter general associations of Gothic orthodoxy with Ulfila and, therefore, with so-called 'Arians'; see below, Chapter 5.

[21]The Greek words, ψάλλων ἐν ἐκκλησίᾳ, might be a purely general reference to worship in church (i.e. to Saba's membership of the congregation), but the comment that this was his 'special concern' implies that something more specific is meant: Saba was *lector*, or possibly *cantor*, of his local church. It makes sense that the persecution should focus on the presbyter and lesser clergy. Ulfila too was *lector* before his consecration as bishop; see the *Letter* of Auxentius translated in Chapter 5, §35[56].

[22]The Greek word μεγιστᾶνες has been discussed as if it referred in some particular way to the Gothic tribal nobility (cf. Thompson, *Visigoths*, 64ff.); in fact it is a general and not uncommon word in Biblical Greek, used for instance of the 'lords' of Herod the Great at *Mark* 6.21. The phase of persecution envisaged is clearly distinct from the 'great persecution' of IV.1ff., but it is not clear by how much it precedes it, or how the two phases are connected; Rubin, for instance, would see a reference to the events of 347/8 (*Mus. Helv*. 38 [1981], at 44). It does however seem very unlikely that the text suddenly jumps 25 years at III.5/IV.1. Furthermore, according to VII.5 of the *Passion* Saba was 38 years old in 372, and so would have

compelling them to eat sacrificial meat, it occurred to some of the pagans in the village in which Saba lived to make the Christians who belonged to them eat publicly before the persecutors meat that had not been sacrificed in place of that which had, hoping thereby to preserve the innocence of their own people and at the same time to deceive the persecutors. **2.** Learning this, the blessed Saba not only himself refused to touch the forbidden meat but advanced into the midst of the gathering[23] and bore witness, saying to everyone, 'If anyone eats of that meat, this man cannot be a Christian', and he prevented them all from falling into the Devil's snare. For this, the men who had devised the deception threw him out of the village, but after some time allowed him to return. **3.** On another occasion when a time of trial was moved in customary fashion by the Goths, some of the pagans from the same village intended while offering sacrifices to the gods to swear to the persecutor that there was not a single Christian in their village. **4.** But Saba, again speaking out, came forward in the midst of their council and said, 'Let no man swear on my account, for I am a Christian'. Then in the presence of the persecutor, the villagers who were hiding away their friends swore that there was no Christian in the village, except one. **5.** Hearing this, the leader of the outrage ordered Sabas to stand before him. When he stood there, the persecutor asked those who brought him forward whether he had anything among his possessions. When they replied, 'Nothing except the clothes he wears', the lawless one set him at nought and said, 'Such a man can neither help nor harm us',[24] and with these words ordered him to be thrown outside.
IV.1 Afterwards, when a great persecution was stirred by the infidels

---

been only 13 or 14 in 347/8.

[23]The nature of the gathering is not defined (at III.4 a village council, or συνέδριον, is mentioned). It has been suggested (cf. Thompson, *Visigoths*, 68f.) that the eating of the meat is intended to represent a communal meal symbolising the social unity of the village, but it is more simply seen as a straightforward test of belief (for another such test, see Sozomen 6.37.13, translated above, p. 108). As on the earlier occasion (II.1-2) the Gothic community seems more anxious to protect its members from harm than to preserve religious solidarity. Sacrificial meat is mentioned in a different context by Gregory Thaumaturgus, translated in Chapter 1.

[24]Thompson, *Visigoths*, 53, makes rather too much of this remark. Presumably Saba's lack of possessions has something to do with his position in the church (above, n. 21); perhaps he is best seen as a Gothic monk, possibly like the 'humiles' seen in the company of a presbyter at Amm. Marc. 31.12.8 (cf. also Chapter 5 n. 1 for the influence of Audius among the Goths). The identity of the 'leader of the outrage' mentioned in this passage is not known; presumably a member of the tribal authorities.

in Gothia against the church of God, as the holy day of Easter approached,[25] Saba resolved to go away to another town[26] to the presbyter Gouththikâs to celebrate the feast with him. As he was walking along the road, the figure of a huge man, radiant in form, appeared and said to him: 'Turn around and return to Sansalâs the presbyter'. Saba replied to the figure, 'Sansalâs is away from home'. **2.** In fact Sansalâs was in flight because of the persecution and was spending time in Romania,[27] but at that time had just come back to his home on account of the holy day of Easter. Saba did not know anything about his return, and that is why he replied in this fashion to the figure that appeared to him, and strove to continue his journey to Gouththikâs the presbyter. **3.** While he was refusing to obey the instruction given him, suddenly, although the weather was fine at that time,[28] a huge fall of snow appeared on the face of the earth, so that the road was blocked and it was impossible to pass. **4.** Then Saba realised that it was the will of God that prevented him from proceeding further and told him to return to the presbyter Sansalâs; and praising the Lord he turned and went back. When he saw Sansalâs he rejoiced and told him and many others[29] of the vision he had seen on the road. **5.** So they celebrated together the festival of Easter. Then, on the third night after the festival,[30] there came at the behest of the impious ones Atharidus, the son of Rothesteus of royal rank, with a gang of lawless bandits.[31] He fell

---

[25]For the date, cf. below, nn. 30, 32ff.

[26]The Greek word is πόλις, but 'city' would here be a misleading translation. What is meant is a village community or small township such as those described in Chapter 3, §2 above.

[27]It is interesting that Sansalas finds refuge from persecution in the Roman empire, presumably with a Christian community there: one thinks of the church at Durostorum (Silistra) on the Danube – or, conceivably, the Gothic Christian settlement of Ulfila at Nicopolis (below, Chapter 5, p. 144 with n. 22). Such a community might well be instrumental in transmitting the known facts about the martyrdom of Saba to the author of the *Passion*.

[28]Perhaps 'at that time (of day)' rather than 'at that season (of the year)'; but the latter is possible.

[29]This phrase, like the incidents of the oath (III.4) and the sacrificial meat (III.1), suggests that there was a considerable number of Christians in the village. For a suggestion as to how Sansalas and Saba were picked out, see n. 21.

[30]The 'third night after the festival' takes us from Easter Sunday to Tuesday night; cf. nn. 32-4, 38.

[31]Rothesteus and Atharidus are otherwise unknown. The 'gang of lawless bandits' looks like a reference to the tribal *Gefolgschaft* ('following'), a Germanic tribal institution mentioned also, for the Goths, by Ammianus (31.5.6). A classic discussion, translated into English, is W. Schlesinger, 'Lord and followers in German institutional history', in F. C. Cheyette (ed.), *Lordship and Community in Medieval*

on the village, where he found the presbyter asleep in his house and had him tied up. Saba also he seized naked from his couch and likewise threw into bonds. **6.** The presbyter they held captive on a wagon, but they took Saba naked as he was and drove him throughout the thickets which they had just burned, following closely behind and beating him with rods and scourges, carried away by pitiless cruelty against the servants of God.

V.1. Yet the harshness of his enemies confirmed the patience and faith of the just man. When day came,[32] Saba, glorying in the Lord, said to those who had persecuted him, 'Did you not drive and beat me across burned wastes, onto the sharp points of thorns, naked and without shoes? See, whether my feet are injured and whether I have weals on my body from this, or from the beatings you inflicted upon me'. **2.** When they looked and no trace was seen on his flesh of the pitiless things they had done, they lifted up the axle of a wagon and put it on his shoulders, and stretched out his hands and tied them to the ends of the axle. In the same way they also stretched out his feet and tied them to another axle. Finally they threw him down on the axles and let him lie on his back upon the ground, and until far into the night went on flogging him without respite. **3.** When the torturers had fallen asleep, a woman came up and set him free; she was a woman working at night to prepare food for the people in the house.[33] Set free, Saba remained in the same place without fear, and joined the woman at her work. When day came,[34] the impious Atharidus ordered Saba to have his hands bound and to be suspended from the beam of the house.

VI.1 A little later came the men sent by Atharidus, bringing sacrificial meat, and they said to the presbyter and to Saba, 'Atharidus ordered these things to be brought to you, that you may eat and save your souls from death'. **2.** The presbyter replied and said, 'We shall not eat these things, for it is not possible for us to do so. Now, tell Atharidus to order us to be crucified, or put to death by whatever method he may choose'. **3.** Saba said, 'Who is it that gave these orders?' They replied, 'Our lord Atharidus'. And Saba said, 'There is one Lord, God in heaven; but Atharidus is a man, impious and accursed. And this food of perdition is impure and

---

Europe (New York, 1968), 64-99.

[32]Viz. Wednesday morning.

[33]This is now the night of Wednesday/Thursday. The woman is possibly a slave or servant of a leading household of the village.

[34]*Sc.* of Thursday, the day of Saba's final inquisition and execution.

profane, like Atharidus who sent it'. **4.** When Saba said this, one of the attendants of Atharidus in a blazing fit of anger seized a pestle and hurled it like a javelin hard against the breast of the saint, so that the onlookers thought that Saba would be shattered by the violence of the blow and die on the spot.[35] **5.** But Saba, his longing for piety overcoming the pain of the inflictions laid upon him, said to the executioner, 'Now, you suppose that you have struck me with the pestle: but let me tell you this, that so far am I feeling pain, that I would suppose you had hurled at me a skein of wool'. **6.** And he provided a clear proof of the truth of his words, for he neither cried out nor groaned as if in pain nor was there any trace whatever of the blow to be seen on his body.

VII.1. Finally Atharidus, learning all this, ordered him to be put to death. Those appointed to perform this lawless act left the presbyter Sansalâs in bonds, and took hold of Saba and led him away to drown him in the river called the Mousaios.[36] **2.** But the blessed Saba, remembering the injunction of the Lord and loving his neighbour as himself [*Mark* 12.33, etc.], said, 'What has the presbyter done wrong, that he does not die with me?' They replied to him, 'This is no concern of yours'. **3.** When they said this, Saba burst out in exultation of the Holy Spirit and said, 'Blessed are you, Lord, and glorified is your name, Jesus, for ever and ever, amen [cf. LXX *Daniel* 3.52, 56]: for Atharidus has pierced himself through with eternal death and destruction, and sends me to the life that remains for ever; so well pleased are you in your servants, O Lord our God'. **4.** And along the entire road he uttered thanks to God as he was led along, thinking 'the sufferings of the present time not worthy to be compared with the glory which would be revealed to the saints' [*Rom.* 8.18]. When they came to the banks of the river, his guards said to one another, 'Come now, let us set free this fool. How will Atharidus ever find out?' But the blessed Saba said to them, 'Why do you waste time talking nonsense and not do what you were told to? For I see what you cannot see: over there on the other side, standing in glory, the saints who have come to receive me'. **5.** Then they took him down to the water, still thanking and glorifying God (until the very end his soul performed worship), threw him in and, pressing a beam against his neck, pushed him to the bottom and held

---

[35] Ammianus describes how some Goths fought at the battle of ad Salices by hurling fire-hardened clubs (31.7.13). The pestle, hurled by a practised arm, would form a somewhat similar implement.

[36] For the river Mousaios as the Buzaŭ, see our Introduction, p. 110.

him there. So made perfect through wood and water,[37] he kept undefiled the symbol of salvation, being thirty-eight years of age. **6.** His consummation took place on the fifth day of the Sabbath after Easter, which is the day before the Ides of April, in the reign of Valentinian and Valens the Augusti, and in the consulship of Modestus and Arintheus (12 April 372).[38]

VIII.1. Then his executioners pulled him out of the water and went away leaving him unburied; but neither dog nor any wild beast at all touched his body, but it was gathered up by the hand of the brethren and his remains laid to rest. These Junius Soranus, *vir clarissimus*, *dux* of Scythia, one who honoured the Lord, sending trustworthy men transported from barbarian land to Romania.[39] **2.** And favouring his own native land with a precious gift and a glorious fruit of faith, he sent the remains to Cappadocia and to your Piety, carrying out the wishes of the college of presbyters, the Lord ordaining matters to please the brethren who obey and fear him. **3.** Therefore, celebrating spiritual communion on the day in which he fought for and carried off the crown, tell also the brethren in those parts, in order that they may perform joyful celebrations in every holy and catholic church, praising the Lord who chooses the elect from among his own servants. **4.** Salute all the saints; those who, with you, are being persecuted, salute you. To him who can gather all of us by his grace and bounty into his kingdom in heaven be glory, honour, power and majesty, with his only-begotten Son and Holy Spirit for ever and ever, Amen.[40]

---

[37] Basil of Caesarea, *Ep.* 164 to ?Betranion of Tomi refers to martyrdoms by 'wood and water' (see below). Execution by drowning under wooden frames is mentioned by Tacitus (*Germania* 12.1) and supported by the discovery in recent times of human remains in bogs and marshes. In this case, the executioners retrieved the body and left it exposed.

[38] The transmitted text, presumably by incorporation of a confused marginal annotation, here reads 'in the [consulship of Flavius] Valentinianus and Valens. [These are found] in the consulship of Modestus and Arintheus'. The translated version incorporates the necessary corrections, by the amendment or deletion of the phrases shown in square brackets. Easter Thursday in 372 did in fact fall on 12 April (Delehaye, 291).

[39] For the role of Junius Soranus (*PLRE* I, p. 848), see below on *Ep.* 155 of Basil of Caesarea. The 'recovery party' here mentioned is no doubt that mentioned by Basil. The 'college of presbyters' mentioned at VIII.2 was presumably that of a church in Scythia, possibly Tomi; 'your Piety' (ἡ ὑμετέρα θεοσέβεια) in VIII.2 is undoubtedly Basil of Caesarea; cf. n. 45.

[40] For the closing allusions to the *Passion of St. Polycarp*, (20.1; 22.3), see above, n. 17.

3. BASIL OF CAESAREA, *EPP.* 155, 164, 165

INTRODUCTION

Further light on the martyrdom of Saba, and on the transfer to Cappadocia of his relics and martyrology, is shed by the three letters of Basil of Caesarea translated here. Two of these letters (*Epp.* 164 and 165) are shown in all printed editions as addressed to Ascholius (or Acholius), bishop of Thessalonica, an attribution for which the manuscript evidence is slender, and which is very likely to be incorrect.[41] The third letter (*Ep.* 155) is addressed to an anonymous correspondent identified in the editions with the Junius Soranus, *dux Scythiae*, mentioned in the final paragraph of the *Passion of St. Saba* as the man who recovered the relics of the martyr and sent them to Cappadocia. Despite the anonymous heading of the letter, this identification is certainly correct. The curious description of the letter as 'concerning a trainer', which has misled at least one of its translators,[42] perhaps derives from an early editor's recollection of a phrase in *Ep.* 164, where Basil's correspondent is described as the 'trainer' (ἀλείπτης) of the martyr. The image of the martyr as an 'athlete' of Christ who struggles in combat against persecution is heavily exploited in this letter, and occurs also in *Ep.* 165, likewise attributed to 'Ascholius'.

The circumstances of the letter to Soranus (*Ep.* 155) are not entirely clear from Basil's oblique references to them. Soranus had evidently complained that he had received no communication from Basil, despite the fact that certain men, apparently including members of his family, were leaving Caesarea to join him in Scythia, and that his name was not mentioned in prayers offered by Basil in church services. It may be that Soranus had some grounds for feeling offended if, as is evident from the last paragraph, he had already formed the intention to recover and send the relics of St. Saba to Caesarea, and if it was to assist him on this project that he had summoned his associates to join him in Scythia. In these circumstances, Basil's silence, and indeed his apparent ignorance of Soranus's plans, did require some explanation. Basil responds by

---

[41] See the article by S. C. Alexe, n. 43 below. The attributions of the three letters in the Loeb ed. by R. J. Deferrari, Vol. II (1928, repr. 1962), pp. 380-5, 420-31, and in the Budé ed. by Y. Courtonne, Vol. II (1961), pp. 80-1, 97-101, largely derive from the Maurist editors, printed in *PG* 32, cols. 611-14, 633-40.

[42] Courtonne, p. 80 n. 2; 'Basile est alors peu précis sur les accusations dont il est l'objet de la part du maître de gymnase.'

blaming Soranus' household for not informing him. The reader will judge how effective an argument this is; in any event, Basil's acknowledgement of the prominence of the family, house and household staff of Soranus, who is himself absent on imperial service, is of some interest in helping us to appreciate the nature of Basil's lay congregation at Caesarea. Nothing is known of the nameless 'brother' of litigious tendencies who is mentioned in the middle paragraph of the letter.

In the first of the letters supposedly sent to Ascholius of Thessalonica (*Ep.* 164), Basil uses the martyrdom of Gothic Christians, as reported in a recent letter from his correspondent, as an opportunity to launch a paean on the days of the early church, which is portrayed as persecuted but unified, in contrast with the contemporary age, in which an accepted and powerful church is riven by heresy and dissension. Apart from its rhetorical force, this is a clever argument, since it enables Basil to evade the likely fact that some at least of these Gothic martyrs were Arians, and so of the party currently responsible, through the Emperor Valens and his supporters, for persecution of the 'orthodox' church of Basil and his colleagues in the east.

It is evident from Basil's letter, and especially from his reference to martyrdom 'by wood and water', that the *Passion of St. Saba* (cf. VII.5) – though not yet the saint's remains – has now reached him and is in his mind as he writes. Beyond this, it is not easy to say whether in his references to a plurality of martyrs and modes of persecution Basil is merely generalising in rhetorical fashion the particular case of St. Saba, or whether other martyr narratives are in question. That there were other martyrs in Gothia is attested by other passages translated below, and Basil may be indicating this without intending a specific reference to other martyrologies.

We saw earlier that the *Passion of St. Saba* emanated, in the form in which we have it, from Christian circles in the Greek-speaking Roman empire rather than directly from within Gothia itself. Saba is specifically claimed as an 'orthodox' Christian (*Passion*, II.1), and the reference to 'persecution' at the end of the *Passion* (VIII.4) conveys the same implication. Christians were being persecuted in both Gothic and Roman territories: that the victims of the Roman persecutions were Nicene Christians at the hands of Arian adversaries is an awkward fact, which Basil avoids confronting directly. These considerations require that Basil's correspondent is an ecclesiastical ally of the orthodox (Nicene) persuasion. Ascholius of Thessalonica is such a candidate, but it is not easy to see what role would naturally fall to a bishop of Thessalonica in the transmission of relics from the Gothic territories by way of Scythia to Cappadocia, and there is much to be said for a different candidate: Betranion (Vetranio) of Tomi (Constanţa) on the coast of the Black Sea, and in the Roman province of Scythia.[43] The suggestion that Betranion was the actual author of the *Passion of St. Saba* is no more than that, but it is easy to assign to such a person an important role in the transmission both of relics and of their documentation, to the Greek churches of Asia Minor.

Whether Betranion was the recipient also of *Ep*. 165 (it is in the editions addressed like *Ep*. 164 to Ascholius, and this might seem a logical inference), is questionable. If the two letters were written to the same correspondent, then one would assume, from the elaborate formality of its opening remarks, that *Ep*. 165 was the earlier of them. This seems incompatible, however, with the actual sequence of the two letters – the arrival of the martyr narrative preceded the relics, not the other way round – and it may be that they were addressed to different recipients. *Ep*. 165 is commonly assumed to have been sent, like *Ep*. 155, to the *dux Scythiae* Junius Soranus, an identification not free from difficulties.[44] To judge by his phraseology, Basil is addressing a clerical colleague; he calls his correspondent 'your true Piety' and 'your Sagacity' – terms most appropriate for a clerical recipient – and at the end of the letter writes of him as his spiritual superior and requests his prayers, in terms that both seem rather distant, and better suited to a cleric than to a senior military officer.[45] We can infer from Basil's letter that his correspondent is located in a part of the Roman empire directly adjoining the Gothic territories, and that he has some influence,

---

[43]S. C. Alexe, 'Saint Basile le Grand et le christianisme roumain au IVe siècle', in E. A. Livingstone (ed.), *Studia Patristica* XVII.3 (1982), 1049-59; cf. Wolfram, *History of the Goths*, 83. The 'orthodoxy' of Betranion is attested by Sozomen, *Hist. Eccl.* 6.21.2; Alexe, at 1052.

[44]Cf. the Loeb and Maurist editions, and *PLRE* I, p. 848 (where the identification is described as 'certain').

[45]The examples of 'Piety' (θεοσέβεια) cited as a form of address by G. W. H. Lampe, *Patristic Greek Lexikon* (s.v., II.C; p. 636), are of clerical/ecclesiastical recipients except one (Athanasius addressing Constantius II). The refs., to which we should add *Passion of St. Saba* VIII.2 (cf. n. 39 above), include Basil, *Ep*. 48 to Eusebius of Samosata (*Ep*. 166, also to Eusebius, in which the address also occurs, is taken to be a letter not of Basil but of Gregory of Nazianzus); so too the uses of σύνεσις ('Sagacity') as a form of address seem to be clerical (Lampe, s.v., §7; p. 1325). The evidence strongly favours an ecclesiastical recipient for *Ep*. 165, but a layman of publicly acknowledged piety is perhaps not totally excluded. *Ep*. 164 to ?Betranion, is addressed to 'your Holiness' (ὁσιότης).

spiritual if not personal, on the progress of Christianity there. He is a person with whom Basil is not in regular contact because of the distance between them, but whom he knew of as a product of his own city of Caesarea. This consideration would favour Soranus rather than Betranion as the recipient of the letter;[46] against Soranus, however, is Basil's statement that his correspondent was 'such as the testimony of all men describes you'. This was evidently someone whom Basil did not know personally.

The recovery and transmission of the relics of a Gothic saint was a complex matter, involving both secular and ecclesiastical authorities, and we would be wrong to assume that we have full information on the matter. The last paragraph of the *Passion of St. Saba* refers to the 'college of presbyters' with whom Junius Soranus arranged the dispatch of the remains to Cappadocia; it was perhaps a member of this college whom Basil was addressing in *Ep*. 165.

TRANSLATIONS

(i) *EP*. 155, TO JUNIUS SORANUS, *DUX SCYTHIAE*

I am at a loss how to answer the many accusations contained in the first and only letter that your Nobility has thought fit to send us; not through lack of a just response, but because among so many reproaches it is difficult to make a choice of the more relevant, and to decide where best to begin dealing with them. Perhaps it will be best to keep to the order in which they were written, and meet them as they arise, one by one.

We were not acquainted until today with the men who are leaving here for Scythia: indeed, none even of the members of your household put it to us that we might address you through them, most eager though I am to salute your Honour at every opportunity. As for forgetting you in our prayers, that is impossible, unless we were first to forget the work to which the Lord has appointed us. Surely you, a man faithful by the grace of God, remember the public declarations of the Church; that we both pray for our brethren who are living abroad, and offer prayers in the Holy Church for those enrolled in military service, and for those who speak out freely on

---

[46] The name (Latin Vetranio, ?cf. *veteranus*) evokes an origin in the lower Danubian rather than in the Cappadocian region; cf. *PLRE* I, p. 954 (Vetranio 1 and 2). In general terms, the letter is an interesting example of the 'Christianisation' of traditional ideas of civic patriotism found, for instance, in the correspondence of Basil's contemporary, Libanius of Antioch.

behalf of the name of the Lord, and for those who display the fruits of the Spirit; and, of a certainty, on most if not on all of these occasions, we reckon that your Honour is also included. And in private life how could we forget you, with so many things to stir us to remember you? – a sister and nephews such as yours, relatives so excellent and loving us so well; house, household staff, friends.[47] All of this, even without our wishing it, would draw us of necessity to remember your good disposition.

On the next matter, the brother whom you mention has caused us no annoyance, nor has any judgment whatever been given by us that might be to his detriment. So turn your annoyance against those who have given you false information, and relieve from all blame both the chorepiscopus[48] and me. If our learned friend is stripping himself for legal action, he has public courts and laws at his disposal. I ask you, therefore, to lay no blame on us in these matters.

As for yourself, whatever good deeds you do, you store up as treasure for yourself; and whatever relief you provide for those suffering persecution for the name of the Lord, this you lay by for yourself on the day of recompense. You will do well, if you send the remains of martyrs to your native city; if indeed, as you have written to us, the persecution in those parts is even now making martyrs to the Lord.

(ii) *EP.* 164, TO ?BETRANION OF TOMI

How great the joy with which we were filled by your Holiness' letter we cannot easily describe, for words lack the power to express it; but you should be able to conjecture it in your own mind, drawing your conclusion from the beauty of the things you wrote. For what was not contained in the letter? Was there not love for the Lord? Was there not admiration for the martyrs, as you described the manner of their contest so clearly that you brought the events before our eyes? Was there not honour and friendship for ourselves? Was

---

[47] The sentence well evokes the physical 'presence' of this leading member of Caesarean society, and its relations with its bishop. Courtonne's translation, 'qui nous aime tant, *nous*, *notre* maison, *nos* familiers, *nos* amis' (our italics) is based on a misunderstanding of the Greek phrase οὕτως ἀγαπῶσαν ἡμᾶς. This is self-contained, and does not govern what follows: the entire sequence 'house, household staff, friends' refers to Soranus' family, not that of Basil.

[48] Chorepiskopoi (χωρεπίσκοποι) were senior clerics with limited episcopal powers enabling them to function in the countryside (χῶρα) of large dioceses, of which Caesarea was certainly one. Numerous disputes arose as to the exact scope of their authority.

there not every fine and good thing one could mention? When we received the letter into our hands and read it time and time again, and observed the grace of the Spirit bursting forth within it, we imagined ourselves to be living in ancient times, when the churches of God were flourishing, rooted in faith and united in love, as harmonious breathing unifies the diverse limbs of a single body. In those days the persecutors stood out in public, and so did the persecuted; the laity, under attack, increased in numbers, and the blood of martyrs, irrigating the churches, brought forth many times over the champions of piety, their successors stripping for action in rivalry with those who went before. Then, we Christians enjoyed peace with each other – that peace, which the Lord left behind for us, of which no trace at all remains to us, so harshly have we driven it from our midst. But now, our souls have returned to that ancient state of happiness. A letter in the full flowering beauty of love arrived from a distant land, and a witness came among us from the barbarians beyond the Ister, declaring in himself the rigour of the faith that is conducted in those parts. Who could express the joy in our souls at this news? What power of words could be imagined, able to make clear the warmth in the depths of our heart? But further: when we saw the athlete, we blessed his trainer.[49] He too will receive from the righteous judge the crown of righteousness, for he has given to many strength for the contest of piety. In bringing to our mind the memory of the blessed man Eutyches,[50] and in glorifying our native land as having herself provided the seeds of piety, you have encouraged us by the reminder of past times, but grieved us when we see the hostile evidence of the world around us. None of us is the equal of Eutyches in virtue; far from taming the barbarians by the power of the Spirit and the operation of his gifts, we have by our excess of sin even made wild those who were gentle.[51] It is to ourselves and our sins that we must assign the blame that the power of the heretics has spread so widely. Almost

---

[49] τὸν ἀλείπτην. Betranion, or whoever else is Basil's correspondent, is by this phrase given part of the credit for the martyr's 'perfection' in Gothia. Again, it is hard to see how the claims of a bishop of Thessalonica could be as strong.

[50] Nothing is known of Eutyches apart from what is in this passage: a Christian evangelist of the Goths, possibly in the aftermath of the third-century invasions in which Ulfila's ancestors were taken prisoner (below, Chapter 5, p. 143f.). The allusion is a re-assertion of the connection between Cappadocia and Gothic Christianity, which is implicit throughout the letter, and in the *Passion of St. Saba*.

[51] For this view of the 'barbarian', cf. sentiments of the orator Themistius, *Or.* 10, translated in Chapter 2 above; e.g. §199/131 and n. 88.

no part of the world has escaped the burning fire of heresy. Your account shows us athletic contests, bodies torn apart for the sake of piety, barbarian fury despised by the resolute of heart, diverse tortures of the persecutors, the resistance through everything of those tested in combat; the wood, the water, the instruments of perfection of martyrs.[52] But our instruments, what are they like? Love has grown cold, the teaching of the Fathers falls in ruins, many are the shipwrecks in the faith, the mouths of the pious are silent; the people are driven from their houses of prayer and lift up their hands in the open air to the Master in heaven. Our afflictions are heavy – but nowhere is there martyrdom, because those who do us harm bear the same name as ourselves.[53] For these reasons, pray yourself to our Lord, and gather together all the noble athletes of Christ to prayer on behalf of the churches: in order that, if any time yet remains for the ordered progression of the universe and everything is not being driven in the opposite direction, God may be reconciled with his churches and lead them again to their ancient peace.

(iii) *EP.* 165, TO ANON.

A long-standing prayer has been fulfilled for us by Holy God, who has thought us fit to receive a letter from your true Piety.[54] The greatest benefit, and that worthy of the greatest effort to achieve it, is to see you in person and be seen by you, and to enjoy face to face the gifts of the Spirit in you; but since we are deprived of this by the distance between us and by the circumstances that personally constrain each of us, it is worthy of a prayer of second choice that our soul should be sustained by frequent letters of your love in Christ. And this has now happened to us, when we took into our hands the letter of your Sagacity. Our spirits have been raised more than twofold by the enjoyment of what you have written. Indeed, it was truly possible to observe your very soul, reflected as if in a sort of mirror of your words. And it increased our happiness many times over, not only that you are such as the testimony of all men describes you, but that the qualities which you possess are the pride of our

---

[52] This whole sentence – and not only the reference to 'wood and water' (cf. VII.5) – is a clear allusion to the circumstances described in the *Passion of St. Saba*.

[53] This passage might well suggest that one aspect of Basil's interest in Gothic martyrs was to strengthen the resolve of his own congregation in the face of the pressure applied by Valens to conform to his non-Nicene settlement.

[54] τῆς ἀληθινῆς σοῦ θεοσεβείας; see above, nn. 39, 45.

city. Like a flourishing branch sprung from a noble root, you have filled with the fruits of the Spirit the land beyond our borders: so that our city rightly exults in her own progeny. And when you were fighting contests on behalf of the faith, our city glorified God, hearing that the good heritage of the Fathers was being kept safe in you.

What, then, are your present achievements? Like a grateful farmer who sends the first fruits of his harvest to those who provided the seed, you have honoured the land that bore you with a martyr who has recently contended for the prize in the barbarian country that is your neighbour. The gifts are truly fitting for the athlete of Christ – a martyr, or witness of the truth,[55] lately wreathed with the crown of righteousness: whom we received with joy, and glorified the God who has from this moment fulfilled the gospel of his Christ among all the gentile nations. Now, I ask you, remember in your prayers us who love you, and earnestly pray to the Lord for our souls, that we too may some time begin to serve God according to the way of the commandments which he has given us for our salvation.

4. GOTHIC MARTYROLOGIES

(i) The first of this group of texts relates to the burning alive of many Gothic Christians in their church, as mentioned in the narrative of Sozomen translated above, and to the later collection of their relics by 'Gaatha', alleged to be a queen of the Goths, and their deposition at Cyzicus by her daughter, who bears the Roman name 'Dulcilla'. It is translated in two parts, as presented by Delehaye (p. 279); these consist of separate but earlier and fuller versions of a notice that appears in the tenth-century *menologium*, or monthly calendar, of the Byzantine emperor Basil II, under the date 26 March (*PG* 117, col. 368).[56] The second part of the passage is

[55]The translation is slightly expanded at this point, in order to show the literal meaning of the Greek μάρτυς as 'witness'.

[56]The date of commemoration of these martyrs is given as 29 October in the fragment of a Gothic calendar translated below. The discrepancy with the *Menologium* might be resolved if one date were that of the martyrdom, the other that of the deposition of the relics. The date of martyrdom of St. Saba was recorded (*Passion* VII.6). In his case that was also recommended as the day of commemoration (VIII.3); in the present case, however, martyrdom and deposition were separated by several years, and a significant change of circumstances (below, n. 60).

suspect in the elaboration of its personal details, but should attest that relics purporting to be of Gothic martyrs were in fact deposited at Cyzicus: as we saw in the case of the *Passion of St. Saba*, it was an essential purpose of such a text to accompany and to authenticate the deposition of relics.

The dating of the martyrdoms to the reigns of Valentinian, Valens and Gratian (367-75) presents no problem in relation to our other evidence. As for the recovery and deposition of the relics, if the dating in the second part of the passage to the reigns of Valentinian (*sc*. II, given his seniority) and Theodosius is authentic, the deposition took place in the period 379-92: if the omission of the name of Gratian is exact, then, more precisely, in 383-92. The recovery of the relics could well have occurred after the treaty of 382 between Theodosius and the Goths, and might indeed form part of the wider history of Romano-Gothic relations of those years; though it has to be said that the circumstances of the journey of 'Gaatha' to the Roman empire and her journey back to Gothia do not seem to envisage that situation. The treaty of 382 was a treaty with the Goths then living inside the empire, but the relics whose deposition is described in this passage are evidently (despite Thompson, *Visigoths*, 159f.) coming from Goths still living outside its borders. The treaty may have created the conditions of peace which made possible the journey of Gaatha, but is not likely to have been relevant in any more direct way.

TRANSLATION.

(a) On the same day (is remembered) the contest of the martyrs in Gothia, among whom are two presbyters, Bathousês and Wêrkas[57] with their two sons and two daughters, and Arpulas the monachos; of laymen, Abippas, Hagias, Ruïas, Êgathrax, Êskoês, Silas, Sigêtzas, Swêrilas, Swêmblas, Therthas, Philgas; and of women, Anna, Alas, Barên, Môïkô, Kamika, Onêkô and Anêmaïs. These lived in the time of Ingourichos, king of the Goths,[58] and of Valentinian and

[57]Bathousês and Wêrkas (or, Ouêrkas) are clearly the Werekas and Batwin mentioned in the Gothic martyrology, and the episode is that described by Sozomen 6.37.14, translated above.

[58]'King' would here seem to stand for the Gothic title *reiks*, which means a leader of second rank rather than of the whole tribe, who was the *iudex*; cf. Wolfram, *History of the Goths*, 94-7. Wingurich can thus be plausibly envisaged as a powerful subordinate of Athanaric, like Rothesteus in the *Passion of St. Saba*; for the possibly similar status of Gaatha the 'queen', see next n. The variation in the form of name,

Valens and Gratian, emperor(s) of the Romans. On account of their confession of Christ they took the crown of martyrdom by fire at the hands of Wingourichos, who set fire to the church of the Christians, in which the holy martyrs were burned to death. It also happened on that occasion that a certain man who was bringing an offering to the same church was seized and, confessing Christ, himself became an offering, burned by the fire.

(b) The remains of these martyrs Gaatha, queen of the race of the Goths,[59] a Christian and orthodox, gathered together, with the help of other Christians, including Wellas, a layman. Leaving the kingdom in the hands of her son Arimênios, travelling from place to place she came as far as the land of the Romans; and her daughter Doulkilla also came with her. Then she informed her son Arimênios and he came to join(?) her, and she went away with him, leaving Doulkilla to come to Cyzicus in the reign of Valentinian and Theodosius;[60] and she [*sc.* Doulkilla] gave part of the relics to venerate in the city. Wellas, departing again for Gothia with Gaatha, was put to death by stoning; and later Doulkilla also was laid to rest.

Ingourichos/Ouïngourichos, is as presented in the Greek text translated here. The form Ou- (W-) is given in both occurrences of the name in the printed text of the *Menologium*, and is intrinsically preferable.

[59]The *Menologium* text describes Gaatha as 'consort [*sc.* widow] of the other leader of the race of the Goths' – as distinct, that is, from Wingourichos. It is unclear whether the compiler of this text had specific information on the point, or whether he is simply providing an explanation that seems required by the logic of the situation – Gaatha as a 'queen', but clearly of someone other than Wingourichos (for the likelihood that there were several such 'kings' within the Gothic lands, see previous note). It thus seems very hazardous to press the reference into service, as does Thompson, *The Visigoths in the Time of Ulfila*, 159f., as evidence for a 'dual kingship' among the Goths, and to describe Gaatha as 'widow of a Judge' (ibid., 54). It may be that 'queen' in the modern sense conveys a somewhat exaggerated impression of her status among the Goths, and that she was really the widow of an important noble.

[60]*Sc.* 379/92. This phase of the story is separated in time from the actual martyrdoms, which Sozomen clearly thought of as having taken place in the early 370s. The recovery and deposition are taken by Thompson, *Visigoths*, 85, 160, to belong to a time after the settlement in Moesia, but the reference to Gaatha's 'coming to the land of the Romans', and her return to Gothia imply that the story concerns a group of Goths still living beyond the Danube. Not all Visigoths fled south of the Danube in 376, cf. Amm. Marc. 31.4.13; Athanaric's group stayed north of the river and, although Athanaric himself fled into the empire in winter 380/1 (*PLRE* I, p. 120f.), this was with only a small group of supporters, the implication being that the majority of those who had followed him in 376 remained beyond the Roman frontier (Amm. Marc. 27.5.10).

𐌺̅𐌲̅ 𐌸𐌹𐌶𐌴 𐌰𐌽𐌰 𐌲𐌿𐍄𐌸𐌹𐌿𐌳𐌰𐌹 𐌼𐌰𐌳𐌰𐌲𐍂𐌹𐌶𐌴 𐌼𐌰𐍂𐍅𐍄𐍂𐌴
𐌾𐌰𐌷 𐍆𐍂𐌹𐌸𐌰𐍂𐌴𐌹𐌺𐌴𐌹𐌺𐌴𐌹𐍃

𐌺̅𐌳̅

𐌺̅𐌴̅

𐌺̅𐌵̅

𐌺̅𐌶̅

𐌺̅𐌷̅

𐌺̅𐌸̅ 𐌲𐌰𐌼𐌹𐌽𐌸𐌹 𐌼𐌰𐍂𐍅𐍄𐍂𐌴 𐌸𐌹𐌶𐌴 𐌱𐌹 𐍅𐌴𐍂𐌴𐌺𐌰𐌽 𐍀𐌰𐍀𐌰𐌽
𐌾𐌰𐌷 𐌱𐌰𐍄𐍅𐌹𐌽 𐌱𐌹𐌻𐌰𐌹𐍆· 𐌰𐌹𐌺𐌺𐌻𐌴𐍃𐌾𐍉𐌽𐍃 𐍆𐌿𐌻𐌻𐌰𐌹𐌶𐍉𐍃
𐌰𐌽𐌰 𐌲𐌿𐍄𐌸𐌹𐌿𐌳𐌰𐌹 𐌲𐌰𐌱𐍂𐌰𐌽𐌽𐌹𐌳𐌰𐌹

𐌻̅

𐌰̅

𐌱̅

𐌲̅ 𐌺𐌿𐍃𐍄𐌰𐌽𐍄𐌴𐌹𐌽𐌿𐍃 𐌸𐌹𐌿𐌳𐌰𐌽𐌹𐍃

𐌳̅

𐌴̅

𐌵̅ 𐌳𐌰𐌿𐍂𐌹𐌸𐌰𐌹𐌿𐍃 𐌰𐌹𐍀𐌹𐍃𐌺𐌰𐌿𐍀𐌿𐍃

𐌶̅ . . . . . . 𐌹̅𐌳̅

𐌹̅𐌴̅ 𐍆𐌹𐌻𐌹𐍀𐍀𐌰𐌿𐍃 𐌰𐍀𐌰𐌿𐍃𐍄𐌰𐌿𐌻𐌰𐌿𐍃 𐌹̈𐌽 𐌾𐌰𐌹𐍂𐌿𐍀𐍀𐌿𐌻𐌰𐌹·

𐌹̅𐌵̅

𐌹̅𐌶̅

𐌹̅𐌷̅

𐌹̅𐌸̅ 𐌸𐌹𐌶𐌴 𐌰𐌻𐌸𐌾𐌹𐌽𐍉𐌹𐌽𐌴 𐌱𐌰𐌹𐍂𐌰𐌿𐌾𐌰𐌹 ·𐌼̅· 𐍃𐌰𐌼𐌰𐌽𐌰

𐌺̅ . . . . 𐌺̅𐌷̅

𐌺̅𐌸̅ 𐌰𐌽𐌳𐌰𐍂𐌹𐌹̈𐌽𐍃 𐌰𐍀𐌰𐌿𐍃𐍄𐌰𐌿𐌻𐌰𐌿𐍃

𐌻̅.

(ii) The scrap of a Gothic calendar which follows is preserved with fragments of the Gothic Bible in sixth-century writing under an eighth-century palimpsest at Milan; a schematic representation of the text, adapted from the publication in Gothic script by Angelo Mai in 1819, is shown opposite. It too commemorates the burning of the martyrs in the church, together with other anniversaries which, in the cases of Constantius II (see n. 64) and bishop Dorotheus, display a strongly Arian tendency. It is possible that the Gothic text itself derives from a Greek original: the reference to Dorotheus (n. 65) shows the text as it stands to have been compiled after 406, presumably in a Gothic Christian community in the Roman empire. For the text see Delehaye, *Analecta Bollandiana* 31 (1912), 276 (also *PL* 18.878-9), and for the conventions of transliteration from the Gothic, the Introduction to our selection of passages in Chapter 7.

TEXT

kḡ þize ana Gutþiadai managaize marytre yah Friþareik[eik]eis
kþ̄ gaminþi marytre þize bi Werekan papan yah Batwin bilaif.
aikklesyons fullaizos ana Gutþiadai gabrannidai

ḡ Kustantei[n]us þiudanis
q̄ Dauriþaius aipiskaupaus [MS aipisks]
iē Filippaus apaustaulus ïn Yairupulai
iþ̄ þize alþyane [MS alþanoine] in Bairauyai, m̄. samana
kþ̄ Andriins apaustaulus

TRANSLATION

[October]

23 (Remembrance of) the many martyrs among the Gothic people, and of Frideric.[61]
29 Remembrance of the martyrs who with Werekas the priest and

[61]Friþareikeis (the MS reading is an obvious case of dittography) is presumably an otherwise unknown Gothic martyr, celebrated on the same day as but not necessarily connected with the other martyrs mentioned in this entry. The emendation 'Friþagairnais' (*sc*. Fritigern) is in our view unlikely (it is supported, with arguments, by Z. Rubin, *Mus. Helv*. 38 (1981), 52f.). The entry might in that case allude to the conversion to Christianity alleged by Socrates of the section of the Goths led by Fritigern in the time of Valens (above, p. 106 with n. 6). The martyrs might then be 'of the Gothic people – that is, of Fritigern', but this interpretation is difficult to work out in detail, and we see no good reason to change the text.

Batwin the minister(?), in a crowded church among the Gothic people, were burned.[62]

[November]

3 Constanti[n]us the emperor.[63]
6 Dorotheus the bishop.[64]
15 Philip the Apostle, in Hieropolis.[65]
19 (Remembrance of) the old women at Beroea, forty in total.[66]
29 Andrew the Apostle.[67]

(iii) The final text is printed by Delehaye (pp. 215-6) from a *menologium* of the month of June preserved in a Paris manuscript of the eleventh century. The narrative is neither very convincing nor very informative of Gothic society, but it adds the names of three more martyrs and of a bishop, 'Goddas'. Again, the function of the text is to provide documentary background to the deposition of relics: unfortunately, the harbour town of Haliscus, where this is said to have happened, is not otherwise known.

---

[62]Our translation differs from all of those put forward by Delehaye, at 278, but seems to relate better to the actual circumstances recorded by other sources. 'Werekas' and 'Batwin' are evidently the 'Bathousês' and 'Wêrkas' mentioned in the text translated above at 4(i)(a), which describes them both as presbyters. The meaning of 'bilaif' is not known. We have translated it to indicate an ecclesiastical rank lower than that of Werekas, who is apparently the leader of the community.

[63]3 November was in fact the date of the death, not of Constantine but of the Arian Constantius II. The textual error might already derive from a Greek source. For the term 'þiudanis' (*sc*. þiudans, 'king') see the selections from the Gothic Bible, below, Chapter 7, on *Matt*. 6.10 (Text III).

[64]Dorotheus was the Arian bishop first at Heraclea, then at Antioch and finally at Constantinople. According to Socrates, *Hist. Eccl.* 7.6, he died on 6 November 406 – at the age of 119 years!

[65]According to the Greek tradition the Apostle Philip died at Hierapolis (here in the form Hieropolis) in Phrygia (cf. Eusebius, *Hist. Eccl.* 3.31.3f. and 5.24.2, citing Polycrates of Ephesus). The date should be 14, not 15 November.

[66]Delehaye, 207-9, prints an unbelievable, and for present purposes irrelevant, *Passion* of the forty old women of Beroea (in Thrace), allegedly martyred in the time of Licinius. Their commemoration might, but need not necessarily, have been taken over by the Gothic church during the period of the Goths' residence in Thrace.

[67]The commemoration of St. Andrew should fall on 30, not 29, November. The presence of the Apostle Philip in the calendar shows that Andrew was not necessarily included because of his supposed connection with the conversion of Thrace and Scythia. The latter connection is however made in the last of this group of texts to be translated.

TRANSLATION

Summary of the trial of the holy martyrs Innâs, Rêmâs, Pinâs, who died in Gothia.

These holy men, who came from the northern land of the barbarians and were followers of Andrew the apostle,[68] converted many of the barbarians to the faith of Christ from the error of the heathen. Brought before the ruler of the barbarians, they refused to yield to his impiety, although he tried to persuade them by blandishments and threats; upon which, on account of their faith in Christ, they were beaten mercilessly. Then, in the depth of a savage winter, while the rivers were frozen solid so that horses might be ridden on them, placing beside one of these rivers upright stakes which they fastened in the ground, they bound the martyrs there; and as the water reached their necks, so they surrendered their souls to the Lord, and their remains were cared for by members of the faithful.[69] Later Goddas, elected as bishop and bearing the relics on his own shoulders,[70] laid them to rest in their own country, seven years after their martyrdom. After this, following a revelation the holy men persuaded the same Goddas the bishop to transport the relics to the place called Haliscus, which is a harbour; where we, not knowing the date of the martyrdom, celebrate the deposition of the relics,[71] to the glory of God and the honour of his holy martyrs, that the all-hallowed name of the Father and of the Son and of the Holy Spirit may be praised for ever and ever, Amen.

---

[68]See n. 67.

[69]How the martyrs drowned in the frozen water is a problem not addressed by the text.

[70]No other information exists on this 'Goddas'. E. A. Thompson, *Visigoths*, 161-5, gives circumstantial reasons (he does not claim proof) for putting the martyrdoms in 347/8 rather than in the 370s, and identifies Goddas as a Catholic bishop among the Goths, on the grounds that there is no room for a second Arian bishop in addition to Ulfila. Goddas should at least be a historical figure, if the harbour-town of Haliscus and its Christian community ever existed, for he apparently took the relics there himself. He might conceivably have succeeded Ulfila in Gothia after the latter's departure for Moesia: despite Thompson's opposition to the idea of suffragan bishops, his election might have seemed a sensible course of action to Gothic Christians who did not leave Gothia and wished to maintain their communities.

[71]Cf. above, passage 4 (i) with n. 56, for a similar question of dating.

CHAPTER FIVE

THE LIFE AND WORK OF ULFILA

INTRODUCTION

By far the best and fullest accounts of the career and work of the famous bishop among the Goths are given in two Arian sources. These are the fifth-century *Church History* of Philostorgius, as epitomised by the ninth-century scholar and patriarch of Constantinople Photius, and a letter of Ulfila's pupil Auxentius, bishop of Durostorum (Silistra) on the Danube, preserved as part of a collection of Arian *scolia* on the council of Aquileia of 381. The precarious survival of these texts is a reflection of the thoroughness with which the victorious 'orthodox' church of the fourth and later centuries succeeded in eliminating the writings, and in large part the reputations, of its opponents. At the end of the extract translated below, Photius accused Philostorgius of excessive admiration for his hero, and the letter of Auxentius is cited in a document of an extremely controversial nature, written into the margins of a single fifth-century manuscript. We catch a glimpse in these texts of the 'alternative ideology' that would have prevailed had the Arian cause in the event been successful. Constantius II would be a Christian hero, and Ulfila a giant of the fourth-century church.

Most of what we know of Ulfila derives from these two texts, and it would be redundant to discuss his life and career at length here. There is, however, further information to be taken into account, and it is particularly worth emphasising the dual context in which Auxentius' and Philostorgius' accounts of Ulfila's life must be seen. Ulfila was both intimately involved in Romano-Gothic relations, and a significant actor in the church disputes of the fourth century.

ULFILA AND ROMANO-GOTHIC RELATIONS

Ulfila's role in diplomatic contacts between the Roman state and the Gothic confederation of the Tervingi was clearly considerable, but is not without its puzzles. Imperial interest in Ulfila is apparent in the fact that he was consecrated, apparently in the reign of Constantius II (see below) by the emperor's leading bishop, Eusebius of

Nicomedia, and in the continuing interest that Constantius took in his work. When Ulfila was forced after just seven years of his mission to leave the Gothic lands, he was received with great honour by the emperor, who (for obvious reasons) styled him 'the Moses of our times', and allowed him to settle with his followers in the province of Moesia.[1] Such imperial interest in the spread of Christianity beyond the Roman frontiers is not unique. Our sources record the same emperor's support for the mission of the 'Indian' Theophilus to the Himyarites at about the same time.[2] Whether this interest simply reflects the view that a Christian emperor should be concerned to spread the Gospel, or whether Constantius thought to gain immediate political benefits from this activity, is hard to say. As E. A. Thompson has shown, however, it later became a common idea that Christianity could help to pacify dangerous peoples, and it is possible that this was part of Constantius' thinking.[3]

Whatever the emperor's motivation, we know that the leaders of the Goths resisted the spread of Christianity in the fourth century in at least two periods of persecution. In the first, Ulfila was driven out of the Gothic lands, probably as part of a more general crisis in Romano-Gothic relations in the late 340s (see our Introduction to Chapter 2). The second followed the peace agreement of 369/70. The aim of this treaty was to draw firm lines between Roman and Goth after a period of closer political and economic ties, and the leaders of the Goths may well have considered themselves free, in its aftermath, to persecute Christians, whereas they had not done so before. It is hard to escape the conclusion that the Gothic leaders, as much as Roman emperors, saw religion as a political issue, equating the spread of Christianity with the advancement of imperial interests in their lands.[4] The strength of the links between Christians north of the Danube and those south of it must sometimes

---

[1]Ulfila's was the most famous, and perhaps the only imperially-sponsored, mission to the Goths, but there is some evidence of others. The heretic bishop Audius, exiled by Constantine to the Roman province of Scythia, is said to have taken an active interest in evangelising the Goths, and to have inspired the foundation of monastic life among them (Epiphanius, *Haer.* 70.14: ed, Dindorf, Vol. III.1, p. 261; *PL* 42.372), and Basil of Caesarea mentions the activities of one Eutyches, who is however otherwise unknown and may belong to this earlier period (*Ep.* 164; cf. p. 123 n. 50 above). For Ulfila as 'Moses', cf. Philostorgius 2.5. and Auxentius §37[59].

[2]A. Dihle, 'Die Sendung des Inders Theophilos', *Palingenesia* IV (1969), 330-6.

[3]'Christianity and the Northern Barbarians', in A. Momigliano (ed.), *The Conflict between Paganism and Christianity in the Fourth Century* (1963), 65ff.

[4]For this and what follows, see Peter Heather, 'The crossing of the Danube and the Gothic conversion', *GRBS* 27 (1986), 289-318, at 315-7.

have worried the Gothic leadership. We saw in the preceding chapter how, in the *Passion of St. Saba*, the priest Sansalas could move easily across the frontier, and Soranus, *dux* of Scythia Minor, was able to procure the martyr's remains.

Ulfila's missionary activity among the Goths must be seen, therefore, in a highly charged political context; he operated with imperial favour, and may well have been perceived by the Goths as some kind of representative of the empire. And up to 376, at least, Christianity continued to play a prominent role in Romano-Gothic relations; despite the many difficulties in the sources, it seems likely that the Tervingi formally accepted Christianity as one of the conditions by which they were allowed to enter Roman territory by the Emperor Valens. As we have seen (p. 106 n. 5), it is also possible that Ulfila was again involved in Romano-Gothic relations at this point. Sozomen reports that Ulfila led the embassy to Valens in 376 which negotiated the entry of Tervingi into the Roman empire. That there was such an embassy is confirmed by Ammianus (31.4.1), and the relevant chapter of Sozomen seems to consist of genuine information which has been misplaced rather than of fabricated material.[5] To accept Sozomen's report would necessitate supposing that Ulfila had kept in contact with people and events in the Gothic world after his expulsion in the late 340s, but given the freedom of movement across the frontier officially sanctioned up to 367 and evident in the *Passion of St. Saba*, this does not seem unlikely. The argument is not conclusive, but leaves open the intriguing possibility that Ulfila's lifetime of involvement in Romano-Gothic relations culminated in the negotiations which allowed the Tervingi to cross the Danube in 376.

ULFILA AND CHURCH DISPUTE

Ulfila's importance in the realm of Romano-Gothic relations may also help to explain why this exiled bishop of the Goths, settled after *c.* 348 around Nicopolis with his followers, should have played such a significant role in the controversies which afflicted the church in the fourth century. All that we know in detail of Ulfila's teaching comes from the letter of Auxentius translated here. Now Auxentius' friendship with Ulfila an extremely close one, which gave him a

---

[5] Cf. Heather, at 298ff.

privileged insight into the work of his master; on the other hand it bears directly only upon Ulfila's later years, and Auxentius' account may well be influenced by the distortions of hindsight as well as by his open partisanship of his cause. We must therefore begin by setting Auxentius' account in the context of contemporary theological debate, and of imperial attempts to find a definition of faith which would bring peace to all, or to all but a minority, of the church.

The set of doctrinal disputes now known as the Arian controversy arose from a conflict between bishop Alexander of Alexandria and one of his priests, Arius, over the relationship of the Father and the Son within the Godhead. What precisely Arius taught is still a matter of debate, but it is clear that he subordinated the Son to the Father in ways that aroused the ire of his bishop, and both protagonists quickly canvassed for support among churchmen of the east. Once he came to power in the east after defeating Licinius, the Emperor Constantine called a general council of the church, held in 325 at Nicaea in Bithynia, as a result of which the key term *homousios* - Greek ὁμοούσιος, 'of the same being, or substance' - was incorporated into more traditional credal statements to define the contested relationship. This term was designed to exclude Arius, who could not accept it and was duly excommunicated.[6]

In its essentials, the Nicene settlement lasted until the death of Constantine (337), though not without a great deal of manoeuvring which saw former supporters of Arius such as Eusebius of Nicomedia increase in influence, and the convinced 'homousian' Athanasius of Alexandria fall into disfavour.[7] With the accession of Constantius II, debate took on a new lease of life. The subsequent half-century or so of theological discussion and political manoeuvre is portrayed in many of our sources as a straightforward clash between orthodox 'homousians' on the one hand and heretical 'Arians' on the other. These sources were largely written after the victory of *homousios*, and reduce what was in fact a very complicated matter into a simple bipartisan clash, in which all opponents of the victorious doctrine, whatever the differences between them, are

[6]There has been much recent literature on Arius and the origins of the dispute. See Rowan Williams, *Arius: Heresy and Tradition* (1987) with refs. to earlier contributions. On the Creeds, J. N. D. Kelly, *Early Christian Creeds* (1952), Chaps. 7-9.

[7]On developments after Nicaea, see L. W. Barnard, 'Church-State Relations, AD 313-337', *Journal of Church and State* 24 (1982), 337-355 at 348ff. and T. A. Kopeček, *A History of Neo-Arianism* (1979), 61ff.

dubbed Arians. A full treatment of this issue would be out of place here, but we may set Ulfila in his theological context by noting the emergence during the reign of Constantius II of four main schools of thought;

(i) The 'homousians', already mentioned, believed that Father, Son and Holy Spirit were of the same or identical mode of being or substance (Greek οὐσία, giving the adjectival termination, -ούσιος), all having existed eternally without priority in time. Athanasius of Alexandria was the leading figure in this group, until it was taken up and refined by the Cappadocian fathers, Basil of Caesarea, and the two Gregorys, of Nazianzus and Nyssa.

(ii) The 'homoeusians' (Greek ὁμοιούσιοι) believed that the persons of the Trinity were not of the same or identical, but of 'similar' (ὅμοιος) substance. This group wanted to exclude Arius, but were still worried by questions that the term *homousios* seemed to leave unanswered: what after all *were* the differences between the Father and Son, and in particular what was the nature of Christ – who had lived as an historical figure in time, and had suffered in a fashion impossible for a supreme God and yet was evidently conceived of as more than human. *Homoeusios* was a compromise formula which left unresolved the whole question of the nature and extent of the differences between the persons of the Trinity. This group began to coalesce after 341 under the leadership of Basil of Ancyra.

(iii) The 'homoeans' were a more conservative group of bishops – they may be regarded as inheritors of the mantle of Ulfila's patron, Eusebius of Nicomedia – who thought, like the homoeusians, that *homousios* confused the persons of the Trinity, but differed from them in believing that all definitions involving the Greek term '-ousios' were unhelpful. Under the leadership of bishops Acacius of Caesarea and Eudoxius of Constantinople, who won the support of the Emperor Constantius, they advanced the compromise view, excluding the term '-ousios', that the Son was 'like' (ὅμοιος, as above) the Father.

(iv) The 'anomoeans', often known as the Neo-, or radical, Arians, advanced the view that the Son was '*un*like' (ἀνόμοιος) the Father, emphasising the separate identities of the Persons of the Trinity. The leaders of this group were

Aetius and Eunomius, and it seems to have emerged in the 350s, in reply to those who wished to distinguish between the Persons of the Trinity, but were willing to accept, under imperial pressure, the compromise formula of the homoeans.

Ulfila's theology shares with Arius its emphatic differentiation between the three Persons of the Trinity. Auxentius further reports his hostility to both of the above groups (i and ii) who wished to use language in '-ousios'; both views, with others, Ulfila denounced as irreligious and Godless heresies, the work of Antichrists (§29[49]). This is firmly in line with Auxentius' repeated insistence that Ulfila's teaching conformed with that of Christ and the evangelists as shown in the New Testament, and with 'tradition'. The New Testament never uses language involving '-ousios' when describing the relationship of Father and Son, and one of the main criticisms of both 'homousians' and 'homoeusians' was that their definitions were non-scriptural. Ulfila based his position entirely on Scripture, and Auxentius' account of it is liberal in its citations.

Ulfila's position also differs from the Nicene position in a rather different respect, in its emphasis on the distinct 'cosmological' roles played by the three members of the Trinity. Indeed, at one point Auxentius presents his teacher (§28[47]), in relation to the 'homoeusian' position, as insisting that the question was not one of identities or similarities between 'things' (*comparatas . . . res*), but of their different 'dispositions' (*differentes adfectus*). 'Adfectus' (or 'affectus') is a highly coloured word, whose meaning extends from a state of body or mind, through love and desire, to will and volition. In using it, Auxentius seems to be emphasising Ulfila's belief that the differences between the Persons of the Trinity were not primarily to be seen in terms of 'substances' at all, but in their functions, or modes of intention.

In considering these issues, we must remember that the history of the Arian controversy as we read it today reflects the way in which the issues were debated in the public arena over a period of more than half a century after the death of Arius. It is a truism, but an important one, that Arius precedes the Arian controversy; we cannot assume that the development of the controversy in the later fourth century reflects what he himself would have found most important in it. The same is true of Ulfila. In his recognition of Christ as an 'only-begotten' (*unigenitus*) God of second order, as 'Lord' (*dominus*) created by the 'unbegotten' (*ingenitus*) Supreme God, or Father, as an act of will and power (§25[43]), and himself the creator, for and on behalf of the Father, of the physical and spiritual universe (*caelestia et terrestria, invisibilia et visibilia omnia*, §26[45]), Ulfila's doctrine certainly resembles what can be perceived of that of Arius;[8] but this is very unlikely to have been its source. The theology belongs to an older world, that of the so-called 'Middle Platonists' of the second and third centuries, with their notion of a creating God or 'demiurge' operating below the Supreme First Principle (*altissimus auctor*, (§24[42]). This is not the place to discuss the constituent features of Middle Platonism, but an affinity may be noted between the theology of Ulfila and surviving fragments of the Platonist Numenius, and even such an ambiguous theological source as the *Chaldaean Oracles*.[9] So too, Ulfila's notion of the Holy Spirit as not a God in the fullest sense, but as an entity created by the Second God to do his service and to assist in the communications of men with the divine world (at §31[51] the Holy Spirit is introduced as the 'advocate' of men and as petitioner on their behalf), also finds echoes in the intellectual world of the Middle Platonists.[10]

It is thus not surprising that in what we may call the politics of church settlement, Ulfila was closest to the 'conservative' grouping within the church (group iii above). As we have seen, he was ordained bishop by Eusebius of Nicomedia, who can be seen as the precursor of this group. After his return to the Roman empire, we hear nothing of Ulfila until 359/60, when he gave his allegiance to the settlement hammered out by Acacius and Eudoxius, with Constantius' approval, at the council of Constantinople. After many preparatory debates, all, except the homousians and Neo-Arians, accepted at this council a Creed incorporating the term ὅμοιος.[11] Now Sozomen 6.37.8, in a section not taken from

---

[8]In the version preserved in the *De Synodis* of his opponent Athanasius; Williams, 101-3.

[9]Cf. R. T. Wallis, *Neoplatonism* (1972), at 34 (refs. omitted); 'Numenius distinguishes Plato's Good (whom he identifies with his First God) from his Craftsman (identified with his Second God). The former is said to contemplate by making use of the latter; hence, though essentially inactive, he is able indirectly to take part in shaping the cosmos'; cf. John Dillon, *The Middle Platonists* (1977), 366ff. The divine 'Craftsman' is the demiurge, the theory being developed in discussion of Plato's *Timaeus*, a fundamental 'Neoplatonic' text. For the *Chaldaean Oracles*, cf. esp. frags. 5, 7, 33 in the ed. of E. des Places, *Oracles Chaldaïques* (ed. Budé, 1971), with his Introduction, 15f.; Dillon, 363f.

[10]In the figure of Ψυχή or 'World-Soul' (although Ulfila's conception is much more personal); cf. Wallis, *Neoplatonism*, 34f., 69, 111, 119, etc.; Dillon, 45f., 282ff. Again, Plato's *Timaeus* is a key text.

[11]Kelly, *Early Christian Creeds*, 274ff.; Kopeček, *A History of Neo-Arianism*, chap. 5. The homoeusians accepted this definition under heavy imperial pressure; in subsequent years many were deposed, although on non-theological grounds.

Socrates (cf. our translation of this passage in Chapter 4), reports that this was the first occasion on which Ulfila joined the 'Arians', as the victorious homousians later dubbed Acacius and Eudoxius, and that up to that moment he had remained in communion with those adhering to Nicaea. A passage in Theodoret might also suggest that he was reluctant to take this step, and did so only because he was convinced that the dispute was about personalities and not doctrine.[12] This may well be so, in the sense that Ulfila was not a positive homoean; the term does not appear in Auxentius' account of Ulfila's teaching or creed, and, as we have seen, Ulfila primarily chose to talk of the Father and Son in terms of different functions or intentions. According to Auxentius, Ulfila was also hostile to the homoeusians (§27[46]), who were part of this settlement, so that there are several reasons why he might have been hesitant to be a part of it. The truth behind all this may be that it was in 359/60 that Ulfila, under pressure to define his position, first formally allied himself with the evolving party of Acacius and Eudoxius. Before that, he had in theological terms been a relatively isolated figure, preoccupied until 347/8 with his mission among the Goths and then with his work of translation and exegesis, with firmly defined views but not so far drawn into the doctrinal disputes of the eastern bishops. To take up Sozomen's second point, the fact that Ulfila was not a declared opponent of Nicaea does not make him a supporter of it - if indeed this whole way of seeing the matter is not anachronistic. One suspects that, in the fluidity of the first 'post-Nicene' generation adherence to that settlement was not the touchstone of orthodoxy that it later came to be.

In the years after 360, however, Ulfila became a determined partisan of the 'anti-ousian' cause. Auxentius reports his fierce denunciations of both homousians and homoeusians, and his last known act, again recorded in the *Letter* (§39[61]), was to attend the

---

[12]Theodoret, *Hist. Eccl.* 4.33. The passage ostensibly deals with the Danube crossing of 376, but describes relations between Ulfila and bishop Eudoxius of Constantinople, who died in 370. Something has gone wrong, and it seems likely that Theodoret has mistakenly combined a notice about 376 with material relating to an earlier incident. This could either be the council of Constantinople in 359/60 (perhaps the more likely view), or Theodoret might alternatively be referring to the creation of the Emperor Valens' church settlement in the later 360s; cf. Heather, 'The Gothic Conversion', 311 (the author now thinks the explanation offered in note 53, rather than that in the text, is the more likely to be correct). Such material is obviously difficult to use; however, Theodoret reports that Ulfila joined Eudoxius and broke with his opponents when he was persuaded that 'the quarrel . . . was really one of personal rivalry and involved no difference in doctrine'.

council of the sects in Constantinople in 383 to attempt to persuade the Emperor Theodosius that his support for *homousios* in 382 had been mistaken. Through Auxentius, Ulfila is also linked to Palladius and the next generation of non-Nicenes who struggled with Ambrose both at Aquileia and at Milan for imperial favour at the courts of the Emperors Gratian and Valentinian II.[13] In both the eastern and western halves of the empire, the struggle to make Ulfila's brand of Christianity the universal faith was lost in the generation after his death,[14] but Goths, Vandals, Sueves and others were to preserve something of his teaching for another two hundred years.

PHILOSTORGIUS, *CHURCH HISTORY* 2.5.

It is difficult to be sure from Photius' summary what was the original context of Philostorgius' account of Ulfila. The passage seems to be safely attributed to the second book of Philostorgius and to belong, in sequence with neighbouring extracts, to the later years of Constantine, who is indeed named in the passage; but if anything is clear, it is that the flight of Ulfila from Gothic territories, which is both the explicit point of departure of Photius' text and the point to which it returns, was under Constantius II. No solution of the problem is free from difficulties.[15] Photius' summary is quite complex, with its 'flash-back' from the departure of Ulfila from Gothia to the third-century Gothic invasions and their consequences, then on to Ulfila's consecration and work among the Goths, finally returning to his expulsion and settlement in Moesia. Much will have been lost in the abbreviation, and the original text may have been still more complex in structure. It is possible that the context of this original version was not the return of Ulfila from Gothia but his consecration as bishop, and hence that this was indeed under Constantine (see below). This interpretation entails, however, that Photius has misunderstood, or has given a misleading impression of Philostorgius. In the passage as it stands, the chronological 'underpinning' is clearly provided by the departure from Gothia, not

---

[13]See the introduction to the translation below, and, on Ambrose and the Arians, McLynn, in the article cited at n. 23 below.

[14]The full history of the 'end of Arianism' remains to be written, but, for an introduction, see Kopeček, *A History of Neo-Arianism*, Chap. 7.

[15]The chronological and other problems attaching to this passage are well outlined by Thompson, *The Visigoths in the Time of Ulfila*, xiv-xvii. See Chapter 4 n. 1 for Philostorgius' time of writing and below, n. 21, for his place of origin.

by the consecration of Ulfila, which functions as an explanatory digression within the text.

Another difficulty is that it is not clear whether the naming of 'Constantine' in the passage is made from the standpoint of the expulsion from Gothia and so looks back from the reign of Constantius, or whether it looks forward to the fourth century from the reigns of Valerian and Gallienus and the third-century Gothic invasions. In the former case, the reading 'Constantine' may stand, to distinguish this emperor from his successor (though Photius himself makes no such distinction between two emperors); in the latter, one might consider emending 'Constantine' to 'Constantius', a very common confusion in the transmission of Greek and Latin texts. This has the virtue of conforming to Auxentius' chronology of the career of Ulfila (see below) and makes good sense of Photius, with the disadvantage that it seems to go against the location of the passage in Philostorgius' original text.

An absolute *terminus ante quem* for the consecration of Ulfila is provided by the death in 341 of Eusebius of Nicomedia, then bishop of Constantinople. Consecration in that or the previous year would give a seven-year mission in Gothia, as described by Auxentius (cf. his *Letter*, §37[59]), ending with Ulfila's departure in 347/8. Some interpreters have, however, argued for an earlier date of consecration in or near 336, when Eusebius was still bishop of Nicomedia; among them, recently, K. Schäferdiek and T. D. Barnes.[16] Preferring the evidence (and the textual reliability) of Photius/Philostorgius to that of Auxentius, they argue the latter to have misrepresented the length of Ulfila's bishopric as 40 years (*sc.* 33 + 7, as explicitly in the *Letter*, §38[60]), rather than what they take to be the true figure of 47 (40 + 7) years, yielding a bishopric of 336-383. Without insisting on the exact total of 40 years, which is certainly influenced by typological requirements (see our nn. 37, 41, etc.), we find the evidence of Auxentius better founded, and his supposed misunderstanding hard to accept.[17]

Just as the dispatch of Ulfila 'with others' on an embassy by the Gothic ruler is likely to have had an overtly political motive, so too,

[16] K. Schäferdiek, 'Wulfila: vom Bischof von Gotien zum Gotenbischof', *ZKG* 90 (1979), at 254ff.; T. D. Barnes, 'The consecration of Ulfila', *JTS* n.s. 41 (1990), 541-5.

[17] Barnes' suspicions of the reliability of Auxentius' text, as transcribed by Maximinus, seem unwarranted (they are based on an unsatisfactory article by B. Capelle published in 1922), and do not ask why Maximinus should have changed such a detail. See also n. 43 below.

on the Roman side, might his consecration as bishop, and this would certainly fit what we otherwise know of the foreign policy of Constantius (see our Introduction and n. 2). If we do give weight to this consideration, there is no compelling need to find a suitable church council, whether at Constantinople in 336 or at Antioch in 341, to provide a context and dating for the consecration; nor, in our view, does the reference to 'Eusebius and the bishops of his party' seem necessarily to entail this.[18] Finally, nothing in our evidence suggests either that Ulfila was consecrated in 336 and went out to evangelise Gothia at a later time, or that he made two visits from Gothia to the Roman empire (one on the embassy, and one other), and we do not favour these means of reconciling Photius' account with that of Auxentius.

The text translated is that of J. Bidez *GCS* (2nd ed., rev. by F. Winkelmann, 1972), pp. 17-18.

TRANSLATION

(Philostorgius) says that at this time[19] Ulphilas led a large body of the Scythians from those living across the Ister (the people whom in olden times they called Getae, but now call Goths) to the land of the Romans, driven through piety from their own homes. Now this people became Christian in the following way. In the reigns of Valerian and Gallienus, a large number of Scythians from beyond the Ister crossed into Roman territory and overran much of Europe. Crossing also into Asia, they reached as far as Galatia and Cappadocia. They took many prisoners, including some who were members of the clergy, and went home with a great quantity of booty.[20] Now the pious band of prisoners, living as they did among the barbarians, converted many of them to the way of piety and persuaded them to adopt the Christian faith instead of the pagan. Among these prisoners were the ancestors of Ulphilas; they were Cappadocians by nationality, from a village near the city of Parnassus

---

[18]As is also observed, for different reasons, by Thompson, *Visigoths*, at xvi.

[19]*Sc*. (on our preferred chronology) in 347/8, on the occasion of the onset of war with Rome and the consequent outbreak of persecution in Gothia; Wolfram, *History of the Goths*, 63f. and 79f.

[20]Cf. Wolfram, *History of the Goths*, 48ff. and 75f. The statement that this happened in the reign (*sc*. the joint reign?) of Valerian and Gallienus would suggest a date before 260, but this should perhaps not be pressed. For the circumstances of the captivity, see Chapter 1 above.

called Sadagolthina.[21] It was this Ulphilas who led the exodus of the pious ones, being the first bishop appointed among them. He was appointed in the following circumstances: sent with others by the ruler of the race of the Goths on an embassy in the time of Constantine (for the barbarian peoples in those parts owed allegiance to the emperor), Ulphilas was elected by Eusebius and the bishops of his party as bishop of the Christians in the Getic land. Among the matters which he attended to among them, he was the inventor for them of their own letters, and translated all the Scriptures into their language - with the exception, that is, of Kings. This was because these books contain the history of wars, while the Gothic people, being lovers of war, were in need of something to restrain their passion for fighting rather than to incite them to it - which those books have the power to do, for all that they are held in the highest honour, and are well fitted to lead believers to the worship of God. The emperor established this mass of refugees in the territories of Moesia, where each man chose to live;[22] and he

---

[21] See S. Salaville, 'Un ancien bourg de Cappadoce: Sadagolthina', *Echos d'Orient* 15 (1912), 61-3; based on the report of an unpublished inscription naming the place. If accepted, the location is near the northern shores of L. Tatta (Tuz Gölü). The site of Parnassus was identified in the region (SSE of Ancyra, 22 m. from Aspuna) by J. G. C. Anderson, *JHS* 19 (1899), 107-9. Philostorgius himself came from the village of Borissos in Cappadocia II (the western division of the province); *Hist. Eccl.* 9.9 (ed. Bidez-Winkelmann, p. 119). Ulfila may have been Cappadocian by descent (cf. Chapter 4, n. 18 on Saba), but his name (Wulfila, 'Little Wolf') is unequivocally Gothic.

[22] The settlement in Moesia, as attested by Philostorgius and referred to by Auxentius (*Letter*, 37[59]) is located near Nicopolis by an intriguing passage of Jordanes, *Getica* 267;

> 'Now there were other Goths as well, who are called the Lesser Goths, a very large people, whose priest and primate Ulfila is said also to have taught them how to write. Today these Goths live in Moesia and inhabit the region of Nicopolis towards the foot of Mount Haemus: a people large in numbers but impoverished and unwarlike, with no resources except for herds of various sort of animal, pasture and the forest for wood. They have little fertile land for growing wheat or other varieties of cereal. As for vines, some of them are unaware even that they exist in other places, and buy their wine from the neighbouring regions. Most of them live on milk'.

There is no obvious reason to disbelieve Jordanes' report. He is describing the fragmentation of the Hunnic empire after the death of Attila, and tracing back phenomena of his own day to this process of fragmentation; he follows his description of the 'Lesser Goths' with a resumption of the history of the Ostrogoths, to which his narrative is primarily devoted. It is remarkable that such a community of Goths, if originally based on the migration of Ulfila and his supporters to the Roman empire, should still exist in the sixth century. (No less remarkable is Jordanes' apparently hazy conception of the true stature and achievement of Ulfila; the Gothic Bible was familiar enough in his own day, and one would expect Jordanes to have known something about it). The comment about wine is expressed rather

held Ulphilas in the highest esteem, so as often to refer to him as the 'Moses of our time'. Philostorgius admires this man to excess, and records that with those in his charge he was attached to the same heretical opinions as himself.

THE LETTER OF AUXENTIUS.

The letter is quoted by the fifth-century Arian theologian Maximinus, in his so-called 'dissertatio' on the council of Aquileia of 381, at which the group of Illyrian Arians led by bishops Palladius of Ratiaria and Secundianus of Singidunum were defeated by Ambrose of Milan and their opinions condemned, despite their vigorous and continuing protests at the unscrupulous tactics of their adversary.[23] Part of a commentary by Palladius on the *Acta* of the council and a criticism of two passages of Book I of the *De Fide* of Ambrose form part of the contents of the fifth-century manuscript in which the 'dissertatio' of Maximinus is also preserved. Palladius' annotations, which do not concern us here, were copied into the margins of a text of the *Acta* at ff.336r-349r of the codex, after the lifetime of their author but clearly not long after the manuscript itself was written. Maximinus' 'dissertatio', including the letter of Auxentius, was written, in up to three later hands, into the margins of a text of Books I-II of the *De Fide* of Ambrose in an earlier part of the codex (ff.298r-311v).[24]

The author is undoubtedly the Arian bishop Maximinus known from his confrontation with Augustine in Africa in 427/8 (Augustine, *Conlatio cum Maximino*, in *PL* 42.709-42).[25] That he compiled his annotations as late as the 440's is shown by his (historically confused)

obscurely. Jordanes must mean that these Goths, if they had known about vines grown elsewhere, would have grown their own and not have been obliged to import their wine.

[23]Neil McLynn, 'The "Apology" of Palladius; Nature and Purpose', *JTS* n.s. 42 (1991), 52-76; M. Meslin, *Les Ariens d'Occident, 335-430* (1967), 85-91.

[24]For this and all matters relating to the MS tradition, see the Introduction of R. Gryson, *Scolies ariennes sur le Concile d'Aquilée* (*SChr* 267, 1980) (on Maximinus, pp. 53ff.); summarily in *CC, series Latina* 87 (1982), pp. xxi-xxii, and at full length in Gryson and L. Gilissen, *Les scolies ariennes du Parisinus Latinus 8907: un échantillonnage d'écritures latines du Ve siècle (Armarium Codicum Insignium*, vol. I; 1980), pp. 5-23.

[25]A. Mandouze, *Prosopographie de l'Afrique chrétienne (303-533)* (1982), s. Maximinus 10, p. 731; '[il] relève par conséquent de la prosopographie de l'Illyricum'.

citation at the end of the text of Palladius (at f.349r of the codex) of two laws from the Theodosian Code, published in the west in 438.[26] It is at least possible that one of the three hands in which the 'dissertatio' and the additional note at the end of the text are written is that of Maximinus himself.[27] The entire codex, which is a compilation of works on the Arian controversy written from the 'Nicene' point of view and also includes works of Hilary of Poitiers, must once have belonged to him or an associate, as part of an annotated library of the writings of his theological opponents.

Maximinus' purpose in citing the letter of Auxentius is to present a version of Ulfila's creed (at §40[63] of the letter) and to demonstrate the connection of Ulfila with Palladius and Secundianus, who were condemned at the Council of Aquileia and who, like Ulfila, presented themselves at the Council of Constantinople of 383, mentioned in Maximinus' introduction to the letter (§23[41]) and at §39[61] of the text. The author of the letter is named as Auxentius at §42[65] of Maximinus' 'dissertatio'. An Auxentius of Durostorum is mentioned at the end of Palladius' tract (§94[140]), and it seems clear that it is the same person, later the leader of the Arian community at Milan.

The text of the letter is most recently edited by R. Gryson, in the *Sources Chrétiennes* volume referred to in n. 22, and, with different numeration of the chapters, in *Corpus Christianorum, series Latina* 87 (Turnholt, 1982), at pp. 160-6; in our translation as in this introduction, chapter numbers are given as in this edition, with the *Sources Chrétiennes* references added in square brackets. Lacunae in the text, which is in places badly damaged, are shown in simplified form and approximately.

TRANSLATION

23[41] And that the aforesaid bishops [*sc.* Palladius and Secundianus] also came to the east with bishop Ulfila, to the court of Theodosius, the following letter testifies [. . . *c.* 65 letters . . .].

24[42] [. . . *c.* 66 letters . . .] a man of great (spiritual) beauty, truly a confessor of Christ, teacher of piety and preacher of truth. To

---

[26] The laws are *CTh* 16.4.2 and 16.4.1 (cited in that order); cf. Gryson, *Scolies Ariennes*, at pp. 97-100 (texts at pp. 324-7).

[27] Gryson, pp. 99f.; cf. the revealing facsimile edition and discussion by Gryson and Gilissen (n. 24 above); Meslin, *Les Ariens d'Occident*, 104f.

those who wished to hear and to those who did not, he never shrank from preaching quite openly and without any room for doubt one single true God, the father of Christ according to the teaching of Christ himself [cf. *John* 17.1-3]; knowing this one true God alone to be unbegotten, without beginning, without end, eternal, heavenly, sublime, above all others, the highest originator,[28] excelling all excellence, better than all goodness, without limit, beyond comprehension, invisible, unmeasurable, immortal, incorruptible, incorporeal, incomposite,[29] simple, immutable, indivisible, immovable, needful of nothing, inaccessible, an inseparable unity, subject to no sovereign, not created, not made, perfect, existing in unique singularity, incomparably greater and better than all things.

25[43] Now this God, since he existed alone, not in order to divide or diminish his divinity but in order to show his goodness and power, by force of will alone,[30] impassive and free from passion, incorruptible and untouched by corruption, immovable and without motion, created and engendered, made and established the only-begotten God.

26[44] In accordance with tradition and the authority of the divine scriptures, he never concealed (the truth) that this God is in second place and the originator of all things from the Father and after the Father and on account of the Father and for the glory of the Father; and furthermore that he is great God and great Lord and great king and great mystery, great light[31] [. . . *c.* 28 letters . . .] Lord, provider and lawgiver, redeemer, saviour [. . . *c.* 50 letters . . .] originator of [. . . . .], just judge of all the living and the dead, **[45]** holding as greater (than himself) God his own Father [*John* 14.28] – this he always made clear according to the holy gospel. The odious

---

28 'altissimus auctor'. Here and elsewhere we translate 'auctor' as 'originator'. Gryson has 'principe suprême' (p. 237).

29 'incompositum', *sc.* not composed of separate parts. A little later 'an inseparable unity' translates 'inscissum', not quite the same as 'indivisible' ('indivisum'): no part can be 'cut' or 'split' off from the whole. This motif is again found in Numenius, cf. Wallis, *Neoplatonism*, p. 34; the idea is of a single God 'split' into different phases of existence by the act of creation and his consequent involvement in physical matter.

30 The word translated as 'power' here and in two occurrences at §26[45], is 'virtus'; this translation is imposed by the Biblical passages at §40[63]. The following phrase 'by force of will alone' (for 'sola voluntate et potestate') is a paraphrase enforced by the lack of a suitable synonym comparable to the French 'pouvoir' and 'puissance' (so Gryson, p. 237), and by the need to keep the sense of the impassivity of God required by the context.

31 'magnum lumen' again finds a parallel in Arius; 'he [*sc.* the Word] is thought of too as radiance and as light'; Rowan Williams, at 103 (line 26).

and execrable, depraved and perverse profession of the homousians he rejected and trampled underfoot as the invention of the Devil and the doctrine of demons [cf. *I Tim.* 4.1]; himself knowing that, if it is truly preached and rightly[32] and faithfully believed by all us Christians that the untiring power of the only-begotten God easily made all heavenly and earthly, all invisible and visible things, why then should not the power of God the Father, which suffers no change, be believed to have made this one Being as his own?

27[46] And he further deplored and shunned the error and impiety of the homoeusians. Being himself carefully instructed on the basis of the divine scriptures and diligently confirmed in many councils of holy bishops, in both his sermons and his tractates he showed that a difference does exist between the divinity of the Father and of the Son, of God unbegotten and God only-begotten, and that the Father is for his part the creator of the creator, while the Son is the creator of all creation;[33] and that the Father is God of the Lord, while the Son is God of the created universe.

28[47] He therefore strove to destroy the sect of homousians, because he held the persons of the divinity to be, not confused and mixed together, but discrete and distinct. The homoeusion too he rejected, because he defended not comparable things but different dispositions,[34] **[48]** and used to say that the Son is like his Father, not according to the erroneous depravity and perversity of the Macedonians that conflicts with the scriptures, but in accordance with the divine scriptures and tradition.

29[49] In his preaching and instruction he asserted that all heretics were not Christians but Antichrists, not pious but impious, not religious but irreligious, not fearful but foolhardy, not in hope but without hope, not worshippers of God but without God, not teachers but deceivers, not preachers but prevaricators, whether Manicheans or Marcionites or Montanists or Paulinians or Sabellians or *anthropiani* or *patripassiani* or Fotinians or Novatians or Donatiani

---

[32] Latin 'iure'; for 'virtus' ('power') in the following line, see n. 30 above.

[33] Again, cf. Arius, in Williams, at 100 (para. (iii)); 'so that through him [*sc.* the Word, or Son] he might make us', and 102 (line 6); '[God] established the Son as the beginning of all creatures'.

[34] For the importance of this phrase, see our Introduction, p. 138. As also explained above, the position adopted by Ulfila in 359/60 involved a temporary and reluctant alliance with the homoeusians; Auxentius is writing here of his attitude as it hardened during his later years.

or homousians or homoeusians or Macedonians.[35] In truth, as an emulator of the apostles and imitator of the martyrs, a declared enemy of heretics, he strove to repel their wicked doctrines and to edify the people of God, putting to flight 'grievous wolves' [*Acts* 20.29] and 'dogs, the evil workers' [*Phil.* 3.2], and like a good shepherd protected the flock of Christ through his grace, with all prudence and care [cf. *John* 10.11].

30[50] The Holy Spirit he furthermore declared to be neither Father nor Son, but made by the Father through the Son before all things, neither first nor second, but set by the first under[36] the second in third place: not unbegotten nor begotten, but created by the unbegotten through the begotten in third place, according to the preaching of the gospel and the apostolic tradition, as in the words of St. John, 'All things were made through him, and without him was not any thing made' [*John* 1.3], and in the assertion of the blessed Paul, 'There is one God, the Father, of whom are all things, and one Lord, Jesus Christ, through whom are all things' [*I Cor.* 8.6].

31[51] Now since there exists only one unbegotten God and there stands under him only one only-begotten God, the Holy Spirit our advocate can be called neither God nor Lord, but received its being from God through the Lord: neither originator nor creator, but illuminator, sanctifier, teacher and leader, helper and petitioner [. . . *c.* 15 letters . . .] and confirmer, minister of Christ and distributor of acts of grace, the warrant of our inheritance, in whom we were 'sealed unto the day of redemption' [*Eph.* 4.30]. Without the Holy Spirit, none can say that Jesus is Lord, as the apostle says; 'No man can say, Jesus is Lord, except in the Holy Spirit' [*I Cor.* 12.3], and as Christ teaches; 'I am the way, and the truth, and the life: no one cometh unto the Father, but by me' [*John* 14.6]. **32[52]** And so they are Christians who in spirit and truth worship and glorify Christ [cf. *John* 4.23], and render thanks through Christ with love to God the Father.

33[53] Steadfast in these and similar doctrines, flourishing gloriously

---

[35]This list of heresies (on which see individually F. L. Cross and E. A. Livingstone [edd.], *The Oxford Dictionary of the Christian Church*, rev. ed. of 1983) is strongly but not exclusively preoccupied with dissenters from Arian theology. Manichaeans, Marcionites, Montanists, Novatians and 'Donatiani' (*sc.* Donatists) are not specifically so connected. That 'homousians' and 'homoeusians' should be tucked away near the end of the list may reflect Ulfila's actual priorities; it may on the other hand be a deliberate part of Auxentius' polemical technique to give them such little prominence. Macedonians are also mentioned at §28[47].

[36]Viz. 'substitutum', expressing the lower position of Son to Father.

for forty years in the bishopric,[37] he preached unceasingly with apostolic grace in the Greek, Latin and Gothic languages, in the one and only church of Christ; for one is the church of the living God, 'the pillar and ground of the truth' [*I Tim.* 3.15]: asserting and bearing witness that there is but one flock of Christ our Lord and God, one worship and one edifice, one virgin and one bride, one queen and one vine, one house, one temple, one assembly of Christians, and that all other assemblies are not churches of God but 'synagogues of Satan' [*Rev.* 2.9, cf. 3.9].[38]

[54] And that all he said, and all I have set down, is from the divine Scriptures, 'let him that readeth understand' [*Matt.* 24.15]. He left behind him several tractates and many interpretations in these three languages[39] for the benefit and edification of those willing to accept it, and as his own eternal memorial and recompense.

34[55] It is beyond my powers to praise this man according to his merits; yet I dare not be silent altogether, for I owe him a debt greater than does any other man, in that he spent upon me a greater share of labour. He received me from my parents as his disciple in the earliest years of my life;[40] he taught me the Holy Scriptures and made plain the truth, and through the mercy of God and the grace of Christ he raised me in the faith, as his son in body and spirit.

35[56] By the providence of God and mercy of Christ, for the salvation of many among the people of the Goths, he was at the age of thirty ordained bishop from the rank of lector,[41] that he should

---

[37] This would seem to be a slight underestimate, in the interests of the symbolism of a forty-year period; cf. §38[60] with nn. 41 and 45. It can probably be taken to mean that Ulfila was bishop for nearer 40 than 50 years; surely not as many as 47, as required by the arguments of Schäferdiek and Barnes (above, n. 16).

[38] A forceful reminder that Ulfila was fighting not merely for toleration of his own beliefs, but that his views should be officially espoused by the whole church.

[39] The translation here stays deliberately close to the Latin, 'plures tractatus et multas interpretationes'; cf. Gryson (p. 245), 'maintes homélies et de nombreux *commentaires*' (our italics). It is possible that 'interpretationes' means 'translations', but that does not seem to be Auxentius' emphasis in this passage.

[40] This is evidently after the settlement of Ulfila and his followers in the region of Nicopolis (cf. n. 22), which is only 100 m. from Durostorum as the crow flies and not much further by road.

[41] On our preferred chronology, this would mean that Ulfila was born *c.* 311. The exact date is however affected by Auxentius' wish to assimilate Ulfila's career to that of king David, who became king at 30 and reigned forty years – seven years and six months in Hebron and thirty-three years 'over all Israel and Judah' (*II Sam.* 5.4f.); to Joseph, who was 30 years old when he interpreted Pharaoh's dreams (*Exodus* 41.46); and to the age of Jesus when he began his ministry (*Luke* 3.23).

not only be 'the heir of God and joint-heir of Christ' [*Rom*. 8.17], but should also in this, through the grace of Christ, be an imitator of Christ and his saints. So, as holy David was appointed king and prophet at the age of thirty years, to rule and teach the people of God and the sons of Israel, so too this blessed man was revealed as a prophet and ordained as priest of Christ, to rule, correct, teach and edify the people of the Goths; and this, by the will of God and with the aid of Christ, was wonderfully accomplished through his ministry. **[57]** And just as Joseph was revealed in Egypt at the age of thirty years [so Ulfila . . . *c*. 45 letters . . .]. And as our Lord and God, Jesus Christ the Son of God, was appointed and baptised at the age of thirty years according to the flesh, and began to preach the Gospel and to nourish the souls of men, so too, by the disposition and ordering of Christ himself, that holy man corrected the people of the Goths, who were living in hunger and dearth of preaching but with no heed to their condition, and taught them to live by the rule of evangelic, apostolic and prophetic truth, and he showed the Christians (among them) to be truly Christians, and multiplied their numbers.

36[58] Then, through the envy and machinations of the Enemy a tyrannical and fearsome persecution of Christians in the barbarian land was aroused by the impious and sacrilegious 'iudex' of the Goths;[42] but Satan, who wished to do evil, did good against his will, for those whom he desired to make abandon and betray their faith, with Christ as their aid and champion, became martyrs and confessors. The persecutor was confounded: those who suffered persecution received the martyr's crown, while he who strove for victory blushed in his defeat and those who were put to the test rejoiced in their victory.

37[59] And then, after the glorious martyrdom of many servants and maidservants of Christ, with threats of persecution growing ever more intense, after completing just seven years in his episcopate the holy and blessed Ulfila, of whom we speak, was driven from the barbarian land with a great number of confessors and, still[43] in the

---

[42]See our Introduction and Chapter 2, p. 19. For 'iudex' as the title of the Gothic king, see Chapter 2, n. 91.

[43]'*athuc* beate memorie Constantio principe'. The chronological argument of Schäferdiek (above, n. 16) is eased by his reading in this passage, from the text of Auxentius published in *PL* Suppl. 1, at col. 706, '*a thunc* beate memorie', etc. The facsimile publication of Gryson and Gilissen (above, n. 24) shows however that 'athuc' (for 'adhuc') is the correct reading. It would imply, either that Ulfila left Gothic territories while Constantius was still emperor (rather than after his death),

reign of Constantius of blessed memory, was received with honour on Roman soil. And as God through Moses liberated his people from the power and violence of Pharaoh and the Egyptians, brought them across the seas and provided that they enter his service, so, through him whom we describe, God liberated from barbarian lands the confessors of his holy son the only-begotten, brought them across the Danube and had them serve him in the mountains,[44] in imitation of the saints.

38[60] Ulfila preached the truth to his people in the land of Romania for thirty-three years, in addition to the seven that went before,[45] so that in this too he was the imitator of those saints who [. . . 14 letters . . .] a space of forty years and time to (convert?) many [. . . 24 letters . . .].

39[61] After the completion of forty years Ulfila (came) by imperial order to the city of Constantinople for the purpose of disputation[46] [. . . 8 lines of 13/15 letters . . .] And entering the aforesaid city, when the conduct of the council had been reconsidered by the impious ones for fear that they might be confuted – men in the depths of wickedness, being 'condemned of themselves' [cf. *Titus* 3.11] and fit to be stricken with eternal punishment – Ulfila at once fell ill; and during the illness he was taken up to heaven in the manner of the prophet Elisha [cf. *II Kings* 13.14]. **[62]** Now it is proper for us to consider for a moment the merit of a man who, with the Lord as his guide passed away at Constantinople – or should I say Christianople[47] – for this purpose, that he, a holy, sinless priest of Christ, a man held worthy, by worthy men, in worthy manner,

---

or that something else had happened to Ulfila earlier in the reign of Constantius (and not before his accession). The second interpretation seems to us, in itself and in its context, to be preferable. The most likely such event is his consecration as bishop (a reference to the emperor and to the date of consecration may well have been lost in the lacuna at §35[57]). This supports the reading of 'Constantius' for 'Constantine' in Philostorgius 2.5, translated and discussed above.

[44] *Sc.* in the Haemus mountains (Stara Planina); see Jordanes, *Getica* 267, translated at n. 22.

[45] The seven years in Gothia are 340/1 to 347/8 (see our Introduction to Philostorgius and nn. 16-19 above). The thirty-three years that follow bring us strictly to 380/1, but Ulfila died at Constantinople in 383. See n. 41 for the explanation of the discrepancy.

[46] See on this council Gryson's introduction, at pp. 158-61; Meslin, *Les Ariens d'Occident*, 91f.

[47] The figure of speech expresses the widespread perception of Constantine's city as the Christian capital of the Roman empire, uncontaminated by 'paganism'. The literal truth of this is critically viewed by Cyril Mango, *Le développement urbain de Constantinople (IVe-VIIe siècles)* (1985), esp. at 34-6.

should be marvellously and gloriously honoured for his merits by holy men, his fellow priests.

40[63] Even in death, he left to the people entrusted to him his faith, inscribed upon his very tombstone[48] in accordance with his testament, in these words: 'I, Ulfila, bishop and confessor, have always so believed, and in this, the one true faith, I make the journey to my Lord; I believe in one God the Father, the only unbegotten and invisible, and in his only-begotten son, our Lord and God, the designer and maker of all creation, having none other like him (so that one alone among all beings is God the Father, who is also the God of our God); and in one Holy Spirit, the illuminating and sanctifying power, as Christ said after his resurrection to his apostles: "And behold, I send forth the promise of my Father upon you; but tarry ye in the city of Jerusalem,[49] until ye be clothed with power from on high" [*Luke* 24.49], and again: "But ye shall receive power, when the Holy Ghost is come upon you" [*Acts* 1.8]; being neither God (the Father) nor our God (Christ), but the minister of Christ [. . . 17 letters . . .], subject and obedient in all things to the Son; and the Son, subject and obedient in all things to God who is his Father [. . . 23 letters . . .] (whom) he ordained in the Holy Spirit through his Christ'.

---

[48]'usque in ipso mortis monumento . . . fidem suam conscribtam'. We have translated this literally, as if the profession of faith really were inscribed on Ulfila's tombstone, without being convinced that this was in fact the case; the description is more symbolic than historical.

[49]The word 'Hierusalem' is an explanatory gloss that has crept into the text. It does not appear in critical Greek texts of the New Testament, nor in the Vulgate. It is however present in other early versions, including the Old Latin text of the Brixian bilingual; cf. below, Chapter 6, Additional Note (ii) and (iii) at p. 173 and Chapter 7, on *Matt.* 6.6 (Text III), for similar signs of the distinctiveness of this text.

𐌰	a	𐌸	þ	𐍂	r
𐌱	b	𐌹, ϊ	i	𐍃	s
𐌲	g	𐌺	k	𐍄	t
𐌳	d	𐌻	l	𐍅	w
𐌴	e	𐌼	m	𐍆	f
𐌵	q	𐌽	n	𐍇	ch
𐌶	z	𐌾	y	𐍈	wh
𐌷	h	𐌿	u	𐍉	o
		𐍀	p		

Figure 16: The Gothic alphabet

Shown above are the 25 letters of the Gothic alphabet, with their conventional transcriptions. Of Latin origin are **q**, **h**, **y(j)**, **r**, **s**; of Runic origin **u** (ᚢ) and **o** (ᛟ), unless this is a simplified form of Greek capital omega, Ω. Since Runic characters are themselves heavily dependent on Latin, either might be the immediate source of Gothic **f** (Runic ᚠ). The characters represented as **u** and **o** appear in the Runic inscription on the gold torque from the Pietroasa Treasure, also illustrated above. Here, the transcription **gutaniowi hailag** clearly displays the Gothic word for 'holy, sacred' (cf. Ger. *heilig*). The first six characters **gutani** may give the old Gothic word for their own people (cf. Latin *Gutones*, *Gotones*), but other texts (cf. p. 129) offer *Gutthiadai* for this, and the interpretation, in particular the connection between the two elements, is very uncertain. Another possibility is that **gutan** is the god Wotan, and the letters **iowi** have been seen as equivalent for Latin *Iovi*; hence 'sacred to Wotan-Jupiter', though the presence of the Latin in this context is not free from difficulties. See briefly R. I. Page, *Runes* (British Museum Publications, 1987), pp. 8-11. Like Page, we take our illustration from G. Stephens, *The Old-Northern Runic Monuments of Scandinavia and England* (1867-8). It is at Vol. II, p. 567.

CHAPTER SIX

THE GOTHIC BIBLE

INTRODUCTION

The texts of Philostorgius and Sozomen describing the invention by Ulfila of Gothic 'letters' and his translation into Gothic of the entire Bible except the Books of Kings, are translated above (Chapter 5). The true situation was evidently more complicated than that envisaged by these writers. The formation of a Gothic alphabet based mainly on Greek letters, with some additional characters of Latin and Runic origin (see the table opposite and facsimiles at pp. 128, 164), is not a very elaborate procedure, and might assume some priority in the thoughts of a bishop appointed to serve the Gothic nation. Nevertheless we saw earlier that the ministry of Ulfila within the Gothic lands lasted only seven years before he was expelled with his followers, received by Constantius II and allowed to live near Nicopolis in Moesia. Seven years is hardly sufficient for the translation of such vast quantities of text, and it is likely that the bulk of this work should be ascribed to the thirty-five or more years in which Ulfila lived quietly in Moesia rather than the much busier and more fraught seven years preceding. Since Ulfila came to the Roman empire with a following of Gothic Christian supporters, it is possible that the whole programme of translation was a collective effort performed by learned members of this community. This may be one explanation of the divergences of style that can be seen between different books translated – though we shall see below that there were other points and circumstances in the history of the text at which such variation could enter the tradition. We can imagine that for much of this period of his life Ulfila will have nourished hopes of returning to Gothia to resume his work of evangelising the Goths, and in one sense might even see the work of translation carried out by him and his followers as a preparation for the resumption of this mission. Until his last years, it would have been a great surprise to Ulfila to learn that his work would be preserved as a consequence of Gothic settlement on Roman soil.

That there was a history of subsequent Gothic exegesis and annotation is indicated by a passage of Salvian and by the preface to the *Codex Brixianus*, both translated below. It is also clear from these and other sources that the actual text of the Gothic Bible in use among Gothic communities in the fifth and sixth centuries was subject to change and adaptation – what a polemical writer like Salvian could describe as corruption and interpolation in the text – and many sources for such adaptation can be found, notably the influence of the 'old Latin' Bible in use among the Roman communities with whom the Goths came into contact. A letter of Jerome (*Ep*. 106) to two Gothic scholars, Sunnias and Fretela, responds to an interest of a very detailed, if unsophisticated, character, in the relationship between the Greek Septuagint and Jerome's revised Latin text of the *Psalms*; Jerome replies to no less than 178 questions on the subject (some of them very simple).[1] There are no grounds for importing Sunnias and Fretela into the history of the Gothic Bible, but if such interest as theirs in the Greek and Latin texts were applied by others to these texts in relation to the Gothic version of the Bible, then one can see how the Gothic text might itself come to be influenced by their researches. The religious integrity of the written word of the Bible, reinforced by familiarity and habit, was a powerful incentive to conservatism in its text: on the other hand there were clear discrepancies in the transmitted text, the Bible was in constant use for comment and exegesis, and it could not be held immune from advances in scholarship. In these circumstances the authority of Ulfila, while profoundly important, was less than canonical.

The most important source for the Gothic Bible is the famous *Codex Argenteus*, a magnificent presentation copy written in silver letters with gold capitals on purple-dyed parchment, which has since 1669 been in the University Library at Uppsala; it was earlier at the monastery of Werden (near Cologne) in the mid-sixteenth century, where it may have been taken from Italy in the late eighth century by the pupil of Alcuin who founded the monastery, and at Prague, from where it was taken by the Swedes in 1648.[2] The codex, of sixth-century Italian (i.e. Ostrogothic) origin, contains substantial parts of all four Gospels (which appear in the 'old Latin' order *Matthew*, *John*, *Luke*, *Mark*), but with extensive lacunae; only 187 of 330 original folios have survived. In the so-called *Codex Carolinus*,

---

[1]See J. N. D. Kelly, *Jerome; his Life, Writings and Controversies* (1975), 285-6, with refs.

[2]For a general account of the Gothic Bible, see M. J. Hunter, in G. W. H. Lampe (ed.), *The Cambridge History of the Bible*, Vol. II (1969), 338-62 – on the manuscripts, briefly, at 340-1; cf. J. Wright, *Grammar of the Gothic Language* (2nd ed. by O. L. Sayce, 1954), 196f. On the *Codex Argenteus*, E. A. Thompson, *The Visigoths in the Time of Ulfila*, xxiii.

now at Wolfenbüttel, survive parts of a Latin and Gothic text of the *Epistle to the Romans*; another bi-lingual version is represented by a double folio of parchment found in 1907 near Antinoë in Egypt, and containing part of *Luke*, chapters 23-24. This fragment, now destroyed, was formerly at Giessen, and is hence referred to as *Codex Gissensis*. In a group of palimpsest manuscripts from the Ambrosian Library at Milan survive respectively: (i) fragments of *Romans*, *Corinthians I* and *II*, *Galatians*, *Ephesians*, *Philippians*, *Colossians*, *Timothy I* and *II*, *Titus*, *Philemon*, and the scrap of a Gothic calendar presented in Chapter 4 above; (ii) more fragments of Pauline epistles, namely *Corinthians I* and *II*, *Galatians*, *Ephesians*, *Philippians*, *Colossians*, *Thessalonians I* and *II*, *Timothy I* and *II*, *Titus*; (iii) a fragment of *Matthew*; (iv) fragments of *Ezra* and *Nehemiah*; and (v) a few sentences of a Gothic homily referring to passages of *Matthew* and *John*. The exact relationship between these fragmentary manuscripts is unclear, but since those here shown as (i) and (ii) (designated A and B in technical discussions) contain text in common - and for other reasons - they evidently represent fragments of two different manuscripts rather than two parts of the same manuscript. If, as is generally accepted, these two fragments, though related to each other, are copied neither one from the other nor from the same archetype, then we must postulate other, now lost, versions of the books of the Bible attested in them. It is noteworthy that all these texts, like the *Codex Carolinus* referred to above, are preserved as palimpsests, that is to say on pages of parchment cleaned of their Gothic texts and re-used, but still decipherable beneath the later writing: we can easily imagine how, as the Gothic kingdom of Italy was replaced by Byzantine domination, copies of the Gothic Bible would become superfluous and join the stocks of discarded books whose materials were available for re-use.

In addition, a manuscript at Turin, originating also in the Ambrosian Library, contains fragments of *Galatians* and *Colossians*, and shared between the Vatican and Ambrosian Libraries is part of a Gothic commentary known since its publication in 1834 as 'Skeireins', or 'elucidation' (*skeinan* is 'to shine, gleam'), of the *Gospel of St. John*;[3] while the preface to the 'old Latin' *Codex Brixianus*, translated below, seems to have formed part of a bi-lingual

[3]Ed. and transl. William Holmes Bennett, *The Gothic Commentary on the Gospel of St. John: skeireins aiwaggeljons þairh iohannen* (1960).

Latin and Gothic version with critical annotations also on the Greek text. All that now survives of the Brixian text itself is the Latin version (known as f in technical discussions), the Gothic and whatever was once included of the Greek text having disappeared. Like the *Codex Argenteus*, to which it is apparently related, the *Codex Brixianus* is written on purple-dyed parchment.

To summarise, no part of the Gothic Bible survives complete, though the relatively extensive remains of the New Testament that we do possess are perhaps the most useful from a historical point of view, because of the Graeco-Roman terminology which they contain; in a manner of speaking, this replicates the Goths' own experience in confronting the Roman empire and its institutions. Enough fragments of the Old Testament survive to attest its existence in Gothic; the absence of the *Books of Kings* from the surviving fragments is consistent with Philostorgius' assertion that these books were not translated by Ulfila, but obviously insignificant as evidence, given the tiny quantity of Old Testament text that does survive. The indications generally suggest a vigorous tradition of use and scholarly interest, generating textual variants and annotations, and a continuing interest in, and consequent influence from, the Latin version of the Bible known to the Roman communities among whom the Goths lived.[4] The extent to which any particular part of what survives represents an 'Ulfilan' original is from every point of view an extremely difficult question, made still more so by the likelihood mentioned earlier that the 'Ulfilan' version was itself the work of several hands. Consistent with 'Ulfilan' origin, however, is the fact that the Greek text used in the translations both of the Gospels and of the Pauline Epistles is the fourth-century text known to the Cappadocian fathers and to John Chrysostom.[5]

PRINCIPLES OF TRANSLATION

The basic principle is of a literal rendering in which each word present in the Greek text, including particles, is represented by a word in the Gothic, and in which much of the original word order is also preserved. The translators were also careful to represent a

---

[4]For possible traces of the Brixian version, cf. the Additional Note to this Chapter, p. 173 (ii) and (iii); Chapter 7 on *Matt.* 6.6 (Text III); cf. Chapter 5, p. 153 and n. 49 (where the Gothic does not survive).

[5]See Chapter 7 below, on *Matt.* 6.13 (Text III).

Greek word occurring more than once by the same word in Gothic (the same principle as in the Revised Version). In *The Gothic Version of the Gospels*, p. 26, Friedrichsen observes that a total of 1,788 different Greek words in the text of the Gospels is represented by 1,878 Gothic words, a limited expansion of vocabulary indicating a very restrictive use of alternative renderings. That the variation of vocabulary which does occur is much greater in *Luke* than in *Matthew* (and, between these extremes, greater in *Mark* than in *John*) may, as we have seen, represent different authorship of the original versions, different influences exercised upon the evolving text, or a combination of these factors. That the same observation is true of the Pauline Epistles in relation to the Gospels in general may in addition reflect the more abstract and complex nature of Pauline language, a more intense theological interest among its readers and, flowing from this, the influence of learned exegesis, for example that of the later fourth-century writer known to us as 'Ambrosiaster'.

The practice of the original translator(s) in staying closely to the Greek text, added to this variety of later influences, means that the language of the Ulfilan New Testament is in syntax not as close as we would like to the spoken Gothic of the fourth century. In their choice of vocabulary, on the other hand, the translators often used Gothic words when transliterations from Greek or Latin might have been employed. Again in *The Gothic Version of the Gospels* (pp. 35-7), Friedrichsen shows in two columns words transliterated from Greek into the Latin of the Vulgate, and in a third column gives the equivalent of these words in the *Codex Argenteus*. It is a limited and no doubt unrepresentative sample, but contains many points of interest and value. In focussing upon the sorts of technical expression where the Greek original was better represented in Latin by transliteration than by translation, the sample tends to highlight those areas where the Gothic translators too had to decide how to manage the elements of Greek, Jewish and Roman culture portrayed in the New Testament. It may therefore be a useful guide to the procedures of the translators and, followed with caution, to the intrinsic resources in vocabulary of the Gothic language.[6] It is in this area that one might also expect to find a high proportion of loan-words from Greek into Gothic; it is therefore of some interest that, in more than half of the 64 cases listed by Friedrichsen, an authentic Gothic word rather than a transliteration of Greek has

[6] See also the extensive discussion of Gothic vocabulary by Wolfram, *History of the Goths*, 90ff. and esp. 112-14.

been chosen.

In the tables set out below, adapted from Friedrichsen with additional commentary of our own, we divide the material into (I) words of religious or liturgical importance, and (II) those referring to secular or everyday objects and institutions. We further list separately (A) words where transliteration from Greek has been accepted, and (B) words where a Gothic alternative has been chosen. We have omitted some cases in Friedrichsen where the Latin transliteration of a Greek word, as used in the Vulgate, was in common general use, and where one would expect the Gothic language to have a word of its own: thus **καθέδρα** – cathedra – **sitls** ('seat, stool'); **κράββατος** – grabbatum – **badi** ('bed'); **θησαυρός** – thesaurus – **huzd** ('treasure'); **παραλυτικός** – paralyticus – **usliþa** (from the negative prefix *us-* [cf. Ger. *aus-*], and *liþa*, 'limb'). It is however of some significance that Gothic offers no word for alabaster, mustard, olive-oil and scorpion, but does produce equivalents for denarius, blasphemy, sponge and tax-collector, and provides both Greek transliterations and vernacular words for demons and the devil: all these examples are included in our selection. Other points of linguistic interest are raised in the notes to the Selected Texts below, to which some reference is made in what follows.

I. WORDS OF RELIGIOUS OR LITURGICAL SIGNIFICANCE

A. TRANSLITERATED WORDS

ἄγγελος (angelus): **aggilus**, 'angel'; **airus** on three occasions in the sense of 'envoy, messenger'.

ἀνάθεμα (anathema); **anaþaima**; see I.B below for ἀναθεματίζειν (anathematizare).

δαιμονίζεσθαι, -σθείς (daemonium habere): **daimonareis**, 'possessed by a devil', etc.; see also I.B below.

διάβολος (diabolus): **diabaulus** (cf. I.B below); Ger. *Teufel*.

εὐαγγέλιον (evangelium): **aiwaggelyo** (see also I.B below); cf. also **aiwaggelyan, aiwaggelista** for εὐαγγελίζειν, -ιστής.

μαμμωνᾶς (mammona): **mammona** (see also I.B below); cf. Chapter 7, Text III.24.

παράκλητος (paracletus): **parakletus**.

παρασκεύη (parasceue), the 'day of preparation': **paraskaiwe**.

πάσχα (pascha): **pascha**; cf. Chapter 7, Text V.39.

προφήτης/-τεύειν (propheta/-izare): **praufetus** (-es), **praufetyan**; cf. Chapter 7, Text IV.9 (and I.B below). For ψευδοπροφήτης, I.B below.

σάββατον (sabbatum): **sabbato**.

συναγωγή (synagoge): **swnagoge** (frequently; but see also I.B below and Chapter 7, Text III.5.

ψάλμος (psalmus): **psalmon**.

B. TRANSLATED WORDS

ἄβυσσος (abyssus): **afgrundiþa**; from *af-* (Ger. *auf-*), **grundus*, 'ground'.

ἀναθεματίζειν (anathematizare): **afaikan**, 'deny'. Cf. I.A.

βαπτίζειν/-ίσμα/-ιστής (baptizare/-isma/-ista): **daupyan**, **daupeins**, **daupyands** (*sc.* John the Baptist); cf. *ufdaupyan*, 'dip', *diups*, 'deep'; Ger. *taufen*.

βλασφημεῖν/-ία (blasphemare/-ia): **wayameryan**, **wayamereins**, from *wai!*, 'woe!', cf. Chapter 7, Text V.40) and *meryan*, 'proclaim, announce'; rarely **naiteins**, cf. *ganaityan*, 'treat shamefully, hold in dishonour'.

δαιμόνιον, δαίμων (daemonium, daemon): **unhulþo**, **unhulþa**, 'evil spirit', frequently; also **skohsl**, 'demon'; also, for δαιμονισθείς (daemonio vexatus): **wods**, 'possessed'; cf. I.A above.

διάβολος (diabolus): **unhulþa** (once only); cf. δαιμόνιον.

ἐγκαίνια (encenia), the feast of the dedication: **ïnniuyiþa**, from *niuyis*, 'new'; Ger. *neu*.

ἐλεημοσύνη (eleemosyna): **armaio**, 'mercy, pity', cf. *arman*, 'to pity'.

εὐαγγελίζειν/-ίζεσθαι (evangelizare): **wailameryan**, from *waila*, 'well', and *meryan*, 'proclaim'; cf. on Chapter 7, Text I.23 and I.A above.

μαμμωνᾶς (mammona): **faihuþraihna**, from *faihu*, 'property, possessions' and **þraihns*, 'heap', cf. *þreihan*, 'throng, crowd'. Cf. I.A above.

μυστήριον (mysterium): **runa**, also in the sense of 'counsel' (συμβούλιον), cf. Chapter 7, Text IV.1.

ὁλοκαύτωμα (holocaustoma): **alabrunsts**, from *alls*, 'all', and *brinnan*, 'burn', cf. Eng. *brand*, Ger. *brennen*, *Brand*, etc. For *gabrannidai*, cf. above, Chapter 4, Text 4(ii).

παραβολή (parabola), 'parable': **gayuko**, i.e. a comparison, cf. *gayuk*, 'yoke, pair'; Tyndale's 'similitude'.

προφητεύειν (prophetare): **fauraqiþan**, from *faura*, 'before', and *qiþan*, 'say, speak', cf. Chapter 7, Text I.12. See also I.A.

σκηνοπηγία (scenopegia), the feast of Tabernacles: **hleþrastakeins**, from *hleiþra* (or, *hliya)*, 'tent', and **stikan*, 'to stick', i.e. 'plant' a tent (Ger. *stechen*), translating Greek πηγνύειν.

συναγωγή (synagoga): **gaqumbs** (5 times); see I.A above and Chapter 7, Text III.5.

σχίσμα (schisma): **missaqiss**, from *missa-* (Eng. *mis-*), and **qiss*, from *qiþan*, 'speak'; i.e. to speak amiss, cause discord.

ὑποκριτής (hypocrita): **liuta**, cf. *liutei*, 'deceit, pretence', *liuts*, 'deceitful'.

ψευδοπροφήτης (pseudopropheta): **liugnapraufetus**, **galiuga-praufetus**; from *liugan*, 'lie', Ger. *lügen*, *Lüge*. Also ψευδό-χριστος (pseudochristus): **galiugachristus**.

II. WORDS OF SECULAR OR EVERYDAY SIGNIFICANCE

A. TRANSLITERATED WORDS

ἀλάβαστρον (alabastrum): **alabastraun**.

δραχμή (dragma): **drakma**; contrast δηνάριος(-ν), μνᾶ, II.B below.

ἔλαιον (oleum): **alew**, 'olive oil'; transliterated from the Latin rather than the Greek.

ἰῶτα (iota): **yota**, the Greek letter, in the phrase ἰῶτα ἓν ἢ μία κεραία (iota unum aut unus apex), where the Gothic for κεραία (the point of a Hebrew letter) is *striks*, a stroke; cf. Ger. *Strich*.

Λεγέων (Legio): **lagaion**, at *Mk*. 5.9 ('my name is Legion'), 15; cf. *Lk*. 8.30 **haryis** (II.B below).

νάρδος πιστική (nardus pisticus): **nardus pistikeins**, 'pure nard (spikenard)', at *John* 12.3 in the phrase λίτραν μύρου νάρδου πιστικῆς (libram unguenti nardi pistici): **pund bals-**

anis nardaus pistikeinis, etc.

πορφύρα (purpura): **paurpura**.

σίναπι (sinapis): **sinap(s)**, 'mustard', in the phrase κόκκος σινapέως, **kaurns sinapis**, *sc*. a grain of mustard-seed. cf. Eng. *kern*, *kernel*, *corn*.

σκορπίος (scorpio): **skaurpyo**, 'scorpion'.

σφυρίς (sporta): **spwreida**, a large basket, distinguished at *Mk*. 8.8,20 (but not in A.V. and R.V.) from **tainyo**, a wicker basket; see also II.B, s.v. κόφινος.

B. TRANSLATED WORDS

ἀγγαρεύειν (angariare), orig. 'press into public service (for transport)', more generally, 'compel': so **ananauþyan** 'constrain, compel'; appropriately at *Mk*. 15.21 **usgreiþan**, 'seize, lay hold of', from *greiþan*, cf. Ger. *greifen*, Eng. *grip*.

βάτος (cadus, batus), a measure of oil: **kas**, 'vessel, pitcher', cf. Chapter 7, Text IV.7.

δηνάριον (denarius): **skatts** (see also, μνᾶ), lit. 'money', Ger. *Schatz*; cf. Chapter 7, on Text III.15.

κόρος (corus), a measure of wheat: **mitaþs**, a bushel; from *mitan*, 'measure' (Ger. *messen*).

κόφινος (cophinus): **tainyo**, a wicker basket (see also II.A. s.v. σφυρίς); from *tains*, 'twig', cf. dial. Ger. *Zain*.

Λεγέων (Legio): **haryis**, 'army, host', Ger. *Heer*; cf. above, II.A.

μνᾶ (mna, mina): **skatts** (see above, s. δηνάριον); occasionally **dails**, 'share, portion'; Ger. *Teil*.

σπόγγος (spongia): **swamms**, 'sponge', Ger. *Schwamm*.

συκομωραία (sychomorus), the fig or mulberry tree: **smakka-bagms**, from *smakka*, 'fig', and *bagms*, 'tree' (cf. Ger. *Baum*). The Gothic makes no distinction between the συκομωραία of *Luke* 19.4 (the mulberry) and the συκῆ of *Mark* 11.13 (certainly the fig).

τελώνιον (teloneum), a customs- or tax-point: **mota**, cf. *motareis*, 'tax-collector', 'toll'; *gemotyan*, 'meet' ; Eng. *meet, moot* (an assembly).

ЄΙΛΝΛΛΛΠΚΛΚΝΛSΤΛΨΛΝSΛΤϚΛΙϿΛΠ:
·ΜΗ·ΝΙhΛΛΛΙSΪSΤΘΛҒΠΛΓΙΝΙSΨΛ
ΤЄΙΝΙΓΛΒΛΙΚhΤϚΛΙϿΛΠ· ΝΙhΥΛΚΨ
ΛΝΛΛΛΠΓΝΛΚЄΙSΥΙΚΠΝΨΥΛΙΚΨΛΙ
ϚΛΒΛΙΘΛShΛΒΛΙΛΠSΧΝΛhΛΠS
ϚΛΝϿΧΝΛΓΛhΛΠSϚΛΙ:
·ΜΛ·ϚΛhUΛΨϿΠΪΜSΛΙΘΙΨΘΛhΛΠSЄΙΨ
ΪΝΨΙΖΛΙЄΙΜΙΤΛΨΜΙΤΙΨΜΙΤΛϿΛ
ΪΖΥΙS· ϚΛhΒΙΛΠΚΛϿΛΪΖΥΙSΨΛΙΜ
·ΜΒ·ΓΛΛΛΠΒϚΛΝϿΛΜ: ΠΝΤЄΨΙSΘΛΜ
ΜЄhSΛЄΙhΛΒΛΙΨΓΙΒΛϿΛΪΜΜΛ·
ϚΛhSΛЄΙΝΙhΛΒΛΙΨϚΛhΨΛΤЄΙhΛ
ΒΛΙΨΛҒΝΙΜΛϿΛΪΜΜΛ:
·ΜΓ·ϚΛhUΛΨSΥΛΪSΤΨΙΠϿΛΝΓΛΚϿΙ
ΓΨSSΥΛSΥЄϚΛΒΛΙΜΛΝΝΛΥΛΙΚΠΙΨ
ҒΚΛΙΥΛΛΝΛΛΙΚΨΛϚΛhSΛЄΠΙΨϚΛh
ΠΚΚЄΙSΙΨΝΛhΤϚΛhϿΛΓΛ· ϚΛh
ΨΛΤΛҒΚΛΙΥΚЄΙΝΙΨϚΛhΛΙΠϿΙΨ
SΥЄΝΙΥΛΙΤΪS· SΙΛΒΧΛΠΚΛΙΚΨΛ
ΛΚΚΛΝΒΛΙΚΙΨҒΚΠΜΙSΤΚΛS·

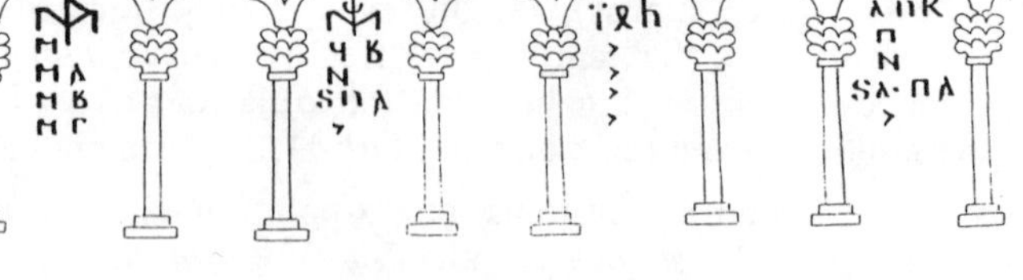

Figure 17: Extract from the *Codex Argenteus*

EXTRACT FROM THE *CODEX ARGENTEUS*

The text shown opposite is *Mark* 4.21-28 as it appears (in somewhat greater splendour) in the *Codex Argenteus*; it is reproduced from H. C. von Gabelentz and J. Loebe, *Ulfilas: Veteris et Novi Testamenti Versionis Gothicae fragmenta quae supersunt* (Leipzig, 1843), Tab. 1. In the last line of the Gothic text, the 't' of 'frumist' is inserted above the line, and in line 15 (v. 26) the abbreviation of 'Guþs' is indicated by a line drawn over the word. Note especially the words for 'candlestick' in v. 21, with its Latin and Gothic elements, and for 'kingdom' in v. 26 (see Chapter 7, Text III.10).

ei ana lukarnastaþan satyaidau?
•M• [22]Nih allis ïst wha fulginis, þa-
tei ni gabairhtyaidau; nih warþ
analaugn, ak ei swikunþ wairþai.
[23]Yabai whas habai ausona haus-
yandona, gahausyai:
•MA• [24]Yah qaþ du ïm, Saiwiþ wha hauseiþ.
Ïn þizaiei mitaþ mitiþ, mitada
ïzwis, yah biaukada ïzwis þaim
•MB• galaubyandam. [25]Unte þiswham-
meh saei habaiþ, gibada ïmma,
yah saei ni habaiþ, yah þatei ha-
baiþ, afnimada ïmma.
•MΓ• [26]Yah qaþ, Swa ïst þiudangardi
Guþs, swaswe yabai manna wairpiþ
fraiwa ana airþa, [27]Yah slepiþ, yah
urreisiþ naht yah daga, yah
þata fraiw keiniþ, yah liudiþ,
swe ni wait ïs. [28]Silbo auk airþa
akran bairiþ, frumist gras . . .

The little arches at the foot of the page are 'canon-tables' of cross-references between the Gospels. In the first arch are repeated the marginal references to the text; in the next three arches are references to the corresponding passages in the other Gospels. These appear in the 'old Latin' order in which the *Codex* presented them, that is, *Matthew*, *John*, *Luke*; *Mark*, here cited first because it is the text referred to, stood last in the series. The absence of a corresponding reference to the other Gospels is shown by a *caret* sign, from which the reader can see that the passage does not occur at all in *John*, and with omissions in *Matthew* and *Luke*. The names of Mark and Matthew are given as monograms, those of John and Luke as orthodox abbreviations. In late antique and early medieval manuscripts, such canon-tables almost invariably precede the Gospel text. Their position here, at the foot of each page, is matched only in the *Codex Brixianus* also described in this Chapter, an early sixth-century manuscript probably from the same north Italian source (Ravenna?) as the *Codex Argenteus*. The arrangement seems to be a specifically Gothic device, perhaps dating from the original production of Ulfila's Bible. It is suggested by Nordenfalk that the manuscripts in which it appears were written for the Arian ascendancy in Ravenna; manuscripts for Catholic patrons had canon-tables in the normal position before the Gospel text. See C. Nordenfalk, *Die Spätantiken Kanontafeln* (1938), I, p. 283 and II, Tafeln 160 (a) and (b), with comparisons of the *Codex Argenteus* and *Codex Brixianus*.

SALVIAN, *DE GUBERNATIONE DEI* 5.2.5-9

Salvian, whose origin was in the Rhineland, became in early adult years a monk at Lérins and, at an unknown date, priest at Marseilles. When Gennadius of Marseilles wrote his *De Viris Illustribus* shortly after 496 (*De Vir. Ill.* 96), Salvian was still living in old age, renowned as a prolific and learned author and, through his writings, as a 'teacher of bishops' (*De Vir. Ill.* 67). His *De Gubernatione Dei* ('On the Governance of God') was written after 439, since it alludes to the capture of the Roman general Litorius in that year (7.10.40); from the absence of any mention of the defeat of Attila the Hun at the battle of the Catalaunian Plains, it has been inferred that the work was completed before 451.

The argument of *De Gubernatione Dei* is that the disasters afflicting Gaul in the fifth century were not evidence for the indifference of God towards the fate of men, but on the contrary were his punishment of the Christian Romans for the personal and public misdeeds arising from the neglect of their faith. The agents of this chastening were the barbarian invaders, whose upright simplicity and ignorance of Christianity exempted them from similar reproach. Salvian is confronted by the fact that the main barbarian agents of Roman misfortune, in the form of the Visigoths, were not pagan like the Huns, Franks and Suebi, but Arian heretics, whose perverse beliefs should have made them still more worthy than Catholic Romans of the punishment of God. He meets this argument, in the passage translated below, by the observation that the Goths' Christian teaching, and their knowledge of Christian texts, were so flawed and incomplete that they were in effect ignorant of the truth of Christianity and so could not be held in contempt of their faith.

This argument is no better than it looks, but has the merit for the historian of eliciting Salvian's comment about corruption and interpolation in texts of the Gothic Bible available to the Visigoths in Gaul. Salvian's references have been used to support Visigothic influence on the Ostrogothic version of the Bible in use in Italy, but this is clearly very hazardous. It is however worth noting the confirmation that the Visigoths did after all use a vernacular version of the Bible. Salvian's allusions to the original 'masters' and 'teachers' of the Arian Goths, and to the 'tradition' of Christian knowledge (or rather ignorance) for which they were responsible (§§7-8), are of course to the work of Ulfila and his associates as translators of, and commentators on, the Bible.

TRANSLATION

5. Now I mentioned above that there are two groups, or sects, of barbarians; pagans and heretics. Since I have already, I think, dealt sufficiently with the pagans, I will now, as the argument requires, add some remarks also on the heretics. For someone might say: It may be that the divine law does not require of pagans that they carry out its mandates, which they do not know, but it certainly does require this of heretics, who do know it: for they read the same things that we read, have the same prophets of God, the same apostles, the same evangelists. It follows that the law is neglected no less by them than by us; in fact their neglect is much greater, because they read the same things as our people do, but their conduct is much worse than ours.

Let us, now, look at each case. **6.** They read the same things, you say, that are read by us. But how can they be the same, when they were written in the first place by bad authors,[7] and are badly interpolated and badly transmitted? They are not really the same, because things can in no sense be called the same when they are

[7]'Authors' ('auctores') is not altogether appropriate, since it is obvious that Salvian has in mind the Gothic translators, rather than the original text, of the Bible. It is quite possible, however, that he believed the translators to have incorporated doctrinal inaccuracy into their work (cf. below, n. 11): in that sense one might call them the 'authors' of false learning enshrined in the translated text.

defective in any part of themselves. Things that have lost their completeness do not keep their integrity, nor do they retain their authority in any way when they are deprived of the power of the sacraments.[8] It is only we who possess the holy scriptures full, inviolate and complete: for we either drink them at their very source, or at least as drawn from the purest source through the service of a pure translation.[9] Only we read them correctly: **7.** if only we fulfilled them in practice as well as we read them![10] I am afraid that we who do not observe well are not good readers either, for it is a lesser fault not to read the holy scriptures than to read and then violate them. As for the other nations, these either do not possess the law, or they possess it in a faulty and damaged form and for this reason, as I said, do not possess at all what they possess in this condition. Even if there are those among the barbarian nations who among their books may seem to possess a sacred scripture that is not interpolated or torn apart, yet they still possess it (in a version) corrupted by the teaching of their masters in the past, and therefore possess a form of teaching rather than the scripture itself: for they do not possess what the truth of the law enjoins, but what the wickedness of bad teaching has inserted into it.[11] **8.** For barbarian people, people without experience of Roman – or, I would rather say, of humane – learning,[12] know nothing at all except for what they hear from their teachers. These people follow what they hear,

---

[8] This observation broadens the argument but begs the question. For the Goths, their Bible was as much a part of their sacraments as was the (Catholic) Romans' Bible a part of theirs. It adds nothing to say that the *Arians'* Bible lacked the authority of the *Catholic* sacraments, though the close connection between Bible and sacraments in Salvian's mind is worth noting. 'Power' here translates 'virtus', cf. above, Chapter 5, n. 28.

[9] That is to say, either in Greek or Latin translation (the Old Testament), or in the original Greek or in Latin translation (the New Testament).

[10] 'Correctly' and 'well' both translate the same Latin word, 'bene'. This is perhaps rather assertive, but the shades of meaning seem helpful in conveying Salvian's argument.

[11] Friedrichsen, *The Gothic version of the Epistles*, at 200, 236f., gives two examples, *Phil.* 2.6 and *I Cor.* 15.26ff., where elements of Arian doctrine may have been incorporated, or at least given emphasis, in the Gothic translation. For Ulfila's own insistence on the authority of Scripture, see our Introduction to Chapter 5.

[12] 'Barbari quippe homines, Romanae, immo potius humanae eruditionis expertes.' Salvian's categorical identification of literary ('humane') culture as by definition Roman is most emphatic and striking. It also permits an extension of the argument: Salvian has hitherto been discussing the integrity of Gothic books, but now goes on to assert the illiteracy and ignorance of Goths in general, totally dependent on the teaching given to them and unable to confirm or challenge anything by their own reading.

and so of necessity, being ignorant of all literature and knowledge, and acquainted with the sacrament of the divine law by learning rather than reading, possess learning rather than the law. So, to these people, the tradition and ingrained doctrine of their masters are as law, because they know nothing apart from what they are taught. They are therefore heretics, but unknowingly. **9.** In fact, they are heretics in our sight, but not in their own: for they judge themselves as catholics, to the extent that they actually dishonour us by marking us with the name of heretic. What they are to us, so are we to them. We are certain that they insult the divine incarnation because they call the Son lesser than the Father. They think we insult the Father, because we believe them equal. The truth lies with us, but they presume it to be with them. We do honour God, but they think that the honour of his divinity rests in what they believe.

PREFACE TO THE *CODEX BRIXIANUS*

This difficult and incomplete text survives on two leaves bound into the sixth-century *Codex Brixianus* described above, containing the Latin text of what was apparently once a bi-lingual Gothic and Latin version. The aim of the Preface, supported by the opening appeal to purported words of St. Peter cited in the Ps.-Clementine *Recognitiones*, is to deprecate innovation in the text of the Bible, while making it clear that even in a literal translation differences of syntax and idiom between languages will occur that do not affect the sense; and – a second point, not very clearly distinguished in the Preface – that choices of vocabulary in translation, which are often bound to be conventional approximations, need not affect the meaning of a text, so long as the reasons for the selection of particular words are understood. To make clear the suitability of conventional equivalents in the Gothic text were inserted the '*vulthres*', or annotations, referred to in the Preface (the only evidence for them). These annotations gave the exact meanings, here called 'etymologies', of the Greek and Latin words that lay behind the Gothic version, comments referring to these two languages being distinguished by signs placed above the Gothic annotations. The sorts of innovation deprecated by the writer of the Preface no doubt included not only the intrusion of the personal preferences of individual translators of which he complains, but of the exegetical influences mentioned above.

The text here translated is that of F. Kaufmann, *Zeitschr. für die*

Deutsche Philologie 32 (1900), pp. 306-11, as reprinted by Streitberg, *Die Gotische Bibel* I (1908), pp. xlii-iii, and by Friedrichsen, *The Gothic Version of the Epistles*, 271, discussed in his *The Gothic Version of the Gospels*, pp. 196-211. Our translation conforms in all respects but one (see n. 18 below) to the punctuation printed by Kaufmann and Friedrichsen; in this and one other place where Friedrichsen himself prefers a different punctuation, a translation of his preference is given in the notes. Kaufmann's text also differs in detail from the critical text of Ps.-Clement, *Recognitiones*, cited in the first paragraph. In the spirit of the Preface, we have also indicated these points of difference in our annotations.

TRANSLATION

St. Peter, the apostle and disciple of the Saviour, our Lord Jesus Christ, instructing the faithful on the question of teaching in diverse languages, advised them all – as is recorded in the eighth book of Clement [*Recognitiones* 8.37][13] – in these words: 'Hear me, beloved fellow-servants. It is good that each one of you should according to his ability be of service to those approaching the faith of our religion. Therefore, do not be ashamed to instruct those who speak against you and to teach the ignorant[14] in accordance with the wisdom which by the providence of God has been conferred upon you: but do so in such a way that to these things which you have heard from me and have been passed on to you, you add only the utterance[15] of your speech, and proclaim no doctrine of your own devising, nor any not passed on to you, even if it should seem to you to bear the signs of truth. But, as I said, follow those things which I myself received from the true prophet and have passed on

---

[13] For the text of Ps.-Clement, *Recognitiones*, as translated by Rufinus of Aquileia, see the ed. of B. Rehm, in *GCS* 51 (1965), p. 240.

[14] This translates Kaufmann's and Friedrichsen's 'disserentes instruere, ignaros edocere', taking 'disserentes' as men who argue or dispute (Kaufmann, 'streitende'). Better as a text is *GCS*, 'quae vobis per dei providentiam conlata est, disserentes, instruere ignaros *et docere*'; 'speaking out in accordance with the wisdom which by the providence of God has been conferred upon you, to instruct and teach the ignorant'. It seems impossible to determine which text the author of the Preface actually had before him.

[15] 'eloquentiam', taken by Kaufmann in the sense of 'elocutionem', *sc.* the simple use of utterance to convey meaning: this well suits the restrained character of Peter's advice.

to you,[16] even if they seem to be less complete as a teaching'.

And therefore, in relation to what is contained inside the book,[17] in case it should seem to the reader that in the translated versions one thing is signified in the Greek language and something else in Latin or Gothic, he should take note that if the text displays a discrepancy arising from the rules of the language, it does nevertheless concur in a single meaning. So, no-one should on these grounds be in any doubt that the true sense of the original text has been determined by careful consideration in accordance with the meaning of the translated language, taking into account differences in the sense of (individual) words: and this the reader will find set out in what follows.[18] This matter requires stating outright, because of certain persons who by erroneous teaching after their own will have through a translation of their own devising introduced falsehoods in the Law and the Gospels. Such falsehoods we here reject: what stands here can be found to be contained in the original authority of the Greek language,[19] and it is demonstrated that the

---

[16] The *GCS* text has 'sed *ea, ut dixi, quae* ipse a vero propheta suscepta vobis tradidi', etc.; this is clearer than Friedrichsen's 'sed *ut dixi quae*', etc., but this is not to say that the author of the Preface had the better text before him. Kaufmann's transcript of the MS text does not suggest that it was fully or consistently punctuated.

[17] 'secundum quae in interiora libri ostenduntur'; 'in relation to what is declared (displayed) inside the book'. This is as it stands sufficiently obscure, without the additional uncertainty whether the 'book' is the Clementine *Recognitiones* just referred to, or (our preference, expressed in the translation) the book - i.e. the translated Bible itself - of which this is the Preface.

[18] Friedrichsen here prints Kaufmann's punctuation, 'quare nullus exinde titubare debet de quod ipsa auctoritas manifestat secundum intentione(m) linguae. propter declinationes sonus diligenti perceptione statuta sunt, ut in subsequentibus conscribta leguntur', but himself prefers to end the first sentence with 'manifestat', with a comma after 'linguae' (according to Kaufmann's transcript the manuscript carries no punctuation after 'manifestat'; the point after 'linguae' can be read as either a comma or a stop, no distinction between them being made in the MS). The meaning would then be, 'no-one need on these grounds be in any doubt as to what the original text declares [*manifestat*]. In accordance with the meaning of the language, taking into account the sense of words [*proper declinationes sonus*], what stands in the following pages has been determined by careful consideration'. We read the whole passage as one sentence, taking the last phrase in the Latin [*ut . . . leguntur*] to refer, not to the text in general, but to the comments, or *vulthres*, which the author goes on to describe and justify. 'Propter declinationes sonus' should have something to do with declension or pronunciation, but we find this sense hard to accommodate to the situation envisaged by the Preface.

[19] 'haec posita sunt quae antiquitas legis in dictis Graecorum contineri inveniuntur'. We have done our best with the rocky syntax of the Latin, and are still uncertain whether 'legis' refers specifically to the Old Testament (as it does above, of people who introduce falsehoods 'in the Law and in the Gospels'; *in lege vel in evangeliis*) or to the general authority of the Greek text.

actual meanings of the words in the languages concerned that have been written down as suitable equivalents do concur in a single sense. Now, since it is appropriate to make clear these meanings, this has been done in the 'vulthres' – which in the Latin language means 'adnotatio' – so that it can be seen why the text stands as it does.[20] Where the sign '.gr.' is found above a vulthre, the reader may know that what is written in this particular vulthre is in accordance with[21] the Greek text. But where the sign '.la.' is found above a vulthre, what is shown in the vulthre is in accordance with the Latin version. The purpose of this form of indication[22] is that readers should not fail to understand the reason why the vulthres are placed in the text. But that [the text breaks off at this point] . . .

ADDITIONAL NOTE ON THE VULTHRES

Without wishing to involve the reader (or ourselves) in technicalities, we select from Friedrichsen's discussion (*Gospels*, pp. 207ff.) three examples of apparent discrepancies in translation where *vulthres* might have been given. The situation is confused by the possibility, pointed out by F. G. Burkitt, 'The Vulgate Gospels and the Codex Brixianus', *JTS* 1 (1900), 129-34, that the Brixian version was itself influenced by the Gothic text, and conceivably, as observed by Friedrichsen, by interpolation from the *vulthres* themselves. It is in any case a corollary of the argument that the *Codex Argenteus*, from which our Gothic examples are drawn, is very closely related to the lost Gothic text of the Brixian bi-lingual; but there are other grounds for thinking this, and there is no particular reason why these texts should not reflect a characteristic Latin version in use in Italy.

(i) at *Matt.* 27.48 the Greek text has ἐπότιζεν αὐτόν ('gave

---

[20] Again, this is Kaufmann's version of the text, to which Friedrichsen prefers an alternative punctuation, 'pro quod in vulthres factu(m) est (latina vero lingua adnotatio significatur). <Ut> quare it [= id] positum est agnosci possit, ubi littera .gr. super vulthre invenitur . . . ', etc.; 'this has been done in the *vulthres* (which means 'adnotatio' in the Latin language). In order that it may be seen why it [*sc.* a *vulthre*] is put there, where the sign .gr. is found . . . ', etc. Our translation, with a small additional change to the text, takes the phrase, '<ut> quare it<a> positum est agnosci possit' as referring, not to the *vulthres* but to the translated text.

[21] I.e. 'is an explanation of'. See Additional Note.

[22] Kaufmann, Streitberg and Friedrichsen read (the MS line divisions indicated by Kaufmann are marked with /), 'et ideo / ista instructio demonstrata / <i>ta est, ne legentes', etc. It is more likely that the MS 'demonstrata/ta' (*sic*) is a simple case of dittography. The omission of 'ita' makes no substantial difference to the meaning.

him to drink'), which is followed closely by the Gothic, 'draggkida ïna' (from **draggkyan** = Greek ποτίζειν, 'to give to drink'). The idiom is not easily translated into Latin, and the Vulgate and Old Latin versions, including the Brixian, read 'dabat ei bibere' ('gave to him to drink'). The Gothic version might be commented on by a *vulthre* such as '.gr. draggkida ïna' or '.la. gaf ïmma driggkyan' (or both), thus indicating that the two versions are in practical terms identical, the differences being merely of syntax.

(ii) at *Matt.* 27.3 (Chapter 7, Text IV below), the Greek has ὅτι κατεκρίθη ('that he was condemned'), the Vulgate and Old Latin (except for the Brixian) versions, 'quod damnatus esset' (some MSS 'est'); the Brixian Latin reads, 'ad iudicium ductus'. The Gothic of the *Codex Argenteus* follows the last version, 'þatei du stauai gatauhans warþ' ('that he was brought to judgment'). This phrase might then be given in a marginal note marked '.la.' to indicate its derivation from the Latin, or there might be one marked '.gr.', giving the literal translation from the Greek, 'gadomiþs warþ' ('was judged': Gothic **gadomyan**, 'to judge', 'condemn'); or, again, both might be given. The reader could then see that the two versions were in practical terms identical.

(iii) *Luke* 19.23 has in Greek ἐπὶ τὴν τράπεζαν (lit. 'onto the table'; A.V. and R.V., 'into the bank'), where the Vulgate and Old Latin versions have 'ad mensam', except again for the Brixian version, which has 'nummulariis'; 'to the money-changers' (*Codex Argenteus* 'du skattyam'). The Gothic version might be shown as deriving from the Latin (unless the influence is the other way round) by the *vulthre* '.la. du skattyam' (Gothic **skattya**, 'money-changer', cf. **skatts**, 'money').

CHAPTER SEVEN

SELECTIONS FROM THE GOTHIC BIBLE

The following extracts from the Gothic translation of the Gospels are chosen for their variety and, in Texts IV and V, to give an opportunity for comparison between parallel narratives. Since it seemed absurd to provide a translation from Gothic of the New Testament, as a companion to the Gothic text is shown the version of William Tyndale, first published in 1526. Apart from the intrinsic interest of the two versions, the comparison between them is apt. Like the Gothic, the Tyndale translation is done from the Greek (rather than the Latin) text of the New Testament; like the Gothic, it is a historic translation into a vernacular; and its relationship to the Authorised Version of 1611, while more complicated (there are several intervening phases), has some similarities with the relationship described in Chapter 6 between the fourth-century 'Ulfilan' version and the surviving sixth-century version of the Gothic text behind which it stands.

The texts are taken from the edition of the Rev. Joseph Bosworth and George Waring, *The Gothic and Anglo-Saxon Gospels in Parallel Columns with the Versions of Wycliffe and Tyndale* (London, 1865). The notes are intended merely to assist comprehension of the text by providing basic information about the meanings of words and, in a few cases, on syntax and accidence. Historical implications are only lightly touched upon; a fuller discussion is given by Wolfram, *History of the Goths*, 90ff. Philological connections are sometimes given with modern English and German words; this again is very selective (many more are self-explanatory) and ignores intermediate forms in, for example, Anglo-Saxon and Old High German, as more appropriate for a learned commentary than for a basic sampler of the Gothic language for those who do not know it at all. The forms of words are given as in the glossary of Joseph Wright, *Grammar of the Gothic Language* (2nd edition with a Supplement to the Grammar by O.L. Sayce; Oxford, 1954, repr. 1981), with the substitution of Wright's conventional 'j' by 'y', as used by Bosworth and Waring; in other transcriptions the symbol 'þ' is sometimes represented by 'th'. We have also consulted W. W. Skeat, *A Moeso-Gothic Glossary* (London and Berlin, 1868), Winfred P. Lehmann, *A Gothic Etymological Dictionary* (1986; for full details see

Bibliography), and standard English and German dictionaries. The meanings of words are given as they are in their context, followed by reference to the root form as given in Wright's *Grammar*. The reader who is in a position to relate the Gothic to the Greek text will see at once how very close it is, both in vocabulary and word order, to the original. In fact, the Greek text itself is by far the best and most economical guide to the meanings of the Gothic words. This too we have tried to indicate at various points of our notes.

TEXT I; THE PRODIGAL SON (*LUKE* 15.11-32)

11 Qaþuþ-þan, Manne sums aihta twans sununs;

11 And he sayde, A certayne man had two sonnes;

12 Yah qaþ sa yuhiza ïze du attin, Atta, gif mis, sei undrinnai mik, dail aiginis. Yah disdailida ïm swes sein.

12 And the yonger of them sayde to his father, Father, geve me my parte of the goodes, that to me belongeth. And he devided vnto them his substaunce.

13 Yah afar ni managans dagans, brahta samana allata sa yuhiza sunus, yah aflaiþ ïn land fairra wisando; yah yainar distahida þata swes seinata libands usstiuriba.

13 And not longe after, the yonger sonne gaddered all that he had to gedder, and toke his iorney into a farre country; and there he wasted his goodes with royetous livinge.

14 Biþe þan frawas allamma, warþ huhrus abrs and gawi yainata, yah ïs dugann alaþarba wairþan.

14 And when he had spent all that he had, there rose a greate derth thorow out all that same londe, and he began to lacke.

15 Yah gaggands, gahaftida sik sumamma baurgyane yainis gauyis. Yah ïnsandida ïna haiþyos seinazos, haldan sweina.

15 And he went, and clave to a citesyn of that same countre. Which sent hym to the felde, to kepe his swyne.

16 Yah gairnida sad ïtan haurne þoei matitedun sweina, yah manna ïmma ni gaf.

16 And he wold fayne have filled his bely with the coddes that the swyne ate, and noo man gave hym.

NOTES

TEXT I; *LUKE* 15.11-32.

11. **qaþuþ-þan**, see on v. 12. **sums**, 'a certain' (Gk. ἄνθρωπός τις), cf. 26, *sumana magiwe*, 'one of his servants' (ἕνα τῶν παίδων).

12. **qaþ**, 'he said' (Eng. *quoth*), cf. vv. 21, 22, 27, 31 and *passim*; 18 *qiþa*, 'I will say'. At v. 11 **qaþuþ-þan** (cf. 25 *wasuþ-þan*) consists of *qaþ* with the enclitic conjunction *-uh* ('and'). This becomes *-uþ* before the *þ-* of *þan*; ('then, thereupon'). **yuhiza**, 'younger', cf. 13; 25 *alþiza*, 'elder'. **du attin**, 'to his father' (dat. case); Cf. **atta**, (nom./voc.) in vv. 18, 28, 29, III.9, etc. **sei undrinnai mik**, 'which falls to me'; from *und-*, 'to' and *rinnan*, 'run, flow'. For *mik*, cf. Ger. *mich*. **aiginis**, from *aigin*, 'goods, property', cf. *aigan*, 'own, possess', Ger. *eigen*, *Eigentum*, etc.

13. **afar ni managans dagans**, lit. 'after not many days'; *manags*, 'much, many'; *dags*, 'day', cf. Ger. *Tag*, Eng. *day*. **brahta samana**, 'brought together', from *briggan*, 'bring', giving past tense (preterite) *brahta*; cf. Ger. *bringen/brachte*, Eng. *bring/brought*. **fairra**, 'far', cf. v. 20. **yainar**, 'there', cf. vv. 14 *and gawi yainata*, 'through that land', 15 *yainis gauyis*, 'of that land', etc. Cf. Ger. *jene*, 'that'. **us-stiuriba**, 'riotously', i.e. 'without control'; *us-* (cf. Ger. *aus-*) *stiuriba*, from *stiuryan*, 'govern, steer', cf. Ger. *steuern*, *Steuer*, etc.

14. **huhrus**, 'dearth', cf. v. 17 *huhrau*. In both passages the Greek word is λιμός. **gawi**, 'land, country', cf. v. 15 *gauyis*; Ger. *Gau*, 'district', as in *Breisgau*.

15. **baurgyane**, 'citizen' (Gk. ἑνὶ τῶν πολιτῶν), cf. Ger. *Burger*, Eng. *burgher*; cf. *baurgs*, 'town, city' (*Burg*, *borough*, etc.). **ïna haiþyos seinazos**, 'to his field'; cf. III.28 *blomans haiþyos*, 'lilies of the field'. Cf. Ger. *Heide*, Eng. *heath*, and on v. 25 below.

16. **gairnida**, from *gairnyan*, 'wish, long for', cf. Ger. *gern*. **sad ïtan**, 'to eat his fill'; *saþs* is 'full, satisfied', cf. Ger. *satt*. **haurne**, from *haurn*, 'horn, husk'. **matidedun**, 'they ate', from *matyan*, 'eat', cf. v. 23 *matyandans*, 'eating'; III.25, V.28, etc.

17 Qimands þan ïn sis, qaþ, Whan filu asnye attins meinis, ufarassau haband hlaibe; ïþ ïk huhrau fraqistna.	17 Then he remembred hym silfe, and sayde, Howe many hyred servauntes at my fathers, have breed ynough; and I dye for honger.
18 Usstandans, gagga du attin meinamma, yah qiþa du ïmma, Atta, frawauhrta mis ïn himin, yah ïn andwairþya þeinamma;	18 I will a ryse, and goo to my father, and will saye vnto hym, Father, I have synned against heven, and before the;
19 Yu þanaseiþs ni ïm wairþs ei haitaidau sunus þeins, gatawei mik swe ainana asnye þeinaize.	19 Nowe am I not worthy to be called thy sonne, make me as one of thy heyred servauntes.
20 Yah usstandands qam at attin seinamma. Nauhþanuh þan fairra wisandan, gasawh ïna atta ïs, yah ïnfeinoda. Yah þragyands, draus ana hals ïs, yah kukida ïmma.	20 And he arose and cam to his father. When he was yett a greate waye of, his father sawe hym, and had compassion on hym. And ran vnto him, and fell on his necke, and kyssed hym.
21 Yah qaþ ïmma sa sunus, Atta, frawauhrta ïn himin, yah ïn adwairþya þeinamma; yu þanaseiþs ni ïm wairþs ei haitaidau sunus þeins.	21 And the sonne sayd vnto hym, Father, I have synned agaynst heven, and in thy sight; nether am I worthy hence forthe to be called thy sonne.
22 Qaþ þan sa atta du skalkam seinaim, Sprauto bringiþ wastya þo frumiston, yah gawasyiþ ïna, yah gibiþ figgragulþ ïn handu ïs, yah gaskohi ana fotuns ïs;	22 Then sayde the father to his servauntes, Bringe forth that best garment, and put it on hym, and put a rynge on his honde, and shewes on his fete;
23 Yah bringandans stiur þana alidan, ufsneiþiþ, yah matyandans, wisam waila.	23 And brynge hidder that fatted caulfe, and kyll hym, and lett vs eate, and be mery.
24 Unte sa sunus meins dauþs was, yah gaqiunoda, yah fralusans was, yah bigitans warþ. Yah dugunnun wisan.	24 For this my sonne was deed, and is alive agayne; he was loste, and ys nowe founde. And they began to make goode cheare.
25 Wasuþ-þan sunus ïs sa alþiza ana akra; yah qimands, atïddya newh razn, yah gahausida saggwins yah laikins.	25 The elder brother was in the felde; and when he cam, and drewe nye to the housse, he herde minstrelcy and daunsynge.

17. **qimands . . . in sis**, from *qiman*, 'come'; lit. 'coming to himself' (Gk. εἰς ἑαυτὸν δὲ ἐλθών). **filu**, 'many', cf. v. 29, etc.; Ger. *viel*. **asnye**, 'hired servants', cf. v. 19; Gk. μισθίοι. Both in Greek and Gothic, this is one of three different words for 'servants' (cf. vv. 22, 26); here equivalent to 'paid (day-) labourers'. **hlaif**, 'bread', cf. III.11; Ger. *Laib*, Eng. *loaf*.

18. **frawaurhta mis**, 'I have sinned', a reflexive construction, cf. IV.4 (Judas); from the negative prefix *fra-* (cf. on III.24 below) with *waurkyan*, 'do, perform'. **himin**, from *himins*, 'heaven', Ger. *Himmel*, cf. III.9, 10, 26. **ïn andwairþya þeinamma**, 'in your presence'; *andwairþi* is 'presence, face', cf. II.14, III.16.

19. **þanaseiþs**, 'henceforth', cf. v. 21; from adv. *þana*, 'then' (cf. Ger. *denn*, *dann*) with *seiþs*, 'late'. **wairþs**, 'worthy', cf. also Ger. *wert*. **asnye**, cf. v. 17.

20. **fairra**, cf. v. 13. **ïnfeinoda**, from *ïnfeinan*, 'take pity on'. **þragyands**, 'running', from *þragyan*. **kukida**, from *kukyan*; Ger. *küssen*.

22. **skalkam**, 'servants, slaves' (Gk. δούλοι, cf. vv. 17, 26), cf. vv. 29 *skalkinoda þus*, 'I have served you', and 32 *skuld was*, 'it was right', Eng. *should*; cf. II.14, III.12, 24, IV.6, V.31, etc. **wastya . . . gawasyiþ ïna**, 'clothing . . . clothe him'; from *wasti*, *(ga-)wasnyan*, cf. Latin *vestis*, etc. See esp. III.25, 29. **frumista**, from *frumists*, 'the (very) best'; formed from the comparative *fruma*, 'prior'.

23. **stiur**, 'calf', cf. Ger. *Stier*, Eng. *steer*. **alidan**, 'fattened', from *alyan*, 'bring up, rear' (Gk. σιτευτόν, *sc*. 'fed'). **ufsneiþiþ**, 'kill' (imper.), from *(uf-)sneiþan*, 'cut'; cf. v. 27 *afsnaiþ*, 'he has killed', and v. 30 *ufsnaist*, 'you [sing.] have killed'; Ger. *schneiden*. **matyandans**, cf. v. 16. **wisam waila**, 'let us be well, make merry'; cf. also Ger. *wohl*. The same sense is conveyed at v. 24 without *waila*; cf. v. 29 *biwesyau*. *Wailameryan* is to preach (*meryan*) good news, *sc*. the Gospel.

24. **dauþs**, 'dead', cf. *dauþus*, 'death', Ger. *Tod*. **bigitans**, 'found', from *bigitan*; cf. V.38.

25. **ana akr**, 'in the field', from *akrs*, cf. Ger. *Acker*, Eng. *acre*. The idea is perhaps of an enclosed (arable) parcel of land; contrast the 'heath' of v. 15 above, where swine are kept. The Greek uses the same word in both passages, but with the plural (εἰς τοὺς ἀγρούς) in v. 15, the singular (ἐν ἀγρῷ) here. **qimands**, cf. v. 17. **atïddya**, cf. v. 29. **saggwins yah laikins**, 'singing and dancing (leaping, jollity)'. *Laik* is OE for 'play'.

26 Yah aþaitands sumana magiwe, frahuh, wha wesi þata.	26 And called one of his servauntes, and axed, what thoose thynges meante.
27 Þaruh ïs qaþ du ïmma, Þatei broþar þeins qam, yah afsnaiþ atta þeins stiur þana alidan, unte hailana ïna andnam.	27 He said vnto him, Thy brother is come, and thy father hath killed the fatted caulfe, be cause he hath receaved him safe and sounde.
28 Þanuh modags warþ, yah ni wilda ïnngaggan. Ïþ atta ïs usgaggands ut, bad ïna.	28 And he was angry, and wolde not goo in. Then cam his father out, and entreated him.
29 Þaruh ïs andhafyands, qaþ du attin, Sai! swa filu yere skalkinoda þus, yah ni whanwhun anabusn þeina ufarïddya; yah mis ni aiw atgaft gaitein, ei miþ friyondam meinaim biwesyau.	29 He answered, and sayde to hys father, Loo! these many yeares have I done the service, nether brake at eny time thy commaundment; and yet gavest thou me never soo moche as a kyd, to make mery with my lovers.
30 Ïþ þan sa sunus þeins, saei fret þein swes miþ kalkyom, qam, ufsnaist ïmma stiur þana alidan.	30 But as sone as this thy sonne was come, which hath devoured thy goodes wyth harloottes, thou haste for his pleasure killed the fatted caulfe.
31 Þaruh qaþ du ïmma, Barnilo, þu sinteino miþ mis wast yah ïs, yah all þata mein þein ïst.	31 And he sayd vnto him, Sonne, thou wast ever with me, and all that I have is thine.
32 Waila wisan, yah faginon skuld was; unte broþar þeins dauþs was, yah gaqiunoda; yah fralusans, yah bigitans warþ.	32 It was mete that we shulde make mery, and be glad; for this thy brother was deed, and is a live agayne; and was loste, and is founde.

26. **magiwe**, 'servants', from *magus*, 'boy, servant', presumably a personal attendant on the elder brother (Gk. ἕνα τῶν παίδων); cf. vv. 17 (and 19), 22.

27. **qaþ du ïmma . . . þatei . . .** represents the Greek ὅτι in a literal translation of the idiom (ὅτι introducing direct speech). **afsnaiþ**, cf. v. 23. **hailana**, from *hails*, 'safe, well'; cf. Eng. *hale*, Ger. *heil*. *Hailyan* is 'to heal'. **andnam**, from *and-niman*, 'take', cf. IV.1; Ger. *annahm*, 'received, accepted'.

28. Note **ïnngaggan**, **usgaggands**, 'to go(going) in(out)'; Ger. *ein/ausgehen*; cf. v. 15 *gaggands*, 'going', *gagga*, 'I will go'. For the past tense *ïddya* see next note. **bad ïna**, 'entreated him', from *bidyan*, 'ask, pray'; cf. III.5ff.

29. **andhafyands**, 'replying', from *andhafyan*; cf. V. 30, 34-6 and *passim*. **filu**, cf. v. 17 above. **skalkinoda**, cf. on v. 22. **anabusn**, 'commandments', cf. *anabindan*, 'order, command'. **ufarïddya**, lit. 'did I go beyond'; from *ufar-* (Ger. *über-*, Eng. *over-*) *ïddya*, used as the past (preterite) of *gaggan*, 'go'. **ni iw**, 'not ever'; adv. from *aiws*, 'time, eternity', cf. Ger. *je*, Eng. *aye*. See also III.13. **friyondam**, 'friends', from *friyonds*, cf. III.5 *friyond*, 'they love', III.24 *friyoþ*, 'he will love'; Ger. *freuen*, *Freund*.

30. **kalkyom**, 'harlots', from *kalkyo*. *kalkinassus* means 'adultery, fornication' at *Matt*. 5.32, *Mk*. 7.21, cf. III.10. **ufsnaist**, cf. v. 23.

31. **Barnilo**, an affectionate diminutive of *barn*, 'child'; cf. Eng. and Scot. *bairn*.

32, cf. vv. 23, 24. **faginon**, 'to rejoice, be glad'; cf. *faheþs*, 'joy, gladness', and Eng. *fain*.

TEXT II; 'RENDER UNTO CAESAR' (*MARK* 12.13-17)

13 Yah ïnsandidedun du ïmma sumai þize Fareisaie yah Herodiane, ei ïna ganuteina waurda.	13 And they sent vnto hym certayne off the Pharises with Herodes servauntes, to take hym in hys wordes.
14 Ïþ eis qimandans qeþun du ïmma, Laisari, witum þatei sunyeins ïs, yah ni kara þuk manshun; ni auk saiwhis ïn andwairþya manne, ak bi sunyai wig Guþs laiseis. Skuldu ïst kaisaragild giban Kaisara? [. . .	14 And as sone as they were come they sayd vnto hym, Master, we knowe that thou arte true, and careste for no man; for thou consydereste nott the degre off men, butt teacheste the waye off God truly. Ys yt laufull to paye tribute to Cesar, or nott?
15 . . .] þau niu gibaima? Ïþ Ïesus gasaiwhands ïze liutein, qaþ du ïm, Wha mik fraisiþ? atbairiþ mis skatt, ei gasaiwhau.	15 Ought we to geve, or ought we nott to geve? He knewe their dissimulacion, and sayd vnto them, Why tempte ye me? brynge me a peny, that I maye se yt.
16 Ïþ eis atberun. Yah qaþ du ïm, Whis ïst sa manleika, yah so unfarmeleins? Ïþ eis qeþun du ïmma, Kaisaris.	16 And they brought hym one. And he sayde vnto them, Whose ys thys ymage, and superscripcion? And they sayde vnto hym, Cesars.
17 Yah andhafyands Ïesus qaþ du ïm, Usgibiþ þo Kaisaris Kaisara, yah þo Guþs Guþa. Yah sildaleikidedun ana þamma.	17 And Jesus answered and sayde vnto them, Then geve to Cesar that which belongeth to Cesar, and geve God that which perteyneth to God. And they mervelled att hym.

TEXT III; THE SERMON ON THE MOUNT (*MATTHEW* 6.5-29)

5 Yah þan bidyaiþ, si siyaiþ swaswe þai liutans, unte friyond ïn gaqumbim yah waihstam plapyo standandans bidyan, ei gaumyaindau mannam; amen qiþa ïzwis, þatei haband mizdon seina.	5 And when thou prayest, thou shalt nott be as the ypocrites are, for they love to stond and praye in the synagogges and in corners of the stretes, because they wolde be sene of men; vereley I saye vnto you, they have there rewarde;

TEXT II; *MARK* 12.13-17.

13. **Herodiane**, 'Herod's men, servants' is a transliteration of the Greek, τῶν Ἡρωδιανῶν.

14. **qimandans**, 'coming', cf. on I.17, III.5. **Laisari . . . laiseis**, 'Teacher [voc.] . . . you teach'; as in Greek (Διδάσκαλε . . . διδάσκεις), the word is the same. For *laisyan*, 'teach' and *leisan*, 'learn', cf. Ger. *lehren*. **bi sunyai**, 'according to truth, truly' (Gk. ἐπ' ἀληθείας), cf. *sunyeins*, 'true'; V.37f. **andwairþya**, from *andwairþi*, 'face, person, presence', cf. I.18; lit. 'you look not to the face of men', i.e. have no regard for them. The Gothic translates the Greek literally. **skuldu ïst**, '(is it) right, lawful', cf. I.22. **kaisaragild**, cf. *gild*, 'tribute-money' and *gildan*, 'pay'; Ger. *gelden*. The Greek has κῆνσον, a transliteration of the Latin *census*. The full text should read '. . . to Caesar [or not? Should we give,] or not give?'

15. **liutein**, 'deceit, hypocrisy', cf. III.5 *liutans* for 'hypocrites' (Gk. ὑπόκρισις/-ν . . . ὑποκριταί). **fraisiþ**, '(you) test', cf. III.13. **atbairiþ**, 'bring', cf. v. 16 *atberun*, 'they brought'. **skatts**, 'money, coin', cf. Ger. *Schatz*, 'treasure, wealth'. The Greek has δηνάριον (cf. above, Chapter 6, II.B).

16. **manleika**, 'image', is self-explanatory. **ufarmeleins**, from *ufar-* (cf. on I.29) with *meleins*, 'writing'; a literal translation of Gk. ἐπιγραφή.

17. **sildaleikidedun**, 'they wondered at', cf. IV.14. The sense is of something rarely seen, cf. **sild*, 'rarely, seldom', and **leiks*, 'like', cf. also v. 16 and Ger. *gleich*.

TEXT III; *MATTHEW* 6.5-18, 24-29.

5. **bidyaiþ**, 'you [sing.] pray', cf. *bidyan*, 'they pray' and vv. 6, 7, 8, 9, etc.; I.28. From *bidyan*, cf. Eng. *bid*, Ger. *bitten*. **liutans**, cf. II.15. **friyond**, cf. I. 29. In addition to the Hebrew *amen* (cf. v. 16), the verse has three examples of words foreign to Gothic, transliterated or translated: **gaqumþim**, 'synagogues' (Gk. ἐν ταῖς συναγωγαῖς), from *ga-* (cf. Ger. *ge-*) *qiman*, 'come together' (cf. Ger. *kommen*); **plapyo** (better, **platyo**?), from Gk. πλατεῖαι 'streets'; **misdon**, 'reward', is a transliteration of Gk. μισθόν (also at v. 16).

6 Ïþ þu þan bidyais, gagg ïn heþyon þeina, yah galukands haurdai þeinai, bidei du attin þeinamma þamma ïn fulhsnya, yah atta þeins saei saiwhiþ ïn fulhsnya usgibiþ þus ïn bairhtein.	6 But when thou prayest, entre into thy chamber, and shutt thy dore to the, and praye to thy father which ys in secrete, and thy father which seith in secret, shal rewarde the openly.
7 Bidyandansuþ-þan ni filuwaurdyaiþ, swaswe þai þiudo, þugkeiþ ïm auk ei ïn filuwaurdein seinai andhausyaindau.	7 But when ye praye bable not moche, as the gentyls do, for they thincke that they shalbe herde ffor there moche bablynges sake.
8 Ni galeikoþ nu þaim, wait auk atta ïzwar þizei yus þaurbuþ, faurþizei yus bidyaiþ ïna.	8 Be not lyke them there fore, for youre father knoweth wherof ye have neade, before ye axe off him.
9 Swa nu bidyaiþ yus, Atta unsar þu ïn himinam, weihnai namo þein;	9 After thys maner there fore praye ye, O oure father which arte in heven, halowed be thy name;
10 Qimai þiudinassus þeins; wairþai wilya þeins swe ïn himina yah ana airþai;	10 Let thy kingdom come; thy wyll be fulfilled as well in erth as hit ys in heven;
11 Hlaif unsarana þana sinteinan gif uns himma daga;	11 Geve vs this daye oure dayly breade;
12 Yah aflet uns þatei skulans siyaima, swaswe yah weis afletam þaim skulam unsaraim;	12 And forgeve vs oure treaspases, even as we forgeve them which treaspas vs;

6. **heþyon þeina**, 'your room, shelter' (Gk. ταμιεῖον, 'inner chamber'), cf. OE *hýdan*, 'to hide'; ?Ger. *Hütte*, 'cottage'. **haurdai**, 'door', cf. Eng. *hurdle*, i.e. a frame used as a barrier. **in fulhsnya**, 'in secrecy'; cf. vb. *filhan*, 'hide' (IV.7). For **atta, attin**, etc., cf. vv. 8, 9, etc. and I.12. The words **in bairhtein**, 'openly' (Gk. ἐν τῷ φανερῷ, Eng. *bright*), repeated here from v. 4 (not printed), are not part of the 'authentic' text, but are often added as an explanatory gloss in Greek, Syriac and Old Latin versions of the New Testament, including the *Codex Brixianus* (cf. pp. 153 n. 49, 173; n. 13 below).

7. **filuwaurdyaiþ . . . filuwaurdein**, A.V. and R.V. 'vain repetitions . . . much speaking'. The Gothic here misses a variation of vocabulary present in the Greek βαττολογήσητε . . . πολυλογίᾳ; 'babbling . . . many-wordiness'. For *filu*, 'many' (Gk. πολύ-), cf. I.17. **þiudo**, pl. of *þiuda*, 'people', here 'gentiles' (Gk. ἐθνικοί) also yields the words for 'king', 'kingdom' etc.; cf. vv. 10, 13; V. 33, 35f.

8. **wait**, 'he knows', from *witan*, 'watch, observe'; Eng. *wit*, Ger. *wissen*, etc. The root meaning is that of 'see'; cf. Latin *videre* and the word for 'bear witness' in IV.13. **þaurbuþ**, from *þaurban*, 'need', cf. Ger. *bedürfen*. **faur-þizei**, lit. 'before that'.

9. **himinam**, pl. from *himins*, 'heaven', cf. I.18, etc. In this passage the uses of the singular (vv. 10, 26) and plural (vv. 9, 14, 26) accurately observe corresponding (not identical) differences in the Greek. **weihnai**, from *weihnan*, 'to be sanctified', cf. *weihan*, 'sanctify'; Ger. *weihen*, *Weihe*, *Weihnacht*, etc.

10. **þiudinassus**, 'kingdom', cf. *þiuda*, 'people' (v. 7), *þiudans*, 'king' (IV.11; V.33), etc. For the abstract form in *-assus*, cf. on I.30. In v. 13 below, *þiudangardi*, 'kingdom', is a less abstract concept; *gards* is a house (Eng. *yard*). The Gothic here implies a distinction not inherent in the Greek, where βασιλεία is used in both passages. **ana airþai**, 'on earth', from *airþa*, cf. also Ger. *Erde*.

11. **hlaif**, 'bread', cf. I.17. **sinteinans**, from *sinteins*, 'daily' (Gk. ἐπιούσιον). For **himma daga**, 'this day' cf. I.13; *himma* is the dative of *his*, 'this'.

12. The construction varies, as in the Greek; **þatei skulans siyaima**, 'that (for which) we are in debt' (Gk. τὰ ὀφειλήματα ἡμῶν) . . . **þaim skulaim unsaraim** (dative), '(to) those (who are) our debtors' (Gk. τοῖς ὀφειλέταις ἡμῶν). For *skulan*, 'owe', cf. Eng. *should*, Ger. *sollen*. **afletan**, 'forgive', is literally Eng. 'let off' (cf. vv. 14, 15).

13 Yah ni briggais uns ïn fraistubnyai, ak lausei uns af þamma ubilin; unte þeina ïst þiudangardi, yah mahts, yah wulþus ïn aiwins, Amen.	13 Leede vs not into temptacion, but delyvre vs ffrom yvell. Amen.
14 Unte yabai afletiþ mannam missadedins ïze, afletiþ yah ïzwis atta ïzwar sa ufar himinam.	14 For and yff ye shall forgeve other men there treaspases, youre father in heven shal also forgeve you.
15 Ïþ yabai ni afletiþ mannam missadedins ïze, ni þau atta ïzwar afletiþ missadedins ïzwaros.	15 But and ye wyll not forgeve men there trespases, no more shall youre father forgeve youre treaspases.
16 Aþþan biþe fastaiþ, ni wairþaiþ swaswe þai liutans gaurai, frawardyand auk andwairþya seina, ei gasaiwhaindau mannam fastandans; amen qiþa ïzwis, þatei andnemun mizdon seina.	16 Moreovre when ye faste, be not sad as the ypocrites are, for they disfigure there faces, that hit myght apere vnto men that they faste; verely Y say vnto you, they have there rewarde.
17 Ïþ þu fastands, salbo haubiþ þein, yah ludya þeina þwah,	17 But thou when thou fastest, annoynte thyne heed, and washe thy face,
18 Ei ni gasaiwhaizau mannam fastands, ak attin þeinamma þamma ïn fulhsnya, yah atta þeins saei saiwhiþ ïn fulhsnya, usgibiþ þus.	18 That it appere nott vnto men howe that thou fastest, but vnto thy father which is in secrete, and thy father which seith in secret, shall rewarde the openly.

[verses 19-23 omitted]

24 Ni manna mag twaim frauyam skalkinon, unte yabai fiyaiþ ainana, yah anþarana friyoþ; aiþþau ainamma ufhauseiþ, ïþ anþaramma frakann. Ni maguþ Guþa skalkinon yah mammonin.	24 No man can serve two masters, for other he shall hate the one, and love the other; or els he shall lene the one, and despise the other. Ye can nott serve God and mammon.

13. **fraistubnyai**, from *fraistubni*, 'temptation', cf. vb. *fraisan*, 'tempt'; cf. II.15. **ubilin** (from *ubels*) is Eng. *evil*; Ger. *Übel*. **þiud-angardi**, cf. v. 10 above. **mahts**, 'power', cf. Ger. *Macht*, Eng. *might*. For **wulþus**, 'glory' (Gk. δόξα) cf. v. 29 below. **aiwins**, from *aiws*, 'eternity' cf. I.29. The concluding phrase *unte þeina . . . in aiwins* is a liturgical addition not found in the versions of the New Testament known to third- and fourth-century patristic writers, nor in general in the Old Latin or Vulgate traditions. It does however occur in the fourth-century Greek text associated with John Chrysostom, and in the Latin text of the *codex Brixianus* (n. 6 above).

14. **afletiþ**, cf. v. 12. **missadedins**, 'misdoings' (Gk. τὰ παρα-πτώματα αὐτῶν) is not the same word as that used in v. 12 ('debtors'). The Gothic follows the distinction in the Greek, which is ignored by Tyndale (it is correctly observed in A.V. and R.V.). The vocabulary of this verse is largely repeated in 15.

16. For the vocabulary cf. v. 5 above. For **gaurai** (*gaurs*), 'sad, sorrowful', cf. *gauryan*, 'grieve', *gauriþa*, 'grief'. **andwairþya**, 'face, presence', cf. I.18, II.14. **frawardyand**, 'disfigure', is stronger than the Greek ἀφανίζουσι, 'hide'. **gasaiwhaindau** (3rd pers. pl.), cf. v. 18 **gasaiwhaizau** (2nd pers. sing.), from *ga-saiwhau*, 'see, behold'.

17. **salbo**, 'salve, anoint', cf. Ger. *zalven*. **haubiþ**, 'head', cf. Ger. *Haupt*. **þwah**, from *þwahan*, 'wash'. The word order closely follows that of the Greek text, the phrase being enclosed by the verbs *salbo . . . þwah*, with the nouns between them. The word for 'face', **ludya**, is different from that in v. 16, where the Greek has the same (though in the plural).

18. For the vocabulary cf. v. 6 above (where *in bairhtein* is added).

[verses 19-23 omitted]

24. **mag**, 'can' (Eng. *may*, Ger. *mögen*) is connected with *mahts*, 'power', cf. v. 13. **twain frauyaim**, 'two masters'; from *frauya*, 'lord, master' (cf. IV.10, V.32). For **skalkinon**, 'serve', cf. I.22. **fiyaiþ**, 'he will hate', from *fiyan*, cf. Ger. *Feind*, 'enemy'. For **friyoþ**, 'he will love', cf. I.29. **ufhauseiþ**, 'he will obey, submit to'. **frakann**, 'despise'; from *fra-kunnan*; *kunnan* is 'to know', the prefix *fra-* (Ger. *ver-*, Eng. *for-*) adding a negative or destructive force (Ger. *verachten*, 'despise', is from *ver-* and *achten*, 'hold in respect'). **mammonin** is of course a transliteration from the Aramaic-Greek μαμμωνᾶς.

25 Duþþe qiþa ïzwis, ni maurnaiþ saiwalai ïzwarai, wha matyaiþ yah wha drigkaiþ; nih leika ïzwaramma, whe wasyaiþ. Niu saiwala mais ïst fodeinai, yah leik wastyom?

25 Therefore I saye vnto you, be not carefull for youre lyfe, what ye shall eate, or what ye shall dryncke; nor yet for youre boddy, what rayment ye shall weare. Ys not the lyfe more worth then meate, and the boddy more off value then rayment?

26 Ïnsaiwhiþ du fuglam himinis, þei ni saisand, nih sneiþand, nih lisand ïn banstins; yah atta ïzwar sa ufar himinam fodeiþ ïns. Niu yus mais wulþrizans siyuþ þaim?

26 Beholde the foules of the aier, for they sowe not, neder reepe, nor yet cary into the barnes; and yett youre hevenly father fedeth them. Are ye not better than they?

27 Ïþ whas ïzwara maurnands mag anaaukan ana wahstu seinana aleina aina?

27 Whiche off you though he toke tought therefore coulde put one cubit vnto his stature?

28 Yah bi wastyos wha saurgaiþ? Gakunnaiþ blomans haiþyos, whaiwha wahsyand. Nih arbaidyand, nih spinnand;

28 And why care ye then for rayment? Beholde the lyles off the felde, howe thy growe. They labour not, nether spynn;

29 Qiþuh þan ïzwis, þatei nih Saulaumon ïn allamma wulþau seinamma gawasida sik swe ains þize.

29 And yet for all that I saie vnto you, that even Solomon in all his royalte was nott arayed lyke vnto one of these.

Figure 18 (opposite): *Matthew* 6.14-16 in the *Codex Argenteus* (cf. text at p. 186)

25. **maurnaiþ**, from *maurnan*, 'mourn'; hence 'to be anxious, troubled about'; cf. v. 27 and on v. 28 below. **saiwalai ïzwarai**, 'for your life', lit. 'soul'; Germ. *Seele*. **matyaiþ**, 'you will eat', cf. I.16. **leik** is 'body' (Gk. τῷ σώματι), seen as a purely physical thing; often in the sense of 'corpse', cf. Ger. *Leiche*. In England a *lichgate* is the covered gate to a churchyard under which the body awaits the clergyman at burials. **wasyaiþ** . . . **wastyam** ('you will wear . . . rayment'), cf. I.22 and vv. 28, 29 below. **fodeinai**, 'food', cf. v. 26 *fodeiþ*, from *fodyan*, 'feed'.

26. **himinis** . . . **ufar himinam**, cf. v. 9 above; here in the senses respectively of 'sky . . . heavens'. **lisand**, from *lisan*, 'gather, collect'; cf. Eng. dial. 'lease, leaze', in the sense of 'glean'. **banstins**, from *bansts*, 'barn'; Ger. dial. *Banse*. **mais wulþrizans**, 'of more worth, consequence', a comparative form derived from *wulþus*, cf. v. 13 above; *mais* expresses the Greek μᾶλλον.

27. **maurnands**, see on 25 above; in the two passages reproducing the Greek μεριμνᾶτε/-ῶν. For **wahstu**, from *wahstus*, 'growth, stature' (Gk. ἡλικίαν), cf. v. 28 *wahsyand*, from *wahsyan*, 'grow'; Eng. *wax*. **aleina**, used here for 'cubit' (Gk. πῆχυν), cf. Eng. *ell*, Ger. *Elle* (*Ellenlang*, 'an elbow's length').

28. **saurgaiþ**, lit. 'sorrow, grieve'; exactly the same extension of sense as found in *maurnan*, cf. v. 25 above (the Greek has the same word in all three passages; here μεριμνᾶτε, again adhering to the Gk. construction). Ger. *Sorge*, 'anxiety, alarm', also 'care, responsibility', displays the same range of meanings.

29. **wulþau**, cf. vv. 13, 26. **gawasida**, cf. v. 25.

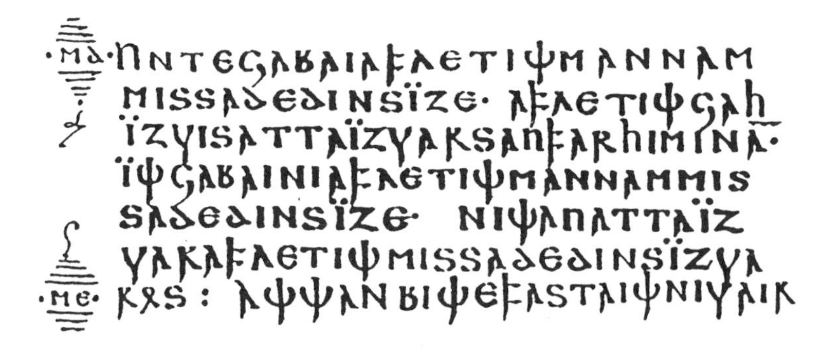

TEXT IV; THE TRIAL OF JESUS (*MATTHEW* 27.1-18)

1 At maurgin þan waurþanana, runa nemun allai gudyans, yah þai sinistans manageins bi Ïesu, ei afdauþidedeina ïna.

1 When the mornynge was come, all the chefe prestes, and senyours off the people helde a counsayle agenst Jesu, to put hym to deth.

2 Yah gabindandans ïna gatauhun, yah anafulhun ïna Pauntiáu Peilatau, kindina.

2 And brought hym bounde, and delyvered hym vnto Poncius Pylate, the debyte.

3 Þanuh gasaiwhands Ïudas sa galewyands ïna, þatei du stauai gatauhans warþ, ïdreigonds, gawandida þans þrins tiguns silubrinaize gudyam, yah sinistam,

3 Then when Judas which betrayed hym, sawe that he was condempned, he repented him sylfe, and brought ageyne the xxx. plattes off sylver to the chefe prestes, and senyoures,

4 Qiþands, Frawaurhta mis, galewyands bloþ swikn. Ïþ eis qeþun, Wha kara unsis? þu witeis.

4 Saynge, I have synned, betraynge the innocent bloud. And they sayde, What is that to vs? se thou to that.

5 Yah atwairþands þaim silubram ïn alh, aflaiþ, yah galeiþands ushaihah sik.

5 And he cast doune the sylver plates in the temple, and departed, and went and hounge hym sylfe.

6 Ïþ þai gudyans nimandans þans skattans, qeþun, Ni skuld ïst lagyan þans ïn kaurbanaun, unte andawairþi bloþis ïst.

6 The chefe prestes toke the sylver plattes, and sayd, It is not lawfull for to put them in to the treasury, because it is the pryce of bloud.

TEXT IV; *MATTHEW* 27.1-18.

1-2. **waurþanana**, from *wairþan*, 'happen, become' (Gk. γενομένης); cf. Ger. *werden*. **runa nemun**, 'they took counsel', again very close to the Greek συμβούλιον ἔλαβον. *runa* is also 'rune, mystery', cf. Chapter 6, I.B; for *niman*, 'take', cf. I.27 (Ger. *nehmen*). **afdauþidedeina ïna**; for *dauþs*, 'dead' (*dauþus*, 'death'), cf. Ger. *Tod*. The first two verses of this chapter should be linked with Amm. Marc. 28.5.14, giving two Burgundian words; *hendinos*, 'king' ('rex'), and *sinistus*, 'high priest' ('sacerdos . . . maximus'). The information does not quite tally with what we find in this passage. *Hendinos* is no doubt connected with *kindins* (vv. 2, 11, 14, 15), used here for the Greek ἡγεμών, 'governor'. **Sinistans** is however used (vv. 1, 3, 12) for 'elders' (Gk. πρεσβυτέροι); it is the superlative of *sineigs*, 'old' (Latin *senex*). The Gothic word used for 'high priests' (ἀρχιερεῖς) is **gudyans** (vv. 1, 3, 6, 12), cf. *Guþ*, 'God' (II.17, etc.).

3. **galewyands**, from *galewyan*, 'give up, present' (παραδιδούς), hence 'betray'; cf. v. 4, V.36. **þatei du stauai gatauhans warþ**, cf. Chapter 6, Additional Note (ii). *Staua* is 'judgment', cf. V.31. **gawandida**, from *gawandyan*, 'turn, return', Ger. *wenden*, Eng. *wend*, *wind*; here in an unusual transitive sense for 'bring back', cf. the Gk. original ἔστρεψε. **þrins tigun**, 'three tens'; **silubreins**, 'of silver', also at v. 9.

4. **frawaurhta mis**, cf. I.18. **swikns**, 'pure, innocent'. **witeis**, cf. III.8; here for Gk. ὄψει, 'you will see'.

5. **alh**, from *alhs*, 'temple'. **ushaihah sik**, 'hanged himself'; cf. *hahan*, 'hang', with prefix *us*- (Ger. *aus*-); *sik*, reflexive, cf. Ger. *sich*.

6. **nimandans**, from *niman*, 'take', cf. vv. 1, 7, 9, etc. **skattans**, from *skatts*, 'money', cf. II.15 and Chapter 6, s. II.B. **ni skuld ïst**, 'it is not possible, lawful', cf. I.22, V.31, etc. **lagyan**, 'put, lay'; cf. also Ger. *legen*. **kaurbanaum** is a transliteration of the Greek κορβανᾶν (Vulgate *corbanan*), itself a transliteration of the Hebrew word for the Temple treasury. **andawairþi**, for Gk. τιμή, 'price'; from *wairþs*, 'worth', cf. Ger. *werth*.

7 Garuni þan nimandans, usbauhtedun us þaim þana akr kasyins, du usfilhan ana gastim.
8 Duþþe haitans warþ akrs yains akrs bloþis, und hina dag.

9 Þanuh usfullnoda, þata qiþano þairh Ïairaimian praufetu, qiþandan, Yah usnemun þrins tiguns silubreinaize, andwairþi þis wairþodins, þatei garahnidedun fram sunum Ïsraelis;

10 Yah atgebun ïns und akra kasyins, swaswe anabauþ mis Frauya.
11 Ïþ Ïesus stoþ faura kindina; yah frah ïna sa kindins, qiþands, Þu ïs þiudans Ïudaie? Ïþ Ïesus qaþ du ïmma, Þu qiþis.

12 Yah miþþanei wrohiþs was fram þaim gudyam, yah sinistam, ni waiht andhof.
13 Þanuh qaþ du ïmma Peilatus, Niu hauseis, whan filu ana þuk weitwodyand?
14 Yah ni andhof ïmma wiþra ni ainhun waurde, swaswe sildaleikida sa kindins filu.
15 And dulþ þan wharyoh biuhts was sa kindins fraletan ainana þizai managein bandyan, þanei wildedun.
16 Habaidedunuh þan bandyan, gatarhidana Barabban.

7 And they toke counsell, and bought with them a potters felde, to bury strangers in.
8 Wherfore that felde is called the felde of bloud, untyll this daye.
9 Then was fullfylled, that which was spoken by Jeremi the prophet, sayinge, And they took xxx. sylver plates, the value of him that was prysed, whom they bought of the chyldren of Israhel;
10 And they gave them for the potters felde, as the Lorde appoynted me.
11 Jesus stode before the debite; and the debite axed him, saynge, Arte thou the kynge of the Iewes? Jesus sayd vnto hym, Thou sayest.
12 When he was accused of the chefe preestes, and senioures, he answered nothinge.
13 Then sayd Pilate vnto him, Hearest thou not, howe many thinges they laye ayenste the?
14 And he answered him to never a worde, in so moche that the debyte marveylled very sore.
15 Att that feest the debyte was wonte to deliver vnto the peple a presoner, whom they wolde chose.
16 He hade then a notable presoner, called Barrabas.

7. **garuni þan nimandans**, cf. v. 1 above. The Gothic closely reflects the Greek construction, with the slight variation *runa/garuni* for the same word, συμβούλιον. For the prefix *ga-*, cf. Ger. *ge-*; it may here be intended to pick up the Greek element συν- in συμβούλιον. **us þaim**, 'from them', i.e. the thirty pieces. **akr**, from *akrs*, 'field', cf. I.25. **kasyins**, from *kasya*, 'potter'; cf. *kas*, 'vessel, pot' (Ger. *Kessel*). **usfilan**, 'to hide completely', cf. III.6, and, for the prefix *us-*, v. 5 above. **ana**, 'in'. **gastim**, from *gasts*, 'stranger', translating Gk. ξένοις; cf. Ger. *Gast*, Eng. *guest*.

8. **yains**, cf. I.13. **und hina dag**, 'until this day' cf. I.13, III.11.

9. For the vocabulary, cf. vv. 3, 6. **usfullnoda**, 'was fulfilled', cf. V.32. **þatei garahnidedun**, from *(ga-)rahnyan*; 'that they counted, valued', Gk. ὃν ἐτιμήσαντο (better therefore would be *þanei*, 'whom . . .'). In Gothic as in Greek, a different word from that for 'bought' (ἠγόρασαν) in v. 7. The reference is in fact to *Zechariah* 11.12f.

10. **Frauya**, 'Lord', cf. III.24, V.32.

11. **kindins**, cf. on vv. 1-2 above. **þiudans Ïudaie**, 'king of the Jews', cf. III.7, 10; V.33.

12. **wroþiþs**, from *wrohyan*, 'accuse', cf. Ger. *rügen* (and archaic Eng. *bewray*); cf. V.29. **ni waiht**, 'not a thing', i.e. 'not a single word'; cf. Eng. *whit*.

13. **filu**, 'many', cf. I.17. **ana þuk weitwotyand**, 'they bear witness against you', Gk. σοῦ καταμρτυροῦσι; cf. V.37.

14. **wiþra**, 'against, in reply to', cf. Ger. *wider*; to be taken with *andhof* (cf. v. 12), 'reply'. **sildaleikida**, 'was amazed at', cf. II.17.

15. **dulþ**, from *dulþs*, 'feast'. **wharyoh** is from *wharyizuh*, 'each, every'; there is no equivalent in the Greek text. **biuhts was**, 'was accustomed', cf. V.39. **managei**, 'multitude, crowd', cf. *manags*, 'much, many'; translating Gk. τῷ ὄχλῳ. **bandyan**, from *bandya*, 'prisoner', i.e. someone fettered, tied up.

16. **habaidedunuh**, plural, accurately representing the Greek εἶχον (contrast Tyndale's 'he'). **gatarhidana**, 'notable' from *gatarhiþs*; Gk. ἐπίσημον. In other contexts, *gatahryan* is 'to note, mark, make a show of', reflecting unfavourably on the thing or person noted. The Greek λεγόμενον (Tyndale's 'called') is not represented in the Gothic.

17 Gaqumanaim þan ïm, qaþ ïm Peilatus, Whana wileiþ ei fraletau ïzwis? Barabban, þau Ïesu, saei haitada Christus?	17 And when they were gaddered together Pilate sayde vnto them, Whether wyll ye, that Y geve losse vnto you? Barrabas, or Jesus, which is called Cryst?
18 Wissa auk, þatei ïn neiþis atgebun ïna.	18 For he knewe well, that for envy they had delyvered hym.

TEXT V; THE TRIAL OF JESUS (*JOHN* 18.28-40)

28 Ïþ eis tauhun Ïesu fram Kayafin, ïn praitoriaun; þanuh was maurgins, ïþ eis ni ïddyedun ïn praitoria, ei ni bisaulnodedeina, ak matidedeina pascha.	28 Then ledd they Jesus from Cayphas, into the housse of iudgement; hit was in the mornynge, and they them selves went not into the iudgement housse, lest they shulde be defyled, butt that they myght eate pascha.
29 Þaruh atïddya ut Peilatus du ïm, yah qaþ, Who wrohe bairiþ ana þana mannan?	29 Pilate then went oute vnto them, and sayde, What accusacion brynge ye agaynste this man?
30 Andhofun, yah qeþun du ïmma. Nih wesi sa ubiltoyis, ni þau weis atgebeima þus ïna.	30 They answered, and sayd vnto hym, Iff he were nott an evyll doar, we wolde not have delyvered hym vnto the.
31 Þaruh qaþ ïm Peilatus, Nimiþ ïna yus, yah bi witoda ïzwaramma, stoyiþ ïna. Ïþ eis qeþunuh du ïmma Ïudaieis, Unsis ni skuld ïst usqiman manne ainummehun;	31 Then sayd Pilate vnto them, Take hym vnto you, and iudge hym, after youre awne lawe. The Iewes sayde vnto hym, It is nott lawfull for vs to putt eny man to deeth;
32 Ei waurd Frauyins usfullnodedi, þatei qaþ, bandwyands whileikamma dauþau skulda gaswiltan.	32 That the wordes of Jesus myght be fulfilled, which he spake, signifyinge what deeth he shulde deye.
33 Galaiþ ïn praitauria aftra Peilatus, yah wopida Ïesu, qaþuh ïmma, Þu ïs þiudans Ïudaie?	33 Then Pilate entred into the iudgement housse agayne, and called Jesus, and sayd vnto him, Arte thou kynge of the Iewes?

17. **gaqumanaim þan ïm**, 'they then being come together'; the past participle with dative absolute corresponds closely to the Greek construction (with genitive absolute). Cf. in both languages the word for 'synagogue' in III.5. **haitada**, 'called', corresponds to the Greek λεγόμενον; Ger. *heissen*.

18. **neiþis**, 'envy'; Ger. *Neid*.

TEXT V; *JOHN* 18.28-40.

28. **praitoriaun**, transliteration of the Greek πραιτώριον (Latin *praetorium*). **bisaulnodedeina**, from *bisaulnan*, 'to be defiled'; cf. **saulyan*, Eng. *soil*. As with **matidedeina** (for the word, cf. I.16), the form is the past subjunctive; the Greek has an idiomatic present subjunctive.

29. **wrohe**, from *wrohs*, 'accusation'; cf. IV.12.

30. **andhofun**, 'they answered', cf. I.29, IV.14 and vv. 34-7 below. **ubiltoyis**, 'evil-doer' (Gk. κακοποιός), cf. III.13 and v. 40 below. **ni þau**; *þau* emphasises the logic; 'in that case'.

31. **nimiþ**, 'take', cf. IV.1, 6, etc. **witoda**, from *witoþ*, 'law'; connected with *witan*, 'know', cf. III.8. **stoyiþ**, from *stoyan*, 'judge'; for *staua*, 'judgment', cf. IV.3. The word order of the Gothic closely follows the Greek; Tyndale reverses the two clauses *bi witoda . . . stoyiþ ina*. **ni skuld ïst**, cf. IV.6. **usqiman**, *sc*. 'deprive of (*us*-, cf. Ger. *aus*-) his being (*qiman*)'. **ni . . . ainummehun**, 'not anyone', again reflecting the Greek word order.

32. Cf. IV.9 for the vocabulary. **Frauyins**, cf. III.24, IV.10. **bandwyands**, 'making, giving a sign', from *bandwyan*, cf. *bandwa*, 'sign, token, bond', and *bindan*, 'bind, fasten'. **dauþau**, from *dauþus*, 'death', cf. I.24, 32; IV.1. **skulda**, v. 31 and I.22. **ga-swiltan**, 'to die'. 'Crimean Gothic' (above, p. 97 n. 87) has *schuualth* for 'death'; cf. Stearns, *Crimean Gothic*, p. 11.

33. **wopida**, 'called', from *wopyan*; cf. Eng. *whoop*. **Þu ïs þiudans Ïudaie?**, as at IV.11.

34 Andhof Ïesus, Abu þus silbin þu þata qiþis, þau anþarai þus qeþun bi mik?

34 Jesus answered, Sayst thou that off thy sylfe, or did other tell ytt the of me?

35 Andhof Peilatus, Waitei ïk Ïudaius ïm? So þiuda þeina yah gudyans anafulhun þuk mis; wha gatawides?

35 Pilate answered, Am I a Iewe? Thyne awne nacion and hye prestes have delivered the vnto me; what hast thou done?

36 Andhof Ïesus, Þiudangardi meina nist us þamma fairwhau; ïþ us þamma fairwhau wesi meina þiudangardi, aiþþau andbahtos meinai usdaudidedeina, ei ni galewiþs wesyau Ïudaium; ïþ nu þiudangardi meina nist þaþro.

36 Jesus answered, My kyngdome is not of this worlde; yff my kyngdome were of this worlde, then wolde my ministers suerly fight, that I shulde not be delyvered to the Iewes; but nowe is my kingdome not from hence.

37 Þaruh qaþ ïmma Peilatus, An nuh þiudans ïs þu? Andhafyands Ïesus, Þu qiþis, ei þiudans ïm ïk. Ïk du þamma gabaurans ïm, yah du þamma qam ïn þamma fairwhau, ei weitwodyau sunyai. Whazuh saei ïst sunyos, hauseiþ stibnos meinaizos.

37 Pilate sayde vnto hym, Arte thou a kynge then? Jesus answered, Thou sayst, that I am a kynge. For this cause was I borne, and for this cause cam I into the worlde, that I shulde beare witnes vnto the trueth. All that are of the trueth, heare my voice.

38 Þanuh qaþ ïmma Peilatus, Wha ïst so sunya? Yah þata qiþands, galaiþ ut du Ïudaium, yah qaþ ïm, Ïk ainohun fairono ni bigita ïn þamma.

38 Pilate sayde vnto hym, What is trueth. And when he had sayde that, he went out agayne vnto the Iewes and sayde vnto them, I fynde in him no cause at all.

39 Ïþ ïst biuhti ïzwis, ei ainana ïzwis fraletau ïn pascha; wileidu nu ei fraletau ïzwis þana þiudan Ïudaie?

39 Ye have a costome amonge you, that I shulde delyvre you won loosse at ester; will ye that I loose vnto you the kynge of the Iewes?

40 Ïþ eis hropidedun aftra allai, qiþandans, Ne þana, ak Barabban. Sah þan was sa Barabba waidedya.

40 Then cryed they all againe, sayinge, Not him, but Barrabas. Barrabas was a robber.

34. **andhof**, cf. vv. 30, 35-7, etc. **þus silbin** (from *selba*), 'your self'; cf. Ger. *selb*, *selbst*, etc. **mik**, cf. Ger. *mich*.

35. **þiuda**, 'people' and (v. 36) **þiudangardi**, 'kingdom', cf. III.10. **gudyans**, cf. on IV.1-2. **gatawides**, from *gatauyan*, 'do'; Ger. *tun*.

36. **fairwhau**, from *fairwhus*, 'world' (Gk. κόσμος). **aiþþau**, 'or, in that case'; perhaps intended to pick up the Gk. particle ἄν; cf. v. 30 above. **andbahtos meinai**, 'my followers' (Gk. ὑπηρέται), cf. *andbahtyan*, 'to serve, minister'. For the Celtic *ambactus*, 'servant', cf. Festus, p. 4.20-1 Lindsay; ultimately yielding *ambassador*, etc. **usdaudideina**, 'they would fight, strive'; *usdaudyan* is 'to strive', in the sense of 'compete, be diligent' (Gk. ἠγωνίζοντο). **galewiþs**, cf. on IV.3.

37. **an nuh**; *an* is an interrogative adverb, *nuh* (*nu-uh*) is 'then', used in questions; Greek οὐκοῦν. **gabaurans**, 'born', from *gabairan*, 'bear'; cf. Ger. *geboren*. **weitwodyau**, cf. IV.13. **sunyai . . . sunyos**, 'truth', cf. II.14. **stibnos**, from *stibna*, 'voice'; cf. Ger. *Stimme*.

38. **fairino**, from *fairina*, 'charge, accusation', hence 'fault' (Gk. αἰτία); cf. *fairinon*, 'blame, accuse'. **ni bigita**, cf. I.24.

39. **biuhti**, cf. IV.15. **pascha**, here for *dulþ* at IV.15.

40. **hropidedun**, 'they shouted out', from *hropyan*; cf. Ger. *rufen*. **waidedya**, 'evil-doer', from *wai*, 'woe!' (exclam.) and **deþs*, **dedya*, 'deed', 'doer'; a different word, as in the Greek (λῃστής), from v. 30 above.

BIBLIOGRAPHY

1. PRIMARY SOURCES REFERRED TO

Ammianus Marcellinus, *Res Gestae* (= Amm. Marc.): ed. W. Seyfarth, 2 vols., Teubner 1978; transl. Walter Hamilton, *Ammianus Marcellinus: The Later Roman Empire (A.D. 354-378)*, with Introduction and Notes by Andrew Wallace-Hadrill; Penguin Books (Harmondsworth, 1986).

Chaldaean Oracles, ed. and transl. by E. des Places, *Oracles Chaldaïques, avec un choix de commentaires anciens*, ed. Budé (Paris, 1971).

Codex Theodosianus (= *CTh*), edd. Th. Mommsen, P. Meyer (Berlin, 1905); transl. Clyde Pharr, *The Theodosian Code and Novels, and the Sirmondian Constitutions* (Princeton, 1952; repr. Westport, Conn., 1969).

Dexippus, *Scythica*, fragments in Jacoby, *FGrH* II.A (Berlin, 1926), pp. 466-75.

Eunapius, *Histories*, fragments in Müller, *FHG* IV, pp. 7-56, and with transl. in R. C. Blockley, *Fragmentary Classicising Historians* II (Liverpool, 1983), pp. 2-127 (we give frag. nos. according to both editions). See also s. Zosimus.

Eusebius, *Ecclesiastical History*, ed. and transl. Kirsopp Lake, ed. Loeb, Vol. I (1926, reprinted); transl. G. A. Williamson, *Eusebius, The History of the Church*; Penguin Books (Harmondsworth, 1965; reprinted).

Gennadius, *De Viris Illustribus*; ed. C. A. Bernoulli (Freiburg i. B. and Leipzig, 1895; repr. Frankfurt, 1968), pp. 58-95; *PL* 58.1059-1120.

Jerome, *Ep.* 106 to Sunnias and Fretela; ed. I. Hilberg, *CSEL* 55 (Vienna and Leipzig, 1912; repr. New York and London, 1961), pp. 247-89; J. Labourt, ed. Budé, Vol. 5 (Paris, 1955), pp. 104-44.

Notitia Dignitatum (= *Not. Dig.*), ed. O. Seeck (Berlin, 1876; repr. Frankfurt, 1962).

Leges Novellae divi Theodosii (= *Nov. Theod.*); see above, s. *Codex Theodosianus*.

Panegyrici Latini; ed. and transl. by E. Galletier, *Panégyriques Latins*, ed. Budé (3 vols., Paris 1949-55); O.C.T. by R. A. B. Mynors (1964).

Passio Polycarpi; text in Knopf-Krüger, *Ausgewählte Märtyrerakten* (4th ed. by G. Ruhbach, Tübingen, 1965), pp. 1-8; with transl. in H. Musurillo, *The Acts of the Christian Martyrs: Introduction, Texts and Translation* (Oxford, 1972), pp. 2-21.

Constitutiones Sirmondianae (= *Sirm.*); see above, s. *Codex Theodosianus*.

Socrates, *Ecclesiastical History*; ed. R. Hussey (3 vols., Oxford, 1853); *PG* 67.33ff.; transl. H. Wace and P. Schaff, in *Nicene and Post-Nicene Fathers* (Oxford and New York, 1891).

Synesius, *De Regno*; transl. with introduction, notes and commentary by Chr. Lacombrade, *Le Discours sur la Royauté de Synésios de Cyrène à l'empereur Arcadios* (Paris, 1951).

Zosimus, *New History*; ed. with transl. and commentary by F. Paschoud, ed. Budé (3 vols. in 5 parts, Paris, 1971-89).

2. SECONDARY WORKS

Alexe, S. C., 'Saint Basile le Grand et le christianisme roumain au IVe siècle', in E. A. Livingstone (ed.), *Studia Patristica* XVII.3 (Oxford, New York, etc., 1982), 1049-59.

Anderson, J. G. C., 'Exploration in Galatia cis Halym, II: topography, epigraphy, Galatian civilisation', *JHS* 19 (1899), 52-134 (§6 'Parnassos', 107-9).

Barnard, L. W., 'Church-State Relations, A.D. 313-337', *Journal of Church and State* 24 (1982), 337-55.

Barnes, T. D., 'Imperial campaigns, A.D. 285-311', *Phoenix* 30 (1976), 174-93.

— — , 'The victories of Constantine', *ZPE* 20 (1976), 149-155.

— — , 'The consecration of Ulfila', *JTS* n.s. 41 (1990), 541-5.

Bennett, W. H., *The Gothic Commentary on the Gospel of John: skeireins aiwaggeljons þairh iohannen; a Decipherment, Edition and Translation* (The Modern Language Association of America: Monographs series XXI; New York, 1960).

- - , *An Introduction to the Gothic Language* (New York 1960; repr. 1980).

Bichir, G., *The Archaeology and History of the Carpi, from the Second to the Fourth Century A.D.*, BAR, Supplementary Series 16 (2 vols., Oxford, 1976).

Bodor, A., 'Emperor Aurelian and the abandonment of Dacia', *Dacoromania* 1 (1973), 29-40.

Bosworth, Rev. J., and Waring, S., *The Gothic and Anglo-Saxon Gospels in Parallel Columns with the Versions of Wycliffe and Tyndale* (London, 1865).

Braund, D. C., *Rome and the Friendly King: the Character of the Client Kingship* (London, 1984).

Burkitt, F. G., 'The Vulgate Gospels and the Codex Brixianus', *JTS* 1 (1900), 129-34.

Burns, T. S., *A History of the Ostrogoths* (Bloomington, Indiana, 1984).

Cazacu, M., '"Montes Serrorum" (Ammianus Marcellinus XXVII.5.3): zur Siedlungsgeschichte der Westgoten im Rumanien', *Dacia*, n.s. 16 (1972), 299-302.

Chrysos, E. K., Τὸ Βυζάντιον καὶ οἱ Γότθοι (*To Byzantion kai hoi Gotthoi*) (Thessalonica, 1972).

Clover, F. M., 'Olympiodorus of Thebes and the Historia Augusta', *Historia Augusta Colloquium, Bonn 1979-81* (Antiquitas 4.15; Bonn, 1983), 127-52.

Cross, F. L., and Livingstone, E. A., *The Oxford Dictionary of the Christian Church* (2nd rev. ed., Oxford, 1983).

Dagron, G., *L'Empire romain d'orient au IVe siècle et les traditions politiques de l'hellénisme: le témoignage de Thémistios*, Travaux et Mémoires 3 (Paris, 1968).

Daly, L. J., 'The Mandarin and the Barbarian: the response of Themistius to the Gothic challenge', *Historia* 21 (1972), 351-79.

Dauge, Y. A., *Le Barbare; Recherches sur la conception romaine de la barbarie et de la civilisation* (Coll. Latomus 176; Brussels, 1981).

Delehaye, H., 'Saints de Thrace et de Mésie', *Analecta Bollandiana* 31 (1912), 161-300.

Dihle, A., 'Die Sendung des Inders Theophilos', in *Politeia und Res Publica; Beiträge zum Verständnis von Politik, Recht und Staat in der Antike dem andenken Rudolf Stark gewidmet*, *Palingenesia* IV (Wiesbaden, 1969), 330-6.

Dillon, J., *The Middle Platonists; a Study of Platonism, 80 B.C. to A.D. 220* (London, 1977).

Downey, G., 'Philanthropia in Religion and Statecraft in the fourth century after Christ', *Historia* 4 (1955), 199-208.

— — , 'Themistius' first oratio', *Greek and Byzantine Studies* 1 (1958), 49-69.

Friedrichsen, G. W. S., *The Gothic Version of the Gospels: a Study of its Style and Textual History* (Oxford, 1926).

— — , *The Gothic Version of the Epistles: a Study of its Style and Textual History* (Oxford, 1939).

Goodenough, E. R., 'The political philosophy of Hellenistic kingship', *Yale Classical Studies* 1 (1928), 55-102.

Grigg, R., 'Portrait-bearing codicils in the illustrations of the *Notitia Dignitatum*', *JRS* 69 (1979), 107-24.

Gryson, R., *Scolies ariennes sur le Concile d'Aquilée* (SChr 267; Paris, 1980).

— — , and Gilissen, L., *Les scolies ariennes du Parisinus 8907: un échantillonnage d'écritures du Ve siècle* (Armarium Codicum Insignium I; Turnholt, 1980).

Heather, P. J., 'The crossing of the Danube and the Gothic Conversion', *GRBS* 27 (1986), 289-318.

— — , *Goths and Romans, 332-489* (Oxford, 1991).

Honigmann, E., and Maricq, A., *Recherches sur les Res Gestae Divi Saporis* (Brussels, 1953).

Hunter, M. J., 'The Gothic Bible', in G. W. H. Lampe (ed.), *The Cambridge History of the Bible*, Vol. II (1969), 338-62.

Joannou, P.-P., *Discipline Générale Antique (IVe-IXe s.)*, t. II; *Les Canons des Pères Grecs* (Pontificia Commissione per la redazione del codice di diritto canonico Orientale: Fonti, fascicolo IX; Rome, 1963).

Kelly, J. N. D., *Early Christian Creeds* (3rd ed., London, 1972).

— — , *Jerome: his Life, Writings and Controversies* (London, 1975).

Klose, J., *Roms Klientel-Randstaaten am Rhein und an der Donau: Beiträge zur ihrer Geschichte und rechtlichen Stellung im 1 und 2 Jhdt. n. Chr.* (Breslau, 1934).

Kolendo, J., 'Une inscription inconnue de Sexaginta Prista et la fortification du Bas Danube sous la Tétrarchie', *Eirene* 5 (1966), 139-154.

Kopeček, T. A., *A History of Neo-Arianism* (Patristic Monographs, 8; Cambridge, Mass., 1979).

Lane Fox, R., *Pagans and Christians* (Harmondsworth, 1986).

Lehmann, Winfred P., *A Gothic Etymological Dictionary* (Leiden, 1986); based on the third edition (1939) of S. Feist, *Vergleichendes Wörterbuch der Gotischen Sprache* (first published in 1909).

McCormick, M., *Eternal Victory: Triumphal Rulership in Late Antiquity, Byzantium and the Early Medieval West* (Cambridge, 1986).

McLynn, N., 'The "Apology" of Palladius: Nature and Purpose', *JTS* n.s. 42 (1991), 52-76.

MacMullen, R., *Paganism in the Roman Empire* (New Haven and London, 1981).

Magie, D., *Roman Rule in Asia Minor, to the end of the Third Century after Christ* (Princeton, N.J.; 2 vols., 1950).

Mandouze, A., *Prosopographie chrétienne du Bas-Empire, I: Prosopographie de l'Afrique chrétienne (303-533)* (Paris, 1982).

Mango, C., *Le Développement urbain de Constantinople (IVe-VIIe siècles)* (Travaux et mémoires du centre de recherches d'histoire et de civilisation de Byzance, Monographies 2; Paris, 1985).

Maricq, A., see under Honigmann, E.

Matthews, J. F., *Western Aristocracies and Imperial Court, A.D. 364-425* (Oxford, 1975; repr. 1990).

— — , *The Roman Empire of Ammianus* (London, 1989).

Mauss, M., *The Gift: Forms and Functions of Exchange in Archaic Societies* (first pub. 1925; transl. I. Cunnison, London, 1954; repr. 1966, 1969, etc.).

Meslin, M., *Les Ariens d'Occident, 335-430* (Patristica Sorbonensia 8, 1967).

Millar, F., 'P. Herennius Dexippus; the Greek World and the Third-Century Invasions', *JRS* 59 (1969), 12-29.

— — , 'Government and Diplomacy in the Roman Empire during the First Three Centuries', *International History Review* 10 (1988), 345-77.

Musurillo, H., *Acts of the Christian Martyrs* (Oxford, 1972).

Nordenfalk, C., *Die Spätantiken Kanontafeln* (2 vols., Gothenburg, 1938).

Page, R. I., *Runes* ('Reading the Past': British Museum Publications; London, 1987).

Roueché, C., 'Theodosius II, the cities, and the date of the "Church History" of Sozomen', *JTS* n.s. 37 (1986), 130-2.

Rubin, Z., 'The Conversion of the Visigoths to Christianity', *Mus. Helv.* 38 (1981), 34-54.

Ste Croix, G. E. M. de, *The Class Struggle in the Ancient Greek World, from the Archaic Age to the Arab Conquest* (London, 1981).

Salaville, S., 'Un ancien bourg de Cappadoce: Sadagolthina', *Echos d'Orient* 15 (1912), 61-3.

Schäferdiek, K., 'Wulfila: vom Bischof von Gotien zum Gotenbischof', *ZKG* 90 (1979), 253-303.

Schlesinger, W., 'Lord and followers in German institutional history', in F. C. Cheyette (ed.), *Lordship and Community in Medieval Europe* (New York, 1968).

Scorpan, C., *Limes Scythiae: topographical and stratigraphical research on the late Roman fortifications on the lower Danube* (BAR, International Series 88; Oxford, 1980).

Skeat, W. W., *A Moeso-Gothic Glossary* (London and Berlin, 1868).

Speidel, M. P., 'The Roman army in Arabia', *ANRW* II.8 (1977), 687-730.

Stearns, MacDonald, Jr., *Crimean Gothic: analysis and etymology of the Corpus* (Studia Linguistica et Philologica, 6; Saratoga, 1978).

Streitberg, W., *Die Gotische Bibel*, Vols. I, Text; II, Wörterbuch (Heidelberg, 1908, 1910).

Syme, R., rev. of Klose, *Klientel-Randstaaten*, *JRS* 25 (1935), 95-99.

Thompson, E. A., *A History of Attila and the Huns* (Oxford, 1948).

— —, *The Visigoths in the Time of Ulfila* (Oxford, 1966).

— —, 'Christianity and the northern barbarians', in Momigliano, A. (ed.), *The Conflict between Paganism and Christianity in the Fourth Century* (Oxford, 1963), 56-78.

Tudor, D., 'Preuves archéologiques attestant la continuité de la domination romaine au nord du Danube après l'abandon de la

Dacie sous Aurélien', *Dacoromania* 1 (1973), 149-161.

Van Dam, R., 'Hagiography and History: the Life of Gregory Thaumaturgus', *Classical Antiquity* 1.2 (1982), 272-308.

Vulpe, R., 'Considérations historiques autour de l'évacuation de la Dacie par Aurélien', *Dacoromania* 1 (1973), 41-51.

Wallis, R. T., *Neoplatonism* (London, 1972).

Whitby, L. M., 'Procopius and the development of Roman defences in Upper Mesopotamia' in P. Freeman and D. Kennedy (edd.), *The Defence of the Roman and Byzantine East* (BAR, International Series 297; Oxford, 1986), 717-35.

Williams, R., *Arius: Heresy and Tradition* (London, 1987).

Wolfram, H., *History of the Goths* (transl. by T. J. Dunlap; Berkeley and London, 1988).

Wright, J., *Grammar of the Gothic Language* (2nd ed. with a Supplement to the Grammar by O. L. Sayce; Oxford, 1954, repr. 1981).

INDEX